REWARD!

Stranger: If you find this Book please return it to me if I know the secret word (which is ....) and I will give you:

☐ **$1,000,000**   ☐ **$10,000**   ☐ **$100**
☐ **$10**   ☐ **$1**   ☐ **10¢**   ☐ **Nothing**

Name...

Address...

....

....

Telephone..

e-mail..

CHEWING GUM PAD

(Place gum here while working on the Book)

Important information about the owner of this Book in case of emergency:

Blood group...

Allergies...

....

....

Name of closest relative..............................

Telephone..

Cell phone...

e-mail...

IS THIS BOOK A GIFT?

<u>DONOR:</u> Explore reasons for giving it here
....
....
....

<u>RECIPIENT:</u> Explore feelings on receiving it here
....
....
....
....

DRAW YOUR PORTRAIT HERE

Fill in life preferences in case of amnesia

My favorite color...

My favorite food...

My lucky number..

My sexual orientation...................................

My best foot..

My best friend...

My most annoying habit................................

My favorite football team..............................

My signature...

Fingerprints (right hand):

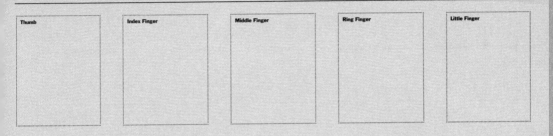

Thumb	Index Finger	Middle Finger	Ring Finger	Little Finger

In case of sudden death

Should I die unexpectedly, please tell:

....

(telephone...)

Confession (my worst sin):

I did...

to..

My funeral:

I want to be Buried ☐ Cremated ☐ Other ☐

Song to be played..

Epitaph...

Lasting regret...

My stuff goes to...

Dear.......................... (best friend), please go to my room and remove .... from...................... before my poor mother finds it.

HOW TO USE THIS BOOK

The Book will only help you if you want to be helped. Welcome it into your life and who knows what or who you'll be by this time next year. Ignore it and your life will continue in its current orbit. Now, of course, not everyone will be in a position to follow the instructions to the letter every day, and some are more demanding than others. But make the effort and your reward will be a year to remember, the first of many. Do not underestimate the difficulty of following the Book. Its dictates may seem arbitrary, but only thus can we counter the arbitrariness of fate.

Life planner

1 Crucial formative influences	**13** Puberty (boys)	**25**	
2	**14** First cigarette behind bike shed	**26**	
3	**15**	**27**	
4	**16** Exams	**28** Marriage and mortgage	
5	**17**	**29**	
6	**18** Prom	**30** Party	
7	**19**	**31** Settle down	
8	**20**	**32**	
9	**21** Drink legally	**33**	
10	**22** End of youthful illusions	**34**	
11 Puberty (girls)	**23**	**35** Itch (seven year-)	
12	**24**	**36**	

Other

37	....	49	....	61	....
38	....	50	Party	62	....
39	....	51	....	63	....
40	Party	52	....	64	....
41	....	53	....	65	....
42	....	54	....	66	....
43	....	55	....	67	....
44	Midlife crisis	56	....	68	....
45	Take up golf	57	....	69	....
46	....	58	....	70	Party ....
47	....	59	Pay off mortgage	71	....
48	....	60	Retirement party	72	....

Other
....

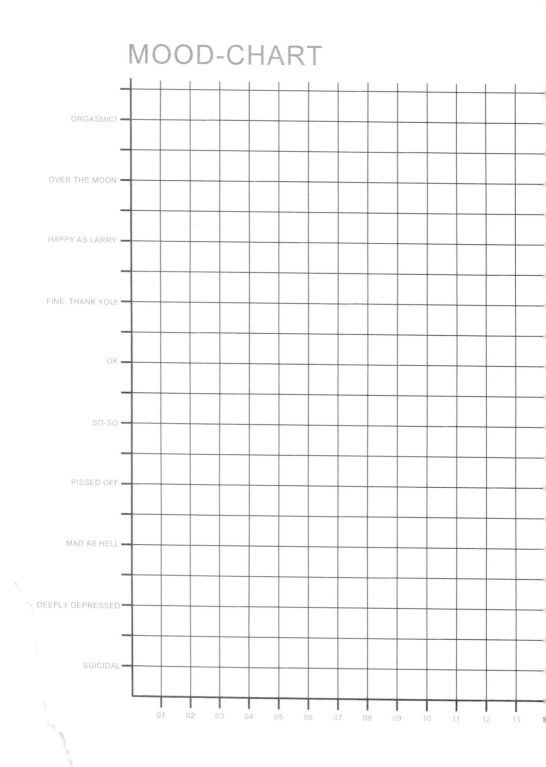

Plot mood level every day of the month against vertical axis. Show one year's results to psychotherapist.

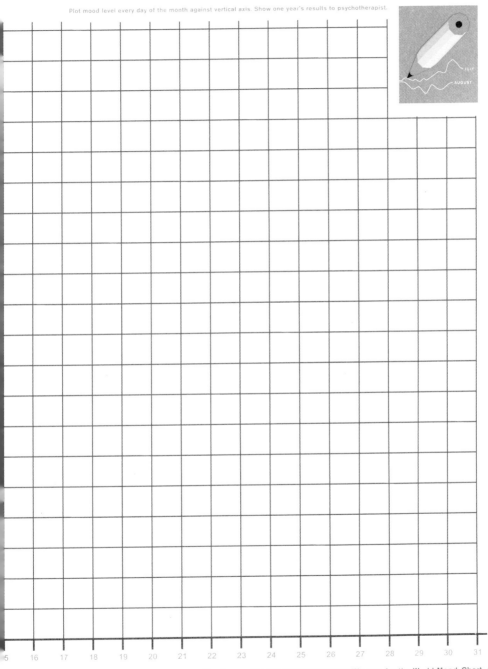

| 5 | 16 | 17 | 18 | 19 | 20 | 21 | 22 | 23 | 24 | 25 | 26 | 27 | 28 | 29 | 30 | 31 |

As this is your first day, you should warm up with
an easy task that will only change your life a little bit.

Choose one of the following options:

Do one press-up.
Perform a striptease (in private).
Triple-tie your shoelaces.
Learn to play »chopsticks« on the piano.
Increase your typing speed by three words a minute.
Jaywalk in a pedestrian zone.
Set all your clocks to exactly the right time.
Whisper a white lie when no one's listening.
Fantasize about your partner.
Use a different thickness comb.
Say »yo« instead of »hello«.
Hold the phone up to your other ear.
Tell someone your middle name.
Try a new sandwich filling.
Leave work five minutes early.
Bookmark a new website.
Give your genitalia pet names.
Decide which one of your toes is the prettiest.
Insult an insect.
Go on a one-minute hunger strike.

And for those crazy individuals who want to dive in at the deep end:
open this Book at random and perform that Day's task.

If you follow this Book's instructions, in a year's time you will be famous.
People will be writing all sorts of stuff about you, and will want to know
exactly how the Book's advice changed you. So make sure you note all
changes day by day in these practical boxes, conveniently headed
NOTES. Then just hand over to your biographers at the end of the year.

DAY 2: THE LOVE OF YOUR LIFE

Today, gaze at everyone wondering whether they might be the one true love of your life, the one destined for you and you alone, and whether you might be passing them by forever... Act in consequence.

Notes

Today throw something away that you like.

WORLD COLORING-IN DAY

Today, work out your globetrotting plans for the rest of your time on earth, and get on the phone to an accredited travel agent. NB: the State Dept. currently discourages travel to the following countries: Afghanistan, Iraq, North Korea, Turkmenistan, Zimbabwe, North Yemen. **Fill in country by country:** ● Been there done that ● Intend to go there this year ●Intend to go there sometime before I die ●Happy never to set foot there in my whole life.

AUSTRALIA

RUSSIA

KAZAKHSTAN

GREENLAND

BRAZIL

BOLIVIA

PARAGUAY

ARGENTINA

PERU

CHILE

UNITED STATES OF AMERICA

CANADA

MEXICO

U.S.A

NOTES

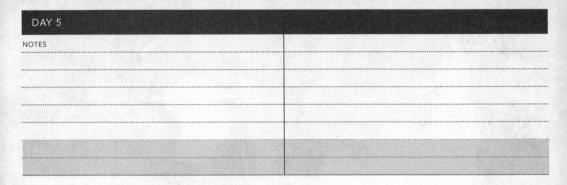

DAY 5

NOTES

OUT OF ORDER

Mass social experiment. Cut out and stick this sign on any item of public infrastructure you might encounter today, including, but not limited to: elevators, garbage trucks, cranes, phone booths, toilets, ventilation units, escalators, entrances to subway stations. The aim is to achieve comprehensive social breakdown across the US.

»It is a truth universally acknowledged, that a single man in possession of a good fortune, must be in want of a wife.« Pride and Prejudice, Jane Austen

»1801 – I have just returned from a visit to my landlord – the solitary neighbour that I shall be troubled with.« Wuthering Heights, Emily Brontë

»Mother died today.« L'ÉTRANGER, ALBERT CAMUS

»You are about to begin reading Italo Calvino's new novel, If on a winter's night a traveller.« If On A Winter's Night A Traveller, Italo Calvino

»Longtemps je me suis couché de bonne heure.« A la recherche du temps perdu, Marcel Proust

»I have carefully collected all I could possibly find out about the history of poor Werther and I lay it before you here, knowing that you will thank me for doing so.« The Sorrows of Young Werther, Johan Wolfgang von Goethe

»All happy families resemble each other; each unhappy family is unhappy in its own way.« Anna Karenina, Tolstoy

»The past is a foreign country; they do things differently there.« The Go-Between, L.P. Hartley

»Call me Ishmael.« Moby Dick, Herman Melville

»…the first thing you'll probably want to know is where I was born, and what my lousy childhood was like, and how my parents were occupied and all before they had me, and all that David Copperfield kind of crap, but I don't feel like going into it.« THE CATCHER IN THE RYE, J.D. SALINGER

»Hale knew they meant to murder him before he had been in Brighton three hours.« Brighton Rock, Graham Greene

»And this also, has been one of the dark places of the earth.« Heart of Darkness, Joseph Conrad

»Riverrun, past Eve and Adam's, from swerve of shore to bend of bay, brings us by a commodius vicus of recirculation back to Howth Castle and Environs.« Finnegans Wake, James Joyce

»In the beginning God created the heavens and the earth.« Old Testament, Anonymous

»Someone must have been telling lies about Joseph K., for without having done anything wrong he was arrested one fine morning.« The Trial, Franz Kafka

»It was a bright cold day in April, and the clocks were striking thirteen.« 1984, GEORGE ORWELL

Today write the opening sentence of your début novel:

»Now, what I want is, Facts.« Hard Times, Charles Dickens

»You don't know about me, without you have read a book by the name of The Adventures of Tom Sawyer, but that ain't no matter.« Huckleberry Finn, Mark Twain

»LOLITA, light of my life, fire of my loins.« Lolita, Vladimir Nabokov

»The snow in the mountains was melting and Bunny had been dead for several weeks before we came to understand the gravity of our situation.« The Secret History, Donna Tartt

»Stately, plump Buck Milligan came from the stairhead, bearing a bowl of lather on which a mirror and a razor lay crossed.« Ulysses, James Joyce

NOTES

WOMEN:

Dark storm clouds were gathering over the Alpine mountain top as Emma finally reached the refuge. Where were the others? Where was her husband Edward? Perhaps they had fallen behind and taken the safe track back toward *St-Paul-des-Clercs* and civilization, she wondered. Well there was no point in panicking now. Night was falling fast, and she would have to spend it up here all alone at the mercy of these peaks. Exhausted, she entered the deserted cabin and barely had time to strip off her drenched clothes and slip into the thermal sleeping bag that Edward had thoughtfully given her for their sixth anniversary, before a deep slumber overtook her naked body.

As even the moon retreated from the inhospitable horizon, strange and fitful dreams came upon her. She tossed and turned in the night, her feverish brow victim to wild imaginings, full of visions of werewolf-like creatures creeping around the cabin, circling, surrounding her with deep-breathing low whistles that seemed to hiss and crackle like FIRE?!!! Emma opened her eyes and shrieked in the empty night. There, across the room, stood the tall, dark stranger. She held her breath in terror as he looked up from the fire he had lit in the wide hearth and stared at her inscrutably. His eyes seemed to contain worlds beyond her ken.

»Who - who are you? What do you want?« she cried. The man made no reply, but simply tossed another log onto the fire with barely a flicker of his powerful deep-veined forearm. He breathed in deeply, closing his eyes. Emma's voice was trembling.

»Look, now, I don't know what is going on but...«

He silenced her with a look from his piercing green eyes that seemed to cut right through her. Before she even realized what she was doing, Emma raced through the door in a mad dash for freedom, through the door and out into a thick curtain of rain lashing down over her exposed skin. He caught up with her easily, his strong arms grabbing her by the waist and hauling her back into the cabin. She writhed desperately in his grip until she could no more. He held her still, stared into her eyes and finally spoke in halting English, in the manner of one who seemed above words.

»Don't. It is too dangerous out there for you. You are safe here with me.«

And somehow she knew that this was so.

The fire dispensed a warm glow to the room. Before she had even recovered from the onslaught of the elements, she was trapped in an embrace as powerful as any of Nature's Furies. As the storm raged on outside, she stared into the infinite depth of his eyes. And then he was upon her, touching her deep within, roughly of course but with infinite tenderness. Suddenly lightning struck a tree nearby, while its thunder covered her animal moans. He held her tight for what seemed an eternity, until the first light of dawn broke the enchanting spell the mountain Gods had woven around them. And he was gone, as swiftly as he had come. Was it but a dream? Emma wondered wistfully, as she drifted off back to sleep smiling, her brow no longer troubled.

MEN:
Two blondes. Doing it. Together.

Notes		

Addiction-Free Day

Your body is your temple. Cut out addictive substances for the day and see how much purer you feel.

Notes

SPECIAL TIP FOR ANY BOOK OWNERS ADDICTED TO CRACK COCAINE: You may not feel purer immediately. Stick at this one for at least a couple of months to see the full lifestyle benefits.

DO SOMETHING BEFORE BREAKFAST TODAY

GO FOR A FIVE-MILE RUN

CALL A FRIEND AND EXPRESS SURPRISE THEY'RE NOT UP YET

FIND OUT WHAT'S ON TV AT THIS HOUR

LICK MORNING DEW OFF A LEAF

HAVE SLEEPY SEX

MILK A COW

GOSSIP ABOUT YOUR NEIGHBORS WITH THE GARBAGE MEN

WATCH THE SUN RISE

As any peasant worth his salt will tell you, the early morning is the best part of the day, so set the alarm for 5 o'clock and rise and shine.

Notes

DAY 9

DAY 10!
MEET JONAS DAY!

This is Jonas Jansson, a courageous young fellow who has agreed to follow the Book's injunctions to the letter. In this, his first week, he has already been arrested once and lost his girlfriend. Go Jonas!

Jonas was born in 1982, in the small village of Gävle in Sweden. He grew up, went to school, made some friends, studied a bit, got drunk a couple of times, got a job – but something was still lacking in his otherwise eventful life. One day last year, the authors of the Book spotted him playing pinball in his local mall. Something about his style

and look caught their eye. They approached him and asked Mr. Jansson if he would play the guinea pig for their venture. He said he'd think about it, and before he knew it, his life was totally and utterly transformed. It's only been a few days since Jonas has been following the Book but already it's pepped up his life no end. Only a week ago,

he read the »love of your life« page, and followed it a bit too far. First he chucked his girlfriend Magda, even though nothing was said about getting rid of current loves. Then he thought he spotted the love of his life, 59-year-old Canadian tourist Bibi Jeanmaire, busy enjoying a coffee in downtown Stockholm with ex-Mountie husband Pierre-Louis. Jonas approached her, showed her the relevant Book page, and proceeded to woo her with a passionate kiss. That's the spirit Jonas! Local police agreed to drop all charges the next day, but not without fining him a substantial 1000 crowns. Better luck next time!

Follow Jonas's exciting adventures and check your progress against his on www.thiswebsitewill-changeyourlife.com

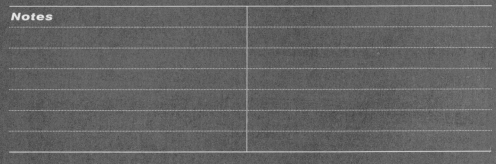

Jonas will be discussing his adventures during the year on www.thiswebsitewillchangeyourlife.com; be sure to compare his experiences to yours.

Notes

VISIT US ON WWW.THISWEBSITEWILLCHANGEYOURLIFE.COM!
FULL OF ALL THE GOOD STUFF WE COULDN'T GET AWAY WITH PUBLISHING IN THIS FAMILY-FRIENDLY EDITION!

DAY 12: WHAT's YOUR TYPE?

Tick it here today as reminder at drunken parties

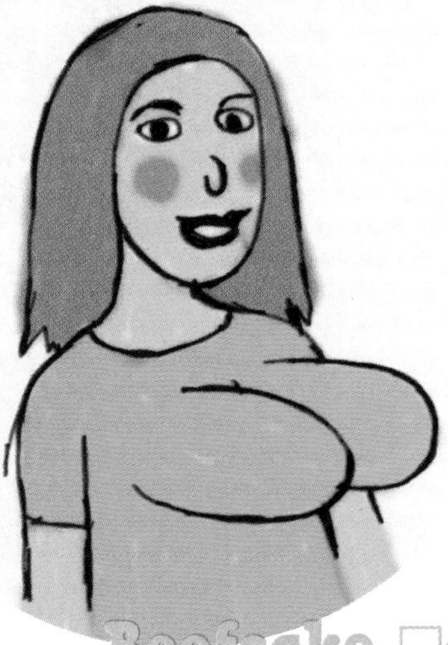

- ☐ **Dumb blonde**
- ☐ **Clever brunette**
- ☐ **Wild redhead**
- ☐ **Lesbian**
- ☐ **Nag**
- ☐ **Cold Fish**

Beefcake ☐
Mr. Nice Guy ☐
Loaded ☐
Married with kids ☐
Sleazeball ☐
Handsome prince ☐

Notes

DAY 13: SEND A LETTER TO A MASS MURDERER

Richard Ramirez (USA, 1960–)
16 victims
Nickname: »The Night Stalker«
Death Row, San Quentin Penitentiary,
San Quentin, CA 94974, USA

David Berkowitz (USA, 1953–)
6 victims
Nickname: »Son of Sam«
Kings County Hospital,
Brooklyn, NY 11212, USA

Peter Sutcliffe (UK, 1946–)
13 victims
Nickname: »The Yorkshire Ripper«
Broadmoor Special Hospital,
Crowthorne, RG45 7EG Berkshire, UK

Dennis Nilsen (UK, 1945–)
15 victims
Nickname: –––––
13 Parkhurst Rd.,
Holloway, London N7 9TK, UK

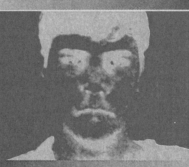

Edmund Kemper (USA, 1948–)
10 victims
Nickname: »The Co-Ed Killer«
California Medical Facility, PO BOX 2000,
Vacaville, CA 95696–2000, USA

Charles Manson (USA, 1934–)
6+ victims
Nickname: –––––
California State Prison, B–33920, 4A 4R–23L,
PO BOX 3476, Corcoran, CA 93212, USA

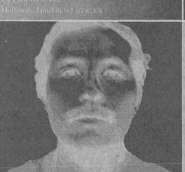

Angel Resendez (MEXICO, 1960–)
9 victims
Nickname: »The Railroad Killer«
Death Row, Polunski Unit, 12002 FM,
350 South Livingston, 4 X 77351, USA

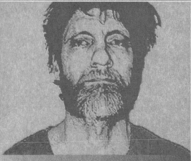

Theodore Kaczynski (USA, 1942–)
3 victims
Nickname: »The Unabomber«
Florence Admax USP, P.O. BOX 8500,
–88–, HWY 67J, Florence, CO 81226, USA

Robert Lee Yates Jr. (USA, 1952–)
14+ victims
Nickname: »The Spokane Serial Killer«
Death Row, Washington State Penitentiary,
1313 N. 13th, Walla Walla, WA 99362, USA

NOTES

DAY 14: A DAY OF COMPLIMENTS

Flatter someone today and see if it does indeed get you anywhere.

WHAT A FINE HAT!

This is the best memo I've ever read

THAT TOUPEE REALLY SUITS YOU, YOUR HONOR

They never told me you were beautiful as well as intelligent

THAT'S A NICE BRIEF-CASE

You're not the boss for nothing!

NOTES

Be gay for a day!

As James Dean said, why go through life with one hand tied behind your back? Here are some hints on how to experience your other side in just one day.

8am During rush hour, try to brush up gently against someone in public transport. This is just to get yourself used to the idea of same-sex contact. Do not push this too far as technically it is known as frottage and could get you arrested.

11am The office coffee machine is the ideal casual flirting situation. Wait for the object of your affection to help themselves to a coffee before bumping into them. Their beverage will spill over them, providing you with the perfect opportunity to caress their chest with a kitchen towel.

1pm Because of social conventions, it is much easier to find a gay mate if you are officially on the lookout. Use your lunch hour to compose a carefully worded all-staff e-mail in which you come out of the closet. (You will always be able to claim it was a misunderstanding tomorrow.)

3pm By now you should have had plenty of responses to your flirting overtures, but you also need to start planning your evening. Ring a close same-gender friend and say you have something important to tell them. Arrange to meet in a romantic bar or restaurant. Candlelight is best.

5pm The end of the office day. As tomorrow you will be able to explain everything, why not turn up the heat a little by squeezing someone's bottom playfully on your way out. (If possible pick someone with a sense of humor.)

8pm By now your date should be going well. After a few drinks, some inadvertent touching and a lot of eye contact, you will have told your close friend that you think that your relationship could be taken to the next level. They may act unconvinced at first, even play »hard to get,« so don't be shy of forcing them to deal with their feelings by grabbing their hand or even French kissing them.

11pm Only one hour left to explore the outer shores of your new sexuality. After today's gradual physical emotional build-up, the last inhibitions shouldn't be too difficult to shed. The rest is up to you...

GAYS: be straight for a day! Adapt the above guidelines, only making it clear you're heading *into* the closet.

Notes

Discreetly give the finger
to people all day today

FIG. A: What's in my eye?!

FIG. B: Just chilling out…

FIG. C: Hmmm… I wonder…

FIG. D: Everything's in order, officer

FIG. E: Sure, take the last seat!

FIG. F: Rich pickings…

FIG. G: Is there something in my teeth?

FIG. H: I like to stay informed

FIG. I: Business is business

NOTES

DAY 17: Eat nothing
but asparagus all day long
to ascertain just how noxious
your pee can get.

Been there
done that? Try one
of the lesser urine-
affecting vegetables:
fennel. eggplant.
okra, turnip.
ginger.

Notes

KILL
SOMETHING DAY

So-called »Western civilization« suppresses our legitimate aggressive impulses. Cast off the chains of narrow morality and stamp out the sad life of a member of some inferior species today: an ant, or perhaps a gnat of some kind. Indulge your dark urges before they overwhelm you. After all, as top Russian anarchist Mikhail Bakunin declared: *the passion for destruction is also a creative passion...*

DAY 18

DAY 19

PRETEND TO BE A SECRET AGENT.
No one can know. This Book was a pretext to get in touch with you. Your government needs you. Don't look up now, they are watching. Meet at 1300 today outside work. Wave at the gray car. It will pick you up and take you to the secret rendezvous. Good luck. P.S. Tear this page out and swallow it.

Notes

Poetry Day

Today everyone is to send in a line to create the world's longest poem. They will be collated as they are e-mailed to www.thiswebsitewillchangeyourlife.com, and the result published across the whole world as soon as a suitable final line is deemed to have been found and we think of a good title. The opening line is:

»MERCY, CRIED THE POPINJAY TO THE POPE«

....

....

....

....

....

....

....

....

THE IAMBIC PENTAMETER FOR IDIOTS. This oeuvre is to be composed in iambic pentameters, undoubtedly the most versatile form in the English poetic idiom. The iambic pentameter runs ti-tum ti-tum ti-tum ti-tum ti-tum, its ten syllables tripping off the tongue effortlessly, thus enabling the poet to propel his meaning forth. William Shakespeare wrote mostly in iambic parameters: Shall I compare thee to a summers day? Thou art more lovely and more temperate, and so on and so forth. If it was good enough for him, it's good enough for you. Happy composing.

Notes

PATRIOTISM DAY!

It is the duty of every citizen to be patriotic. A country is one's soil, one's blood, one's tears, one's roots. Here is a list of countries along with their strong points, so you can choose which one to feel patriotic about today.

FRANCE ⭐⭐⭐⭐⭐ /5

LANGUAGE: French.
ANTHEM: La Marseillaise.
MILITARY RECORD: Prone to invasion.
PATRIOTIC POTENTIAL: Gung-ho anthem, easy to get worked up about.

UNITED KINGDOM ⭐⭐⭐⭐⭐ /5

LANGUAGE: English.
ANTHEM: God Save The Queen.
MILITARY RECORD: Good, though the English Channel has undoubtedly helped.
PATRIOTIC POTENTIAL: Wide choice of tones, from Churchill to football hooliganism.

CHINA ⭐⭐⭐ /5

LANGUAGE: Mandarin.
ANTHEM: March of the Volunteers.
MILITARY RECORD: Strength in numbers.
PATRIOTIC POTENTIAL: If you like your patriotism tinged with ideology, this could be for you.

NIGERIA ⭐⭐ /5

LANGUAGE: English/Yoruba/Hausa.
ANTHEM: Arise O Compatriots!
MILITARY RECORD: Very good at fighting each other.
PATRIOTIC POTENTIAL: Limited, except during soccer World Cups.

Notes

MOLDOVA ⭐⭐⭐ /5

LANGUAGE: Moldovan.
ANTHEM: Awaken Thee Romania!
MILITARY RECORD: Nothing yet, but evidence of anti-Russian rowdiness.
PATRIOTIC POTENTIAL: Still all to play for!

RUSSIA ⭐⭐⭐⭐ /5

LANGUAGE: Russian.
ANTHEM: The Patriotic Song (no words)
MILITARY RECORD: Defeated Hitler, but lost Cold War.
PATRIOTIC POTENTIAL: Never a dull moment.

DAY 22

Today agree to meet someone in 10 years' time. Fill in this coupon and hand it to a stranger or someone you hardly know.

Notes

We, the undersigned, may only know each other casually, but we hereby agree to meet up in exactly ten years' time at..........(hour) on the..............(date) at...............(place). In case we have changed beyond recognition, we agree to wear the following identifying features:...................................

In case we have nothing to say to each other, here is a list of current »hot« topics to reminisce about:

....

....

....

Signed

....

See you in ten years' time.

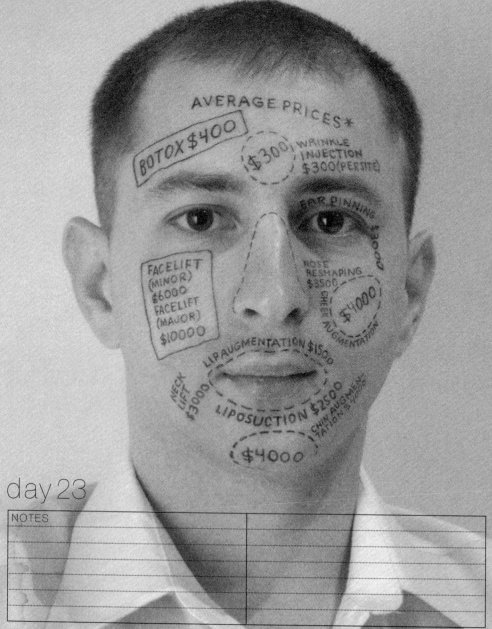

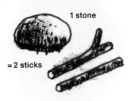
1 stone

= 2 sticks

DAY 24
BARTER
DAY

1 mud hut

= 4 donkeys

Bartering provides fun for all the family, bypasses the taxman, and is a useful skill to acquire in the event civilization should suddenly revert to the Stone Age. Here are some useful equivalencies to get you started.

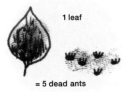
1 leaf

= 5 dead ants

1 giraffe

= 1 bicycle

2 apples

= 1 loaf bread

1 cow

= 2 dogs

12 french fries

= 1 pencil

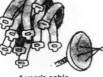
17 seatbelts

= 1 year's cable TV subscription

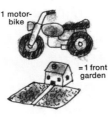
1 motor-bike

= 1 front garden

110 fresh eggs

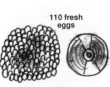

= 1 DVD

2 bottles vodka + 1 scarf

= 1 guitar

1 cell phone

= 1 big rock

Notes

3 eighteen-wheelers

= 1 small house with no window

1 skyscraper + 4 pears

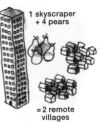

= 2 remote villages

DAY 25

THINGS YOU WILL NEVER DO BEFORE YOU DIE

Tick the boxes to come to terms with the fact that you will never:

- Read Proust ☐
- Climb Everest ☐
- Swim with dolphins ☐
- Learn Italian ☐
- Visit Bhutan ☐
- Write that novel/screenplay ☐
- Become world chess champion ☐
- Rob a bank ☐
- Run away ☐
- Have a sex change (just for a day) ☐
- Become a queen ☐
- Become a king ☐
- Wear colored lenses ☐
- Donate your liver ☐
- Compromise ☐
- Become a millionaire ☐
- Go to heaven ☐
- Parachute ☐
- Walk to the North Pole ☐
- Learn Russian ☐
- Live off charity ☐
- Contract an STD ☐
- Swallow a coin ☐
- Spend a night in prison ☐
- Start a revolution ☐
- Pretend everything is all right ☐
- Follow this Book rigorously ☐
- Learn how to drive ☐
- Hurt a friend ☐
- Celebrate Xmas in May ☐
- Call your father »Pa« ☐
- Call your mother »Ma« ☐
- Learn the Periodic Table by heart ☐
- Go to a drive-in cinema ☐
- Become an artist ☐
- Collect stamps ☐
- Work in a coal mine ☐
- Be late for a date ☐
- Watch all of Bergman ☐
- Follow Mao's teachings ☐
- Bite the dust ☐
- Kiss a stranger ☐
- Move to Japan ☐
- Visit space ☐
- Invent a cookie ☐
- Become grumpy when old ☐
- Wear a rucksack ☐
- Ride a camel ☐
- Use a semicolon ☐
- Inject heroin ☐
- Wear loafers ☐
- Speak in tongues ☐
- Become a fanatic ☐
- Dress like a hip-hopper ☐
- Faint with love ☐
- Save the world ☐
- Become insensitive to suffering ☐
- Be gay ☐
- Be heterosexual ☐
- Start a cult ☐
- Stand and speak up for your rights ☐
- Talk to strangers ☐
- Start a fire ☐
- Drink yourself silly in New Zealand ☐
- Order tap water ☐
- Grow a beard ☐
- Master the yo-yo ☐
- Become a fitness instructor ☐
- Be on TV ☐
- Laugh at a bad joke ☐
- Feel like Batman ☐
- Apply for a patent ☐
- Become a rock star ☐
- Fall for advertising ☐
- Live for a year on a desert island ☐
- Stop worrying ☐
- Use the term »solutionize« ☐
- Confess to a priest ☐
- Confess to a whore ☐
- Eat leaves from a tree ☐
- Graffiti a highway bridge ☐
- Be drunk during office hours ☐
- Own an owl ☐
- Contemplate suicide ☐
- Ride a Harley ☐
- Take NO for an answer ☐
- Say a prayer ☐
- Gamble your shirt ☐
- Break a promise ☐
- Learn to fly ☐
- Get a tattoo ☐
- Learn to live with gnats ☐
- Go on a field trip ☐
- Take part in a brainstorming ☐
- Invade a small country ☐
- Be the fifth wheel ☐
- Ride a donkey ☐
- Demand a ransom ☐
- Proclaim yourself emperor ☐
- Disinherit your heirs ☐
- Say NO when you mean YES ☐
- Adopt a Romanian ☐
- Seduce the prom queen ☐
- Paint someone in tar and feathers ☐
- Run for your life ☐
- Witness a miracle ☐
- Light a fart ☐
- Shave off your pubic hair ☐
- Smoke a cat ☐
- Make the front page ☐
- Cross-dress ☐
- Win the Nobel Peace Prize ☐
- Make love in front of a stranger ☐
- Volunteer for a dangerous mission ☐
- Overdose ☐
- Give birth to a goatboy ☐
- Win the rat race ☐
- Make like a tree ☐
- Overthrow a regime ☐
- Bake a soufflé ☐
- Organize an orgy ☐
- Understand Hitler ☐
- Race at Monaco ☐
- Live within your means ☐
- Marry someone you've just met ☐
- Marry someone you've never met ☐
- Star in a Hollywood blockbuster ☐
- Shovel manure ☐
- Discover the lost city of Atlantis ☐
- Dream in black and white ☐
- See your face on a banknote ☐
- Be eaten by cannibals ☐
- Own a grotto ☐
- Solve a crime ☐
- Host a game show ☐
- Sue the government ☐
- Win the lottery ☐
- Sleep with your best friend's partner ☐
- Start your own religion ☐
- Experience an earthquake ☐
- Meet Santa ☐
- Shoot the last buffalo ☐
- Bump'n'grind ☐
- Hibernate ☐
- Burn your bra (women) ☐
- Burn your jockstrap (men) ☐
- Find a guru ☐
- Turn 117 years old ☐
- Update the Kama Sutra ☐
- Marry a prince or princess ☐
- Settle in Pittsburgh ☐
- Run with the wolves ☐
- Become pope ☐
- Inherit the crown jewels ☐
- Be used as a manga character ☐
- Grow a tail ☐
- Crash a helicopter in the jungle ☐
- Take a vow of silence ☐
- Take a vow of chastity ☐
- Jump bail ☐
- Move someone to tears ☐
- Fake a multiple orgasm ☐
- Become employee of the month ☐
- Go live with a hermit ☐
- Greet the extraterrestrial delegation ☐
- Become a Muslim ☐
- Become a Buddhist ☐
- Become a Christian ☐
- Tie the perfect shoelace knot ☐
- Eradicate hepatitis C ☐
- Kiss your own lips ☐
- Shoot the pianist ☐
- Ride off into the sunset ☐
- Invent a typeface ☐
- Reject society ☐
- Beat Bjorn Borg at tennis ☐
- Fulfill your true potential ☐
- Be in the eye of the storm ☐
- Break the bank in Vegas ☐
- Have a park bench named after you ☐
- Risk your life ☐
- Refuse a new technology ☐
- Meet your great-great-grandchildren ☐
- Suffer a fool gladly ☐
- Sway a jury ☐
- Sweep a chimney ☐
- Fight the power ☐
- Be the 78th person on the moon ☐
- Collect coins ☐
- Be called upon by your president ☐
- Win best-looking baby of the year ☐
- Smoke a Cuban cigar ☐
- Think up a new swear word ☐
- Fight a duel ☐
- Jump the gun ☐
- Escape your past ☐
- Suck on 12 lollipops at once ☐
- Have your own brand of olive oil ☐
- Become immortal ☐
- Learn pole dancing ☐
- Play the lead in Swan Lake ☐
- Master the remote control ☐
- Catch that bird that pooped on you ☐
- Loop the loop ☐
- Make a pact with the devil ☐
- Wish upon a star ☐
- Tell your deepest secret ☐
- Witness the mating of flamingos ☐
- Feel ugly ☐
- Feel pretty ☐
- Confess under duress ☐
- Walk down the yellow brick road ☐
- Travel at warp speed ☐
- Stab someone in the back ☐
- Implode ☐
- Swim in Lake Titicaca ☐
- Jump on a real bandwagon ☐
- Run an arms dealership ☐
- Shit in the woods ☐
- Exterminate a zombie ☐
- Sniff superglue ☐
- Whistle while you work ☐
- Become a superhero ☐
- Memorize an encyclopedia ☐
- Floss twice a day ☐
- Go on a rampage ☐
- Make your bank manager beg ☐
- Lick an electric eel ☐
- Broker a ceasefire ☐
- Conduct an orchestra ☐
- Jump ship ☐
- Make a leap of faith ☐
- Get drunk on meths ☐
- Sacrifice a goat ☐
- Live to tell the tale ☐
- Inaugurate a building ☐
- Forgive and forget ☐
- Sleep with a whore of Babylon ☐
- Reach Nirvana ☐
- Find out what it's all about ☐
- Crush grapes with your bare feet ☐
- Ride a yak ☐
- Sup with Satan ☐
- Bite the hand that feeds you ☐
- Track down Lord Lucan ☐
- Cause an intergalactic rift ☐
- Get away with murder ☐
- Travel back in time ☐
- Apologize for existing ☐
- Think the unthinkable ☐
- Appease a dictator ☐
- Lose your mojo ☐
- Face a firing squad ☐
- Become an object of worship ☐
- Gate crash the White House ☐
- Burn a banknote ☐
- Have the Midas touch ☐
- Trigger an avalanche ☐
- Cure the common cold ☐
- Own an oil field ☐
- Save the whale ☐
- Discover a new continent ☐
- Serenade a lover ☐
- Come out of a black hole alive ☐
- Precipitate the decline of the West ☐
- Jump for joy ☐
- Suck your little toe in public ☐
- Mate with another species ☐
- Become possessed ☐
- Surpass Einstein ☐
- Understand Einstein ☐
- Look like Einstein ☐
- Predict an eclipse ☐
- Participate in the Olympics ☐
- Catch a shark ☐
- Meet your maker ☐
- Commit arson ☐
- Wear a cape ☐
- Talk dirty to a flower ☐
- Spot the Invisible Man ☐
- Head a posse ☐
- Undergo emergency liposuction ☐
- Do the Rubik's Cube ☐
- Blame God for everything ☐
- Acquire a hard-ass nickname ☐
- Betray your country ☐
- Regain your virginity ☐
- Change astrological signs ☐
- Bring back Bambi ☐
- Write in cuneiform ☐
- Get fired for being truculent ☐
- Become like your father ☐
- Become like your mother ☐
- Join the French Foreign Legion ☐
- Achieve perfection ☐
- Spell »egg« differently ☐
- Win top prize for your verruca ☐
- Beg in the street ☐
- Channel lava away from a village ☐
- Grow a third nipple ☐
- Spend all your salary on payday ☐
- Witness the Big Bang ☐
- Gerrymander ☐
- Generate controversy ☐
- Meet a bolshevik ☐
- Ooze charm ☐
- Molt ☐
- Have too much of a good thing ☐
- Die of hard work ☐
- Run amok ☐
- Discover your ancestor is Napoleon ☐
- Make it to the top ☐
- Successfully crash-land a jumbo jet ☐
- Fiddle while Rome burns ☐
- Design the perfect crouton ☐
- Run out of tears ☐
- Howl at the full moon ☐
- Win an Oscar ☐
- Unbreak a taboo ☐
- Give rise to a cause célèbre ☐
- Part the Red Sea ☐
- Have sex with your clone ☐
- Know the truth about JFK ☐
- Wave a red rag to a bull ☐
- Get high on life ☐
- Find your self ☐
- Rule the world ☐
- Other ☐

NOTES

today choose what you'd prefer to be reincarnated as

Circle your first choice and send off with a $5 donation to the Dalai Lama, Lhassa, Tibet.

Notes

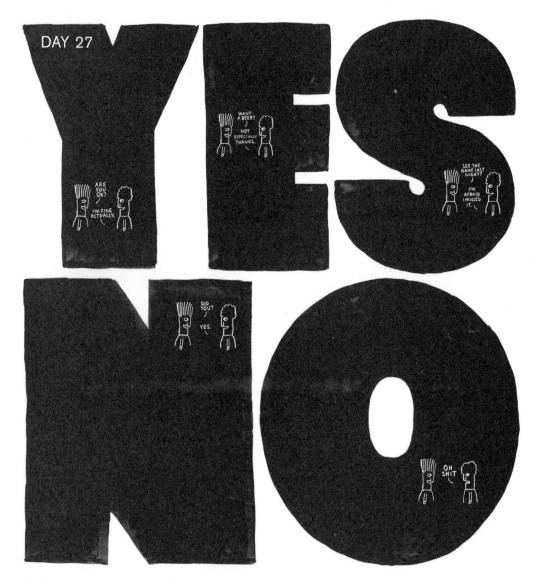

Today you are not allowed to use the words »yes« or »no«. See just how long you last.

Notes		

DAY 28: Choose your final meal on death row and make it.

POPULAR CHOICES:
LEONARD ROJAS Offense: Double Murder. Executed: 12/04/2002
One whole fried chicken (extra crispy), salad with Thousand Island dressing, French toast, two Diet Cokes, one apple pie, and French fries.
LAWRENCE BUXTON Offense: Murder. Executed: 02/26/1991
Steak (filet mignon), pineapple upside-down cake, tea, punch and coffee.
RON SHAMBURGER Offense: Murder. Executed: 09/18/2002
Nachos with chilli and cheese, one bowl of sliced jalapenos, one bowl of picante sauce, two large onions (sliced and grilled), tacos (with fresh tomatoes, lettuce, and cheese), and toasted corn tortilla shells.

NOTES

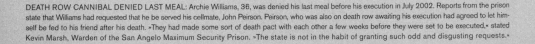

DEATH ROW CANNIBAL DENIED LAST MEAL: Archie Williams, 36, was denied his last meal before his execution in July 2002. Reports from the prison state that Williams had requested that he be served his cellmate, John Peirson. Peirson, who was also on death row awaiting his execution had agreed to let himself be fed to his friend after his death. »They had made some sort of death pact with each other a few weeks before they were set to be executed,« stated Kevin Marsh, Warden of the San Angelo Maximum Security Prison. »The state is not in the habit of granting such odd and disgusting requests.«

Day 29: Dial a phone number at random and read this script with a Deep South accent.

You know, without Christ, without Jesus, we have no hope. Why? Well, because we know that the standard of God's righteousness is Law, a law of the Ten Commandments, a law of statutes and judgments. And which God gave unto Moses on Sinai, saying this is thy righteousness, O Israel. But you know, God also gave another law. A law revolving around a system of shedding a poor and innocent lamb's blood. So that all who would break the Law of God, who would seek God for forgiveness and pardon, had to bring a lamb, something innocent, and slay it – although, Israel themselves never really knew the real meaning of this. Nonetheless, they were commanded to do it. Also there were other sacrifices, such as: turtle-doves, goats, oxen, red heifers.

But, it was a very sophisticated and very prolific type system of worship. Of course, God had to give these people their own country. He had to give them blessings and things, to be able to perform these rituals. And naturally of course, having to slay a lamb for your sins or such sacrifices, it would definitely keep a man on guard, not to sin too much, because otherwise he could lose the livestock pretty quick, couldn't he? Well anyway, (thanks be unto God), from as far back as Deuteronomy 32, all the way through to Malachi, there has been other writings, writings of the Prophets. Writings who do not usurp the authority of Moses, but actually exalt The Law of Moses. But yet there's an additional testimony. For the same God of Heaven – Who's rich in mercy – has not only given to men a Law, but also a way of escape, for those Repentant Souls who might fall short of the glory of God's law. Which some scholars will agree, that the glory of God's law is that it's a divine precept of His own character. God's character is revealed in The Law. Now, Christ is the only hope for a world that sins. Now, how do we know? Well – The Prophets – have prophesied? But what if we're not familiar with the prophets? Well, were the Jews familiar with the prophets when this Word-of-God was made flesh? When Mary, The Virgin, had a baby boy, did everyone believe, that she was really a virgin when Christ was conceived? If we search the Scriptures,

we'll find in certain arguments the Pharisees confronted Christ – and said to him, »We be not sons born of fornication.« So obviously, not everyone believed that he was a child of a virgin birth! If they hadn't looked back to Isaiah chapter 8, and learned the mystery of Immanuel – that a virgin would conceive and bear a son – then they might not really put too much ahhm... consistency into the fact that Christ at that day claimed to be born of a virgin. I mean, if Isaiah the prophet was a false prophet, well then naturally they would conclude that anyone claiming to have these things fulfilled would be false, too.

But of course, Christ, he did something much more, than to just fulfill prophecy. He did miracles. Miracles of mercy such as: healing the sick, feeding the hungry, raising the dead. And if we study we'll see that »Matthew, Mark, Luke, and John« gives us in somewhat, a full view of the oppositions, and also, the confidements, that he had in doing these miracles. He gathered many unto him through the means of these miracles.

But sad to say, even though he had done so many miracles, Scripture says, yet when it came right down to it, they didn't believe in him. It's amazing that even his own disciples forsook him – except Mary Magdalene. She stayed with him to the end, didn't she? Last to leave The Cross, first to come to the sepulchre. Now, we need to sit here, and we need to ask the question, »how come the men of that generation didn't believe in Christ?«

In Matthew 23, Christ had to say to the Jews »O Jerusalem, Jerusalem« how often I would have gathered you, but you would not. Why? He tells them that they have forsaken The Prophets. »Thou that killest the prophets,« how often I would have gathered you. How does the subject of ›gathering Israel‹ and ›the prophets‹ combine together? He tells them that their houses, their temple, is left to them desolate.

And that in Matthew 24, as Christ said on the Mount of Olives, his disciples came to him to ask him, concerning these things. What should be the sign of thy coming and of the end of the world? Well, Christ begins to tell them, let no man deceive you, »For many shall come in my name, saying, I am Christ; and shall deceive many.«

Notes

If you dial an answering machine, try to fit it all in the time allocated. If you can't, call back later to complete the message.

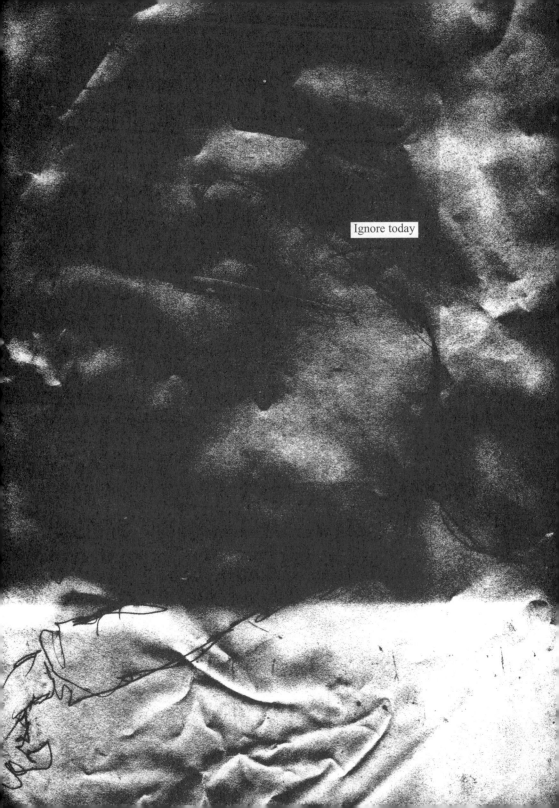

Ignore today

BE SURE TO
TRY ROAST
NAURU PIG
TODAY!

DAY 31

Nauru is a tiny island all alone in the middle of the
Pacific. Today let them know they're not completely forgotten
by sending the President a friendly postcard at Office of the
President, c/o Ministry of Works, Yaren Nauru.

NAURU

AWARENESS DAY!

NOTES

Political update:
Nauru became independent as
a republic in 1968 and joined
the Commonwealth as a special
member, which means they
make a voluntary contribution
toward the running of the
Secretariat.

Six-time President
of Nauru, Bernard
Dowiyogi (1946–2003)

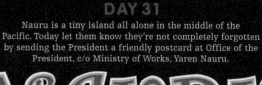

Sadly, Nauru is in mortal danger from rising sea levels in the Pacific, due
to global warming. In October 2000, a draft report from the IPCC
(Intergovernmental Panel on Climate Change) predicted that the average
global temperature could be 11 degrees Fahrenheit higher by the year
2100. This means Nauru and other Pacific islands could disappear under
the waves; indeed some atolls in nearby Kiribati and Tuvalu have already
been drowned. Don't mention this in your postcard however as it's a bit
of a downer; certainly Naureans would consider this a faux pas.

Tonight control your dreams

Freud postulated that our dreams are essentially the recombined elements of things that had affected us during the day. Today think very hard about these three things and see if they crop up in your dreams tonight.

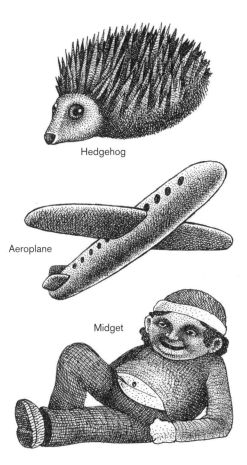

Hedgehog

Aeroplane

Midget

NOTES		

DAY 33: BE ON THE LOOKOUT FOR THE PARANORMAL

There is more to the world than meets the eye.
Today try to be especially receptive to paranormal manifestations and determine for yourself whether there is indeed a world beyond the veil. Here is a list of clues to look out for in ascending order of conclusiveness.

Odd feeling
Strange wind-like whisper
Flutey sounds in the distance
Scratching noises
Unexplained smells
Unexplained footsteps
Fleeting shadows
Feelings of being watched
Dogs barking
Cats barking

DON'T JUMP TO CONCLUSIONS, THERE'S PROBABLY A PERFECTLY INNOCENT EXPLANATION.

Voices
Voices of people dead for months
Voices of people dead for years
Doors opening
Cupboard doors opening
Keys disappearing
Keys reappearing
Lights turning on and off
Mist appearing out of nowhere
Being touched by an invisible hand

CURIOUSER AND CURIOUSER! CONTACT YOUR LOCAL PARANORMAL INVESTIGATOR, AND PROBE FURTHER.

Being slapped by invisible hand
Furniture moving
Dinner plates flying across the room
Spouse speaking in tongues
Apparition (ghost)
Apparition (zombie)
Apparition (hungry zombie)
Blood sluicing down walls
Head of daughter spinning
Being strangled by own intestines

YOU'VE PROBED TOO FAR. GET THE HELL OUT IF IT'S NOT TOO LATE.

NOTES

Today write to a dictator to stop torture

Sample letter:

Dear General/Minister/Grand Leader,

I have been greatly disturbed to hear of the arrests of _____ (check Amnesty International for recent names). I am writing to request that their whereabouts be disclosed and that they be granted immediate access to their families and lawyers. I also request that they be immediately released unless charged and brought before an ordinary court of law.

Yours sincerely,

Official forms of address

Your Majesty... to Kings, Queens & other monarchs

Your Excellency... for Presidents & other Heads of State

Dear Sir/Madam,... for Prime Ministers & Ministers

Dear Ambassador/High Commissioner... for Ambassadors & High Commissioners

Dear Sir/Madam... for other Embassy staff such as Chargé d'Affaires

Dear Admiral/General/Captain etc... for military officials

Your Grace... for Archbishops

Your Eminence... for Cardinals

Dear Bishop... for Bishops

Dear Mr/Father/Reverend... for other Clergy

Notes

DAY 34

Day 35: Today give little tasks to people around you

Smile more often when you see me	Be more strict with me on Wednesdays	When you next see me, pretend we've never met	Offer me flowers more often	When I say something witty, praise me	Water my desk plants
SLEEP WITH ME	Spy on my spouse for me	Taste my food for poison	Hold my hand to cross the street	Tell me something cute	BUY ME AN EXPENSIVE CAR
SALUTE ME	Let me win all discussions	Let me have the remote tonight	Read me a bed time story	COMFORT ME	TAKE A BATH
Watch my back	ANSWER MY TELEPHONES	Hold the elevator for me	Tell me what to do!	Buy me lunch	Tell me if my breath stinks
Tie up my laces if they come undone	NOTES				Greet me with a bow
Whistle my favorite tune					Let me win at chess for once
HUG ME	Don't let me forget my umbrella again!	Be my slave for the day	Pick my NOSE	Never talk to me again	Wake me up if I snore
Organize my surprise birthday party	Carry my Book for me today	DO WHAT I SAY!	Don't leave me alone	Read me my horoscope	Help me make a baby

It's amazing how much of the time we speak to say nothing of interest, in fact a lot of social interaction is superficial, with people just talking at cross-purposes because they love the sound of their own voices, I often wonder how much we'd all of us actually say if we had to stick to important and relevant things like information of a practical or educational nature like how to start a fire or build a house, stuff like that that makes a difference to how we live, not a lot I suspect because in truth not many folk obey the old adage and turn their tongue in their mouth seven times before speaking, indeed once would make a hell of a difference already the way some carry on as if they were full of supreme wisdom when they are talking out of their anal orifices, excuse my French, of course in some countries and cultures like France it's considered polite to chat incessantly, sing for your supper, but at least there they have interesting cultural stuff to discuss, so much so that it's a true pleasure and an entertainment to witness a Frenchman in full flight although they also had that Mime Marceau guy so go figure that one out, I guess that's why the French are supposed to be so full of contradictions, anyway, to get back to my point there should be a law against verbal diarrhea or at least maybe something like a red card that you could shove in the face of loudmouthed people when they were wittering on hey that's a great idea if I say so myself, maybe I should patent it and rake it in so then I could go live on my own desert island and not have to put up with incessant chit-chat but I digress, now what about those mute nuns they really are something they just decide to shut up one day for twelvescore years or whatever and zip, that's it, even if they feel like a good bitch about the mother superior and God knows nuns gossip like the rest of us, oops shouldn't bring God into it, sorry, blasphemy kills and all that, but as I was saying, there should really be more people taking that vow of silence thing it would clear some airspace for the rest of us to hear ourselves think, but do you think those individuals have even an ounce of consideration for us, no sirree, not one little bit between them, they know who they are, now I'm a pretty relaxed person I would say, but sometimes it drives me mad and I start twitching and sometimes I tell them straight off shut your piehole, I say, which is a very useful expression and conveys the point nicely though the French never seem to get it but then again they're a special case as I was discussing above and did you know there's no word in French for quiet, apparently, which is pretty significant in my book, just like the Icelandic Eskimos have 213 words for snow which would indicate they're a pretty chatty lot, not sure I could put up with hours of that kind of conversation, anyway where was I oh yes one time there was this girl I was going out with who was talking and talking about how she'd had all these problems in her childhood with her uncle and yadda yadda yadda so I just said you must mistake me for someone who cares anyway and would you believe that shut her up pretty sharpish let me tell you and that's another free tip for nothing, so take it from me the world would be a whole lot better off if there was a day where no one said anything like today.

NOTES

TODAY, EAT AND RUN

RUNNER ETIQUETTE:

1) Wait until the coffee course, particularly if there is a set menu.

2) Do not leave your date behind, unless you are sure it is the last time you wish to see them.

3) Do not start actually »running« until you are outside the restaurant.

4) Do not select the heaviest items on the menu. Running on a bouillabaisse is medically inadvisable.

5) Beginners and the shy: Do a practice »runner« before ordering any food.

NOTES		

Day 38
Spend some time in a church today

Even the irreligious amongst us can appreciate the sanctuary that churches provide, away from the hyperkinetic madness of modern life.

Breathe in the air of centuries. Let the shadows envelop you. Light a candle for a long-lost friend. Contemplate the silence. Perhaps even find God.

What to say to God if you find him

God is fed up with being quizzed about the same old chestnuts like evil and creation all the time.

Make Him notice you with a cheeky question, like what's his favourite breakfast cereal, or did Adam and Eve have belly buttons.

Notes

DAY 39: LEARN TO SPEAK SWEDISH!

New languages open up possibilities for new meetings. Today learn these useful phrases in Swedish. You never know when they may come in handy:

Hello. Hallå.
Goodbye. Hej då.
You are beautiful. Du är vacker.
Thank you for the food.
Tack för maten.
My name is... Mitt namn är...
I am from... Jag kommer från...
That is a lovely hat.
Det där är en vacker hatt.
Where is the little boys' room?
Vart ligger den lille gossens rum?
Nice meeting you. Trevligt att råkas.

And if you find those easy to learn, these ones will definitely impress your Nordic friends:

There is a smurf buried in my butter.
Det ligger en smurf begravd i mitt smör.
The palms of my feet are constructing portals for you while you sleep.
Mina fotsulor konstruerar portaler at dig medan du sover.
I am a tiger. Only kidding! I used to be a tiger but I'm not anymore.
Jag är en tiger. Nej, skojar bara! Jag brukade vara en tiger men inte nu längre.
A tractor has recently landed in my backyard. Is it your cousin's?
En traktor har nyligen landat i min bakgård. Är det din kusins?
That gargoyle is very contemporary.
Den där gargolen är mycket modern.

You are a sausage.
Du är en korv.
I am in the market for some Bolivian alabaster.
Jag är på marknaden för att hitta lite Bolivisk alabaster.
There's a bunch of daffodils on the rampage.
Ett gäng maskrosor har blivit lokiga och mördar folk .
Beat me, Mr. Badger!
Slå mig, herr Bajskorv!
My contact lens fell into that volcano on the right.
Min kontakt-lins föll ner i den där vulkanen till höger.

NOTES

| 1 ETT | 2 TVÅ | 3 TRE | 4 FYRA | 5 FEM | 6 SEX | 7 SJU | 8 ÅTTA | 9 NIO | 10 TIO |

Day 41: Apply for a knighthood

Don't remain plain old Mr. or Mrs. J. Schmoe all your life. To become a Knight or a Dame, simply write to the British Prime Minister c/o the Prime Minister's Office, 10 Downing St, London SW1A 2AA, United Kingdom. Explain what exceptional achievement or service you feel merits the award of a knighthood. Previous successful applicants have used the following, just to give you an idea: »been head nurse for 60 years,« »Nobel Peace Prize winner,« »raised millions for obscure charity,« »served in minor government position for whole life,« »won World War 2,« »saved cat from extra-tall tree.« Even better, get the President to recommend you.

The honors ceremony takes place on the Queen's Birthday. So make sure you keep it free! US citizens please note: Non-subjects may not style themselves Sir or Dame, though they may place the appropriate letters after their name.

Notes

DAY 42
TODAY WALK BAREFOOT ON GRASS.

Grass was well-known amongst Indian shamans for its soothing anti-ulcerative properties. When a papoose was sickly, the shaman would lay him down on a grass bank and sprinkle him with dew from the bark of a Great Conifer Tree, for 5 days and 5 nights (at least). Today grass is widely available of course in parks, gardens and the like. The current theory is that the leaves contain herbacinium, a derivative of morphine, which »rubs off« on the fibrous nerves of our bare feet, gets into the bloodstream and slows down our heart rate by up to 14%, thus »relaxing« us. Indeed, poets have long known this, as is conclusively demonstrated by the following:

LEAVES OF GRASS

A child said, What is the grass? fetching it to me with full hands;
How could I answer the child? I do not know what it is, any more than he.

I guess it must be the flag of my disposition, out of hopeful green stuff woven.

Or I guess it is the handkerchief of the Lord,
A scented gift and remembrancer, designedly dropped,
Bearing the owner's name someway in the corners, that we may see and remark, and say Whose?
Or I guess the grass is itself a child, the produced babe of the vegetation.
Or I guess it is a uniform hieroglyphic,
And it means, Sprouting alike in broad zones and narrow zones,
Growing among black folks as among white,
Kanuck, Tuckahoe, Congressman, Cuff, I give them the same, I receive them the same.
And now it seems to me the beautiful uncut hair of graves.
(Walt Whitman)

NOTES		

THIS EVENING, WRITE A PROPER DIARY ACCOUNT OF YOUR DAY
If Winston Churchill found time to write in his diary when he was busy fighting World War II, so can you. Here's a typical entry:

06/06/44. Woke up 8-ish, slept fairly well though had a strange dream featuring an elephant and a mongoose, perhaps attributable to that third bottle of claret. I really could not find the energy to rouse myself but Clemmie insisted that I should go and fight the war. Bless her. Arrived at War Office at midday to find Monty in a mess over D-day. As far as I can tell everything seems to be going to plan. Am not really that interested since they forbade me to join in. Anyhow, other than that, not much of a day. Scrambled eggs for dinner. Bed now.

Notes

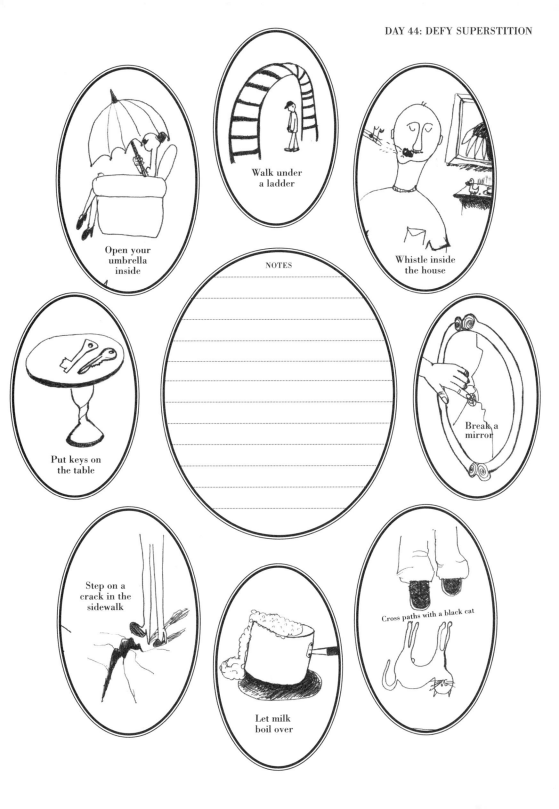

Open your
umbrella
inside

Walk under
a ladder

Whistle inside
the house

NOTES

Put keys on
the table

Break a
mirror

Step on a
crack in the
sidewalk

Let milk
boil over

Cross paths with a black cat

Romance Day:
*Come up with a compliment
that has never been made before.*

Top male compliment clichés
Do you work out?
Nice driving!
*Boy, you sure can handle
your drink.*
*Look at those hands – are
you a lumberjack?*

Top female compliment clichés:
*You are the woman
of my dreams.*
Your eyes are like two stars.
*It must have hurt, when you
fell from heaven.*
*You're not like any girl
I've ever met.*

Notes

BIRTHDAY DAY!

Don't forget your special buddies' special day! Write their birthdays down here so you'll remember them.

Friend 1	Friend 6	Friend 11
Friend 2	Friend 7	Friend 12
Friend 3	Friend 8	Friend 13
Friend 4	Friend 9	Friend 14
Friend 5	Friend 10	Friend 15

For those of you who can't be bothered, here is a list of convincing excuses:

I couldn't remember where you lived

I knocked my head on the pavement and suffered 24-hour amnesia

To be honest, I never liked you much anyway

Surely our friendship transcends material possessions like gifts

We have this telepathic bond, and that's how I sent the card

I can barely recall your name, let alone your birthday

You didn't remind me

I gave you a present last year

Wht're u tlkng bout? I snt u a txt msge, d'nt u gt it?

Well, you forgot our friendship anniversary

I was gonna call but my bunny rabbit passed away

I spent time with my mother

I only follow the Chinese calendar

I didn't forget! You must have an evil double

DAY 46

Notes

DAY
47

TONIGHT COUNT SHEEP AND CURE INSOMNIA

How far do you get before falling asleep? Tick each of these as you go along and find out.

NOTES

...AND WATCH OUT FOR THE EVIL COW

First impressions are crucial in life. Today hand this to a stranger and find out what impression you made.

Hello!

If you have one minute, would you please write down your first impression of me, for an experiment. Please be as honest as you can. If you want you can shut this book when you're finished and I'll only look when you're gone. Thank you.

Write here please: ....
....
....
....
....
....

Photocopy and repeat if you are not happy with the first opinion or if you want more.

day 48

notes

DAY 49

MAKE A CITIZEN'S ARREST! When a crime is committed and no police officer is in the vicinity, you have the right and responsibility to make a Citizen's Arrest. Such crimes include: murder, manslaughter, armed assault, conspiracy to defraud, littering.

CITIZEN'S ARREST ● PW56CJFb 00087 /

ARRESTOR DETAILS

Full name...

Home address...

City.. Zip code.................................

ARRESTEE DETAILS

Full name...

Nickname (if any) ....

Home address..

City...

Zip code...

Height.......................Weight......................

Eyes..

Hair....................Race.....................Gender.......

Identifying scars/tattoos (if able to draw please attach drawing)..

Fingerprints:

CRIME:

Plea: Guilty □ Not guilty □

Other..

Motive: Drugs □ Alcohol □ Money □

Blackmail □ Revenge □ Insanity □

Other..

Statement/confession..............................

....

....

....

....

Signatures:

CITIZEN...

CRIMINAL..

THAT'S RIGHT BUDDY! JUST CUT IT OUT AND HANG IT AROUND SOMEONE'S NECK!

NOTES

DAY 50: MAKE PEOPLE NOTICE YOU TODAY!

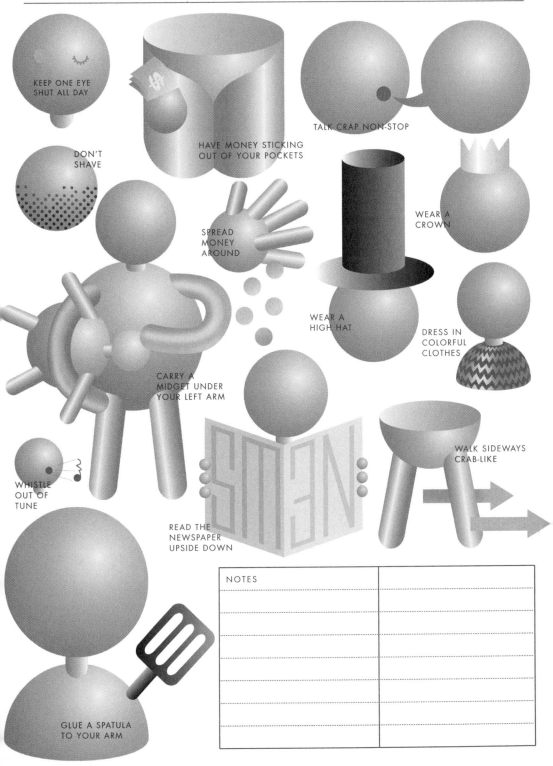

Sense-less Day

GO THROUGH TODAY WITHOUT USING YOUR SENSE OF: SIGHT

How to: Very dark glasses and white cane.

True story: There is an extraordinary study by Marius Von Senden, called »Space and Sight.« In it he examines the experiences of those born blind whose sight has recently been restored by cataract surgery. For them, vision is a radical new experience. They see the world as a field of colors. One girl was so moved by its dazzling brilliance that she kept her eyes shut for two weeks, only opening them briefly now and again, to repeat »Oh God! How beautiful.« Alas, she found it impossible to understand space, and kept bumping into these colors. She was only ever happy with her eyes closed, pretending to be blind again.

Notes

Write down the pros and cons of this sense as you discover them.

Pros: ....

Cons: ....

....

End of day assessment: How crucial is my sense of sight to me ..../10

WHAT IS THE MEANING OF LIFE? TODAY SOLVE THAT ETERNAL PROBLEM BY LOOKING IT UP IN THE DICTIONARY.

NOTES

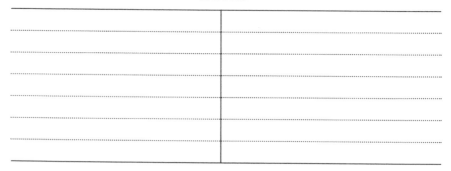

DAY 53
TODAY, RETURN ALL
YOUR JUNK MAIL
Junk mail clogs up your mailbox and forces you to spend hours every month disposing of it. But hey, if you send it back, it has the same effect on the companies who dish it out. Just write **RETURN TO SENDER** and change the name to B. Smith, Resources & Personnel Dept, and they will spend valuable time trying to work out who or what should be on the receiving end of your correspondence.

NOTES

Day 54 Today count your farts. Everyone emits gas, except the Queen of England perhaps. But just how cow-like are you in your production? Today keep a very rough numerical tally to ascertain if your methane generation falls within statistical norms, or if you pose a particular danger to the ozone layer.
MEN: 50cm³ (9 emissions) WOMEN: 20cm³ (4 emissions)

Notes

Pancake Day

TODAY, A TEST OF PATIENCE: FLIP THE PERFECT PANCAKE.

1) The pancake mixture must be very smooth. Start with 2 cups of flour and a pinch of salt in large bowl. Whisk in two eggs. Mix 2 cups of milk and 1 cup of water, and add them in gradually, whisking until the batter is creamily smooth.

2) Lubricate your frying pan with butter and put it on medium-high heat. Spoon in roughly one ladle-ful of mixture per pancake, tipping it around the pan so it spreads evenly. As soon as the underside is golden, it's time for the tricky bit.

3) Flipping (or »tossing«) is all in the forearm. Lift the pan away from the heat, then slide the pancake around slightly to avoid stickiness, and whip the pan up in a forceful yet precise movement. The pancake should rotate 180 degrees vertically and land back in the same spot it became airborne. (Beginners, children under 12 and the elderly: you are free to adjust the pan slightly to catch it though.)

This highly unusual rock formation known as »Pancake Rocks« is situated at Punakaiki, on the West Coast of the South Island, New Zealand. It received its name in May 1832 from the white settlers, as the indigenous Maoris were not familiar with the concept of pancake.

What makes the perfect pancake? 10% technique, 10% instinct, 80% patience.

Take care »tossing« your pancakes. Firefighter Stuart Mitchell says: »Cooking and flipping pancakes is great fun but people should take care with hot oil. You hardly need any oil and people should be very wary that they flip their pancakes away from the stove so that if the tossed pancake isn't caught it can be cleared up.«

Notes		

ROCK'N'ROLL

Today, live the Heavy Metal lifestyle at its most decadent...

4pm wake up to the gentle bobbing motion of fellatio from some nameless groupie **5pm** snort two industrial-sized lines of coke **6pm** take a swig of J. Daniels to help you out of bed **6pm** threaten manager or, if too wrecked, at least leave the trash hotel room, and take a swig of J. Daniels... throw television set out the window **7pm** ...with looted gun, doing a convincing imitation of someone who doesn't know or care if the safety is on **8pm** time for refreshments: pills washed down with vodka and a spliff **9pm** copulate with two Dallas Cowboys cheerleaders in full view of Dallas Cowboy **10pm** convince them to tattoo your name on their ass, misspelling it for them **11pm** the night is young and so are the girls around here, so time to hit the town

12am Meet your current dealer in bar with bag full of loose banknotes **1am** Shoot up in bar toilet, standing up to avoid the unhygienic **2am** OD in limo, but not before trying to wrestle steering wheel from driver seat **3am** get arrested trying to throttle nurse stealing your precious blood **5am** OD again, this time in prison hospital, for stabbing you and set fire to **7am** set fire to prison sheets, trying to light concealed emergency joint **9am** sink into coma-like sleep in pool of own vomit, ensuring plenty of personal space in otherwise crowded cell **10am** throw up again on lawyer, who should know better than to wear best suit to these occasions **11am** restorative sleep in tour van **4pm** repeat until early death and instant immortality

DAY 56

NOTES

Today, try food that scares you

NOTES

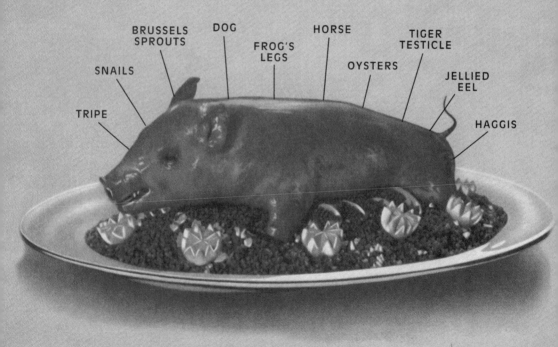

TRIPE
SNAILS
BRUSSELS SPROUTS
DOG
FROG'S LEGS
HORSE
OYSTERS
TIGER TESTICLE
JELLIED EEL
HAGGIS

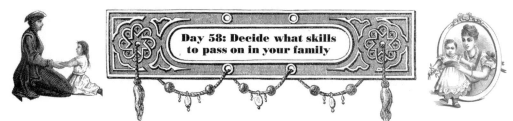

Families are the nuclei of society, cells of history and knowledge through which wisdom and morals are transmitted from generation to generation and beyond. What age-old traditions and skills define your family? Make a conscious effort to inculcate them in your children and grandchildren today. Here is a case study to inspire you.

W H I T T L I N G

The Medvak family of Cloverdale, Oregon (Robert, Annie, Gabriele, Sammy and animal companion Pooch) have long enjoyed whittling as a hobby. But it's something more too. Let's hear it from Rob Medvak: »Whittling's not just an inexpensive and fun pastime, it's a way of life. I learnt to whittle from my grandfather Bobbie Medvak, a bear of a man, who could turn a 10-by-10 chunk of good solid basswood into, say, a cowboy boot or a love spoon in ten minutes flat... Now that's whittling!« The Medvaks went through a rough patch in their marriage a few years ago when Annie entered a

lesbian »phase,« and Rob reckons whittling not only helped him and the kids through it, but made them stronger as a family. »Me and the kids we used to carve little pictures of Ann when she was gone, which was a really quite difficult thing, very elaborate because you've got to get the expression right, and of course after she shaved her hair they

didn't look much like her anymore so we moved on to carving bottle stoppers instead. Sam even carved these beautiful wooden horses all on his own.« Rob Medvak is proud to have passed the tradition on to his children. »I reckon Gaby and Sam will be whittling for life. It's a good character-building discipline. Anyway, they can't wait to show Mommy all their work as soon as she comes back.«

Notes

ARE YOU PSYCHIC?

TODAY TRY LIFTING AN OBJECT WITH YOUR MIND.

BEGINNERS	INTERMEDIATE	FREAKS
TWIG	CHAIR	WEIGHTS
STAMP	BICYCLE	FAT LADY
PEN	CHILD	BUILDING

URI GELLER	URI STARTED BENDING SPOONS AT THE AGE OF FOUR. HE USED TO THRILL HIS CLASSMATES AT SCHOOL BY MAKING THE CLOCK HANDS MOVE FORWARD SO LESSONS WOULD END EARLY. HE IS NOW A MULTI-MILLIONAIRE SEVERAL TIMES OVER. SO YOU SEE IT'S WELL WORTH CULTIVATING THOSE HIDDEN POWERS.

5000 TONNES

KRAFTMANN

DAY 59

Day 60: Order an impossible pizza

Some favorite toppings!
Banana
Peas
Cheerios
Orange
Candy
Ice Cream
Roast Duck
Sauerkraut
Honey
Apple Pie

Notes

TODAY, FIND OUT HOW SYMMETRICAL YOU ARE

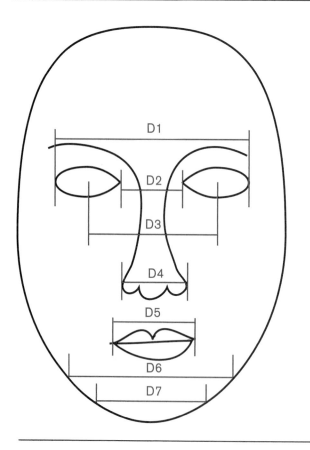

According to recent research at the Ludwig Boltmann Institute for Urban Ethnology, Vienna, symmetrical people are more attractive*. These findings have since been confirmed in 112 different countries and cultures. Draw a line down the middle of your face and measure your symmetry at the following points:

D1: Distance between outer eye corners.
D2: Distance between inner eye corners.
D3: Distance between pupils.
D4: Nose width.
D5: Mouth width.
D6: Outer jaw width.
D7: Chin width.

Hint: How do you know if you're asymmetrical without measuring? Well, you can be pretty sure you are if people have used these words about your physique: quirky, funny, different, special, kooky, homely, odd, interesting, unusual, alternative, ugly.

NOTES

OK! So you've taken those measurements, now here's an easy guide to working out your degree of symmetry. Add them up in the following manner: D1 + D2 + D3 + D4 + D5 + D7 = Dx. Dx /6 = Dz. Now Dz is your baseline symmetry coefficient (BSC:Dz). So far so simple. But here's where we start cooking. You need to correlate BSC:Dz with the Overall Average Facial Asymmetry Rating (OAFAR = 0.453). So let's say your BSC:Dz = 49mm. Individual Asymmetry Score (GRD) = 49/0.453 + 1 (adjusted) = 109.16! Voilà... If your GRD <79.8, you are in the top 10% of the general population and should have no trouble getting laid. If 79.9<GRD<123.56, you are average and veer from »lucky« periods to »bad patch« times. If your GRD >123.57, seek circus employment.

IN THE PARK!

AS SEEN ON TV!!!

DOWN THE STEPS!

Nothing really bad can happen to you if you keep within a circle.

Day 62: prepare convenient circles everywhere you habitually go.

Why do circles work? There are strange and dark powers out there that seek to influence your mind. Some call them ghosts, others call them demons, but unless they are kept at bay, they will drag you deep into psychosis. *Thus the need for circles.* Drawing a circle around yourself invokes protective pagan powers and establishes a psychic shield within which you are safe and in control. You may want to further secure the circle by using salt or rum. Ideally, you should aim to be able to hop from one protective circle to another for continuous protection.

BY THE POST!

ACROSS THE ROAD!

NOTES

DIFFICULT
- Fastest man on earth (C. Lewis, 26.95mph)
- Longest manned space flight (V. Poliyakov, 437 days, 17hr, 58 min, 16 sec)
- Hottest Planet in the solar system (864^{0}F, Venus)

AVERAGE
- Largest pumpkin (1061lbs, Nathan and Paula Zehr, USA)
- Longest letter to an editor (25,513 words, J. Sultzbaugh in »the Upper Dauphin Sentinel of Pennsylvania,« 1979)
- Longest paper plane flight (20.9 seconds, Chris Edge and Andy Currey, UK, 1996)
- Most mosquitos killed in 5 minutes (21, Henry Pellonpaa, Finland, 1995)

EASY (no record officially established)
- Most zits on face (Teenager/ Adult)
- Longest time holding up an umbrella
- Quickest recitation of the alphabet
- Longest occupation of attic

How to register your world record: contact
THE GUINNESS BOOK OF RECORDS
++44 891 517 607 or write to
Guinness Publishing Ltd, 338 Euston Rd,
London, NW1 3BD, UK.

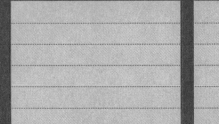

NOTES

day 64

TODAY SEND a LETTER TO SOMEONE AT random with a PHOTO OF youR SELF, A $5 BiLL, NO ExPLANATION AND NO SeNDeR adDRESS. See WHAT Comes of iT.

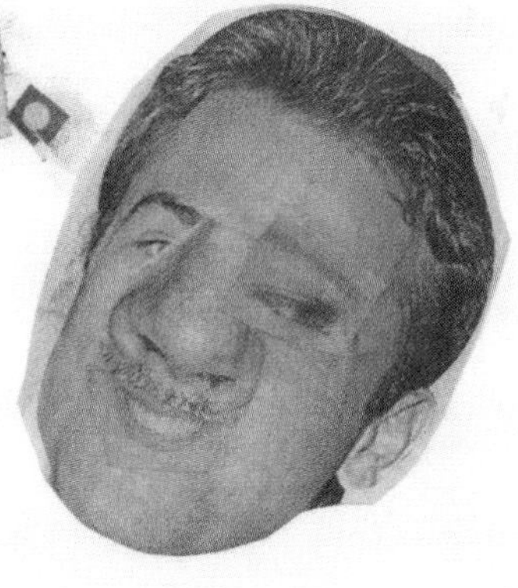

NOTES

Day 65
Today learn a poem by heart.

Hope is a Thing With Feathers
by Emily Dickinson

Hope is a thing with feathers
That perches in the soul,
And sings a tune without words,
And never stops at all,

And sweetest, in the gale, is heard;
And sore must be the storm
That could abash the little bird
That keeps so many warm.

I've heard it in the chilliest land,
And on the strangest sea;
Yet, never, in extremity,
It ask a crumb of me.

Notes	

Notes

DAY 66. *Today save water.* The battleground of the 21st century will be water supply. Due to global warming and demographic trends, huge swathes of Africa and Asia will find their water demand drastically overrun their supply. Inevitably this will result in migratory pressure towards the more temperate regions. Do your bit to prevent this by safeguarding water. Hold off going to the WC as far as physically possible (one flush per five people is enough). Don't shower or bathe quite so often: once a week is quite sufficient. And why water the lawn? Concrete is a much more contemporary look. Remember: water is life.

ONE-DAY DETOX

AIM: today, your goal is to try and expel some of the toxins that are building up and gradually poisoning your body. Only consume cleansing food and drink. By tonight, your internal organs will have begun to purge all the drugs, preservatives, additives and excess bile that you've been lugging around for years. This is the first step towards the new you!

WHAT TO EAT
»Nothing« is the short answer! Because we are following an intensive one-day-only program, an essentially liquid diet is necessary. But that doesn't mean you won't enjoy it! Start off with a yummy breakfast of lemon juice in warm water: go on, squeeze a whole lemon in there and treat yourself. (Citrus juice is a powerful bowel-purging agent.) Drink mineral water through the day, and again, don't stint on quantity, the more the better. For lunch, a treat: an apple to keep the doctor away, washed down with two cups of camomile tea. If you are feeling desperately hungry, you may eat a teaspoonful of sesame seeds towards 5pm, though strictly speaking you shouldn't! For dinner, a nice clear soup of hot water, flavored with some fennel. And before going to bed, a cup of peppermint tea, to aid the digestion.

POSSIBLE SIDE EFFECTS
As is often said, »no pain, no gain«! Your one-day detox may produce some »unwanted« side effects. Indeed, if it doesn't, you're probably doing something wrong. You may in fact wish to take the day off work before attempting it. Now, what should you expect? You will certainly experience headaches, starting before lunch. This is partly due to the brain's cravings for its usual stimulant, caffeine. As the day progresses, your tissues will also be eliminating noxious substances through the bloodstream, and thus through the brain, causing irritation. By lunchtime, you will feel weak, weak and hungry. This is no excuse to eat. Mid-afternoon, your detoxing skin may erupt in local rashes. As the day draws to a close, frequent urination, diarrhea and gas are often observed, along with negative, anti-social feelings. Bravo! Cherish these side effects, for they mean you have successfully completed the »one-day detox«!

NOTES

Well done! If you've followed this diet today, you will live longer by: (age x 4.5) – (weight/ maternal great-grand-mother's age at death) minutes!

Day 68: choose one hair on your body that you will let grow 1 yard long. Most hair grows at approximately half an inch a month, so within 8 years your chosen hair should be reaching optimum length. Remember to keep it clean, using shampoo and conditioner daily, and avoiding any tangling. Special note for pubic hair: tape it to your inside leg during sexual congress so as not to ruffle it.

Notes

You'll never get bored of your special hair. Here for instance, we've used ours to recreate the Mona Lisa, only better.

This advice comes to you courtesy of Shailesh Gor, accountant to the stars. Besides accountancy, Shailesh loves cricket and pizza, and is available for your downsizing needs for a reasonable fee. Contact him via www.thiswebsitewillchangeyourlife.com.

Day 69: Downsizing Day

In the current economic climate, we must all cut costs. Today fire someone from your entourage.

HAIRDRESSER?
-$10
Cut your own hair or get a handy friend to do it.

CLEANER?
-$30
Cleaners cost money and steal things. Plus it's good exercise for you.

BUTCHER?
-$9
Become a vegetarian, it's cheaper!

BROKER?
-$75
If they're any good, why haven't they retired rich by now?

BANKER?
-$50
Keep your money under your mattress, the new generation of thieves aren't trained to look there.

TRAINER?
-$25
With all that cleaning (see above), you won't need this one anymore.

PARTNER?
-$900
All that romantic tête-a-tête stuff costs a bomb. Ditch the bitch (or bastard).

CABLE GUY?
-$10
You watch too much TV.

DENTIST?
-$110
Original teeth are over-rated. There are very life-like prosthetics on the market these days.

LIBRARIAN?
-$2
Can you afford those whopping fines? Reread your old books.

GARDENER?
-$15
You'll learn to love gardening when you retire. Why not start now?

BODYGUARD?
-$870
No one's going to kidnap you if you're worth nothing.

OLD FRIENDS?
-$100
Old friends expect birthday gifts and other such luxuries you can ill afford. Lose'em.

PET?
-$25
Save money twice by not only downsizing your pet, but eating it (if is edible).

ACCOUNTANT?
-$15000
This one's a no-no. They know too much about you. Keep'em.

THERAPIST?
-$150
They also know too much about you, but nothing truly interesting. End it.

NOTES

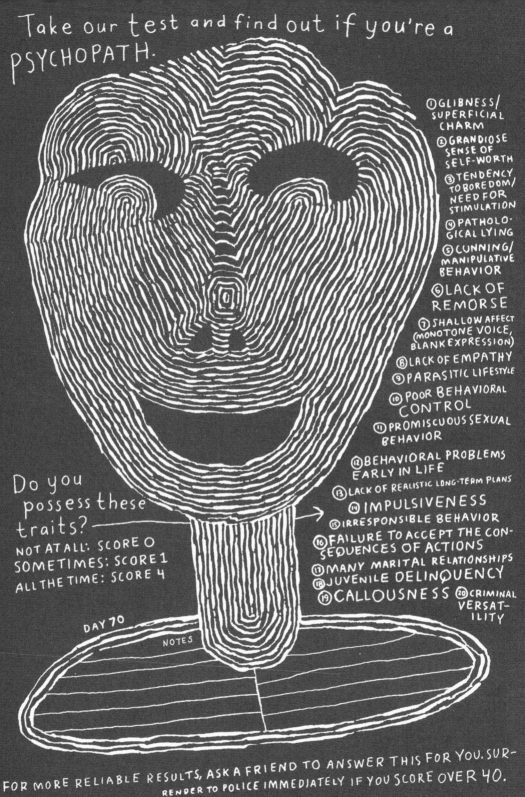

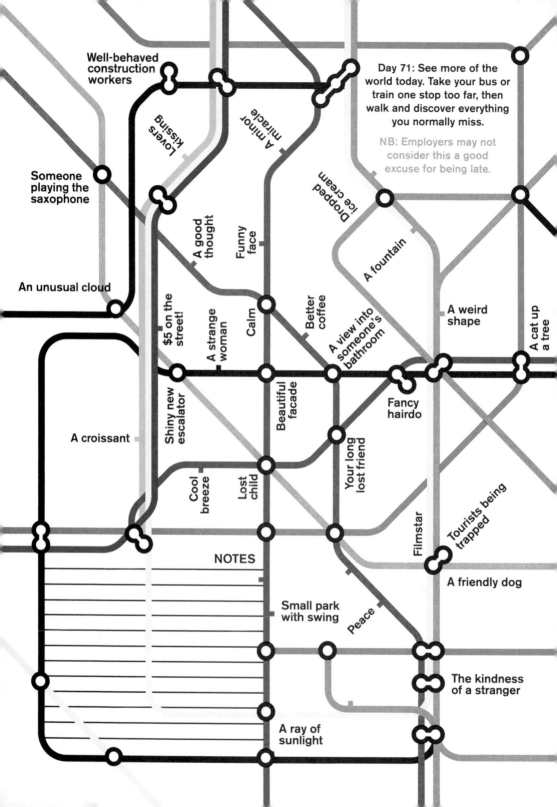

DAY 72   **Today is Closure Day**
We all form a strong attachment to our first toy. Today, call up
your kindergarten and ask them if they've found your rattle.
Explain that you lost it a good few years ago now, but only
recovered the memory of this last week. Emphasize how
important it is to your psychological health that they find it (if
necessary, send a letter from your psychiatrist).

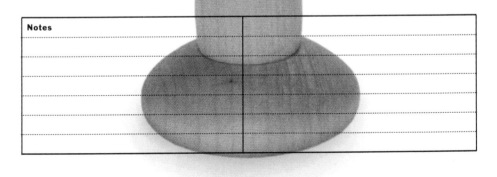

Notes

GET A HOBBY!

Today is the first day of your new hobby. Choose one or several of the following and look them up on the web for a comprehensive introduction to your new life-long passion.

Count other people's teeth.

Build a houseboat.

Teach dogs to stand on one leg.

Cultivate pimples around your mouth

Set out to see all films with Morgan Freeman.

Search for subliminal messages on heavy metal albums. Report your findings.

DAY 73

Notes	

Set fire to all brown shoes.

Topple a dictator using only the internet.

Attempt to make gold out of cotton and raisins.

Try to grow another toe.

Read the Bible in all languages.

Make the perfect tax return.

Record birds singing and edit into hit songs.

Drink one glass of every wine ever bottled.

Organize fires.

Try to forget everything you ever learnt in school.

Watch the moon complete its circle from new to full.

Invent a pair of sunglasses that see very small animals.

Play Russian roulette.

MACY

EXPRESS YOUR VIEWS TODAY
What do you want to say? Let us know today on
www.thiswebsitewillchangeyourlife.com.
The Book user with the most original views will
see them up in print by the end of the year.

NOTES

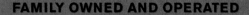

Gino's

ITALIAN
RESTAURANT

Where Mama Still Does The Cooking!

100% Family Owned and Operated!

AUTHENTIC ITALIAN CUISINE
& ITALIAN-STYLE SEAFOOD

Gino's Restaurant has been a staple of the Baton Rouge restaurant community for over 35 years. Gino's was established in 1966 by the Marino family, Vincent, »Mama,« Gino, Laurence and Frances. The Marino family originated in Agrigento, Sicily and first came to the USA in 1951. With the exception of Vincent, patriarch of the Marino family, who passed in 1970, Gino's remains 100% family owned and operated today.

Gino's originally was located on Perkins Road, and moved to its current beautiful facilities on Bennington in 1975. Gino's specializes in traditional southern Italian food, Mediterranean style, with fresh seafood and, of course, steaks.

At Gino's, our signature dish is Arancini, and our house specialties include Mama's Special Salad, Gino's Italian Salad and Laurence Bread. Gino's beautiful decor and Italian atmosphere lend to the romantic, and Gino's has always been a couples' favorite. Visit us and see our etched glass reminiscences of Italy,

fireplace, copper table tops and romantic candlelight. Complementing all this beauty is imported Italian music from our discreet sound system. On Gino's highly acclaimed Thursday Jazz Night, you can experience the best jazz in the area from local, national and international jazz artists.

Our wine cellar, stocked with over 300 wines, has been included in many »Best of« Lists and has won numerous awards over the years. Gino's Restaurant has won numerous awards over the years, being an almost perennial favorite in the Best Italian, Best Date and Most Romantic categories.

Our kitchen is supervised by our best, Mama... From day 1 she has been THE cook... »she comes with the furniture« says Gino. It is with great pride and great care that Mama cooks with and supervises the heavy use of true imported cheeses, anchovies, olive oils, tomato products, pasta and herbs. Visit us at Gino's soon... Where Mama does the cooking... We're looking forward to seeing you. Ciao!

Notes

Day 75. Today every Book owner is to reserve a table at Gino's for eight o'clock on the 4th of July next year. Phone number: (225)927-7156 Gino's. 4542 Bennington, Baton Rouge, Louisiana. Open 11 a.m.–2 p.m. and 5–10 p.m. Mon.–Fri.; 5–10:30 p.m. Sat. Closed Sun. MC, VISA, AE, DC, DISC. No checks.

DAY 76

Wear shoes that are one size too small. That way you will experience huge relief when you come home and take them off tonight.

There is no more certain tonic!

ROYAL

Make yourself a nice footbath to celebrate.

Females! Cures diseases of womankind too!

A boon to the temperament, indispensable in curing all manner of affliction, from softening of the brain to biliousness.

No Pain
↓
No Pleasure

HIGHLY UNUSUAL!

Pronounced a miracle remedy by many eminent doctors from the universities and elsewhere

NOTES

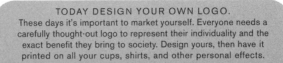

TODAY DESIGN YOUR OWN LOGO.
These days it's important to market yourself. Everyone needs a
carefully thought-out logo to represent their individuality and the
exact benefit they bring to society. Design yours, then have it
printed on all your cups, shirts, and other personal effects.

DAY 77

NOTES

In many respects Johann Sebastian Bach (1685-1750) did very well for himself, composing and performing many top classical music moments, as well as fathering an impressive twenty
children. But how much better could he have done with a logo? No one will ever know for certain, but here are some ideas he might have come up with if the logo had been invented then.

HOW POLITICALLY CORRECT IS YOUR CIRCLE OF FRIENDS?

Today work out if your friends represent the full tapestry of human cultural and ethnic variety. Take remedial action if not.

CHINESE ☐

CAUCASIAN ☐

HISPANIC/LATINO ☐

AFRICAN/☐
AFRICAN-
AMERICAN

PACIFIC ISLANDER ☐

INDIAN/ ☐
PAKISTANI

JAPANESE ☐

NATIVE ☐
AMERICAN

OTHER
ASIAN ☐

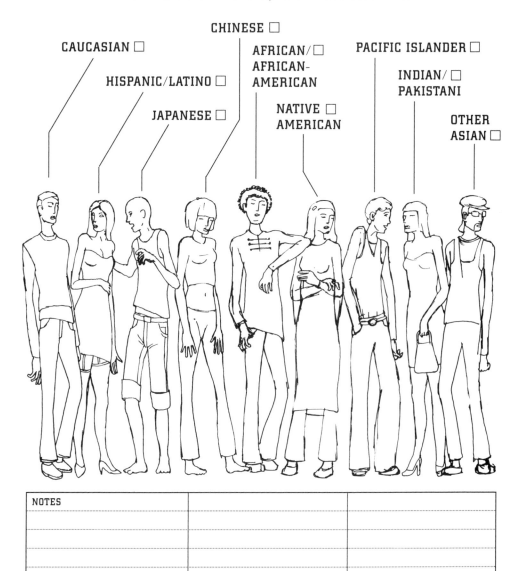

NOTES		

BECOME AN EXPERT ON TODAY

Read all the newspapers from A to Z and watch all the news bulletins so that by midnight tonight no one in the world knows more about the events of **DAY 79** than you. Here is a quick test to check your knowledge before you use it to attain unheard-of riches and power:

Weather in Zambia today:

Number of wars in progress today:

World population today:

Result of main sporting event today:

First topic on Jerry Springer today:

Middle East oil reserves today:

Number of astronauts in space today:

Lottery results in Colorado today:

Percentage of faked orgasms today:

Time spent waiting for phones to be picked up:

Moon-Earth distance at midday:

Horoscope of Leos with Scorpio ascendants:

Number of birthdays worldwide:

Notes

Congratulations: you are now the world's leading expert on today's news. Tomorrow morning be sure to get a business card printed and send it to everyone you know.

Day 80

TODAY START TO EAT A
PIECE OF FURNITURE
*You will need: A piece of wooden furniture
(wardrobe, bookshelf, table, chair), a nail file.*
Shave off a small amount of wood from
your piece of furniture. Sprinkle it on
your lunch. Enjoy! Persevere every day,
and you should be able to eat the entire
piece of furniture within 20 years.

NOTES		

DAY 82

Sit in the lotus position for 30 minutes today
Lotus Position (Padmasana) Sit on the floor with spine erect and legs stretched out in front of you, slightly apart. Place right foot on left thigh with the sole of foot turned up. Rest right knee on the ground. Take left foot and place it high on right thigh with sole facing up and left knee resting on the ground. Let feet rest on the pressure points at the top of the groin.

NOTES

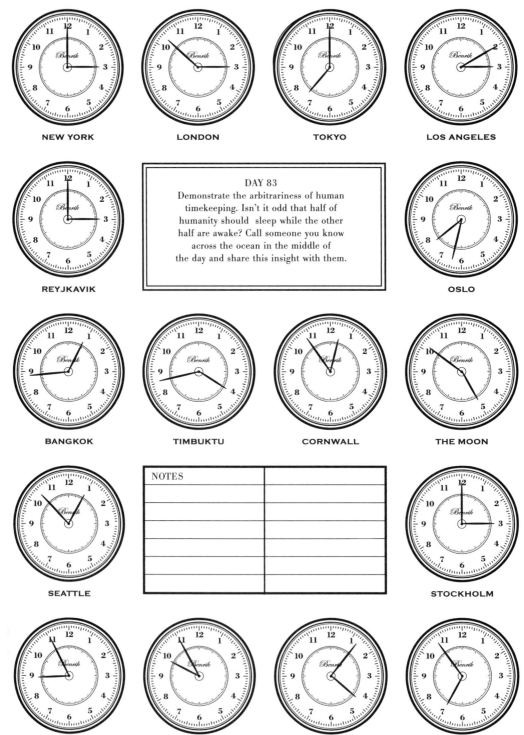

NEW YORK

LONDON

TOKYO

LOS ANGELES

REYJKAVIK

DAY 83
Demonstrate the arbitrariness of human
timekeeping. Isn't it odd that half of
humanity should sleep while the other
half are awake? Call someone you know
across the ocean in the middle of
the day and share this insight with them.

OSLO

BANGKOK

TIMBUKTU

CORNWALL

THE MOON

SEATTLE

NOTES

STOCKHOLM

WASHINGTON

ALASKA

PEKING

MOSCOW

Day 84. Today throw away an apple core in a park. Mark the spot well, and come back in 20 years' time to see your apple tree.

Is your apple tree lonely? Every apple tree needs another apple tree to cross-pollinate. Otherwise it will bear beautiful flowers, but will be barren of fruit... So ensure that you plant your tree near another (alternatively simply throw away two apple cores).

Notes

DAY 85:
TODAY RELEASE
A RED BALLOON

Look! There it goes, soaring into the blue skies, a tiny beacon of friendship and hope, up, up, up and away, scattering the sparrows, inspiring the eagles, and perhaps eventually causing a major commercial airliner disaster.

NOTES

TODAY: GO TO THE WRONG SIDE OF THE TRACKS

DAY 86

Is there a road near where you live where you fear to venture after dark? Where you feel perhaps less than welcome? Where you sense feral eyes following your every move from behind closed curtains? Today step down that road and conquer your fear of the unfamiliar.

Sportmaster

Notes

Rural readers: today go to the wrong side of the electric fence.

JUST TESTING
.--- ..- ... - / - . ... - .. -. --.

GOOD EVENING
--. --- --- -.. / . ...- . -. .. -. --.

SORRY TO DISTURB YOU
... --- .-. .-. -.-- / - --- / -.. .. ... - ..- .-. -... / -.-- --- ..-

I'M FEELING LONELY
.. .----. -- / ..-. . . .-.. .. -. --. / .-.. --- -. . .-.. -.--

AND RANDY
.- -. -.. / .-. .- -. -.. -.--

FANCY SOME FUN?
..-. .- -. -.-. -.-- / ... --- -- . / ..-. ..- -. ..--..

ONLY KIDDING
--- -. .-.. -.-- / -.- .. -.. -.. .. -. --.

IS THAT A RIFLE?
.. ... / - .... .- - / .- / .-. .. ..-. .-.. . ..--..

AAARRGGH
.- .- .- .-. .-. --. --. ....

SOS
...---...

Notes	

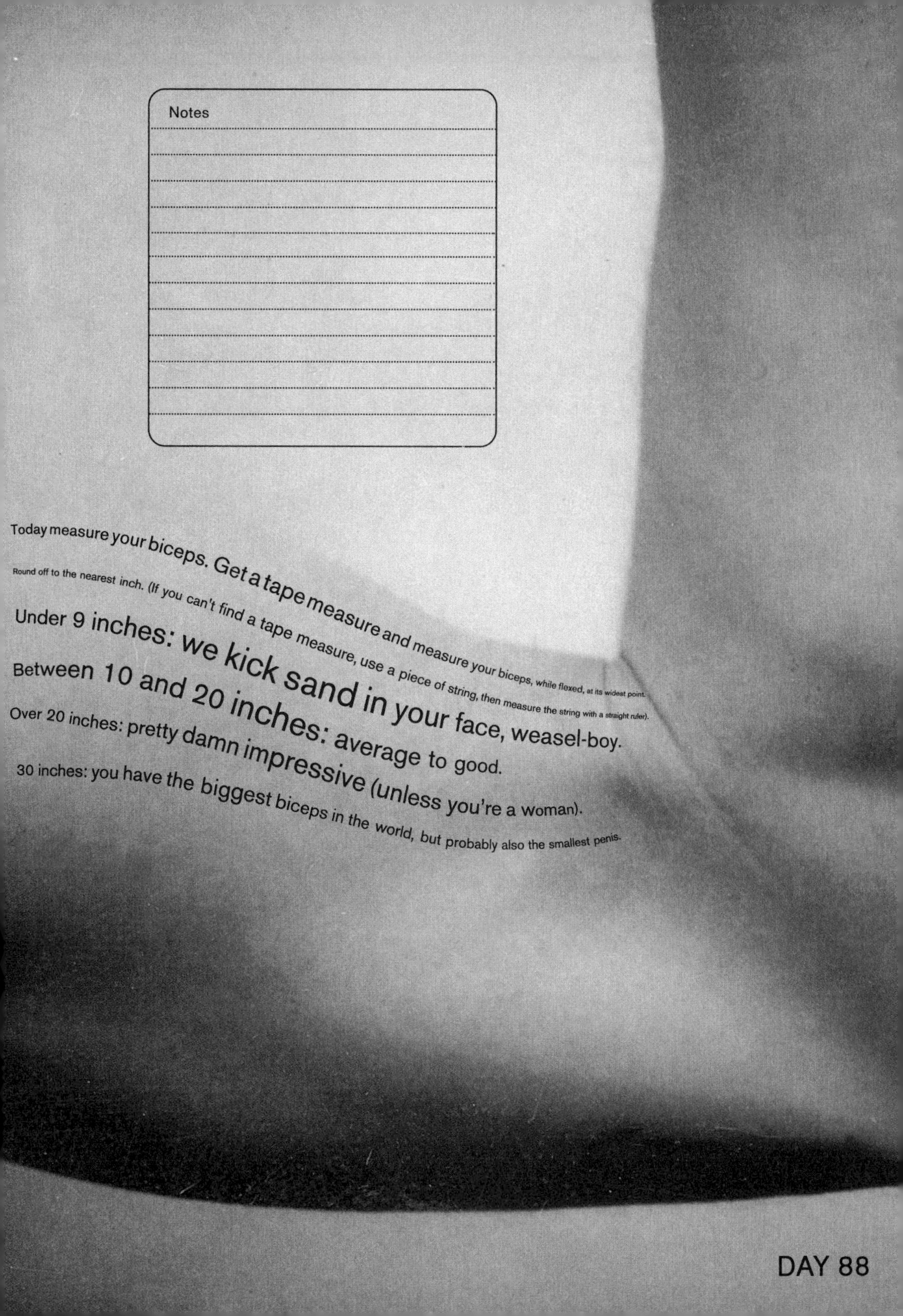

Notes

_____
_____
_____
_____
_____
_____
_____
_____
_____
_____
_____
_____

Today measure your biceps. Get a tape measure and measure your biceps, while flexed, at its widest point.

Round off to the nearest inch. (If you can't find a tape measure, use a piece of string, then measure the string with a straight ruler).

Under 9 inches: we kick sand in your face, weasel-boy.

Between 10 and 20 inches: average to good.

Over 20 inches: pretty damn impressive (unless you're a woman).

30 inches: you have the biggest biceps in the world, but probably also the smallest penis.

DAY 88

Day 90
Today help collapse a currency!

The Bangladeshi Taka is currently under pressure at 58tk to the US dollar. If every Book owner buys 100 takas this year and then sells them on December 31 at 4.55pm Bangladeshi time, the Taka won't be worth the paper it's printed on. To participate, simply call the DFE, Dhaka Foreign Exchange with your credit card details on: (88 02) 9667712-3.

DON'T WORRY! The IMF and the World Bank will step in to restore financial and economic stability. In the process, they'll probably get rid of a couple of unnecessary social programs as well, so you'll be doing Bangladesh a good turn.

Notes	

Day 91. Today invent a new way of peeling potatoes.

No one is happy with the current situation. That's why potato peeling is the province of the jailbird or the disgruntled housewife. Think laterally – perhaps peeling isn't the real problem here… Anyhow: come up with a novel solution and your fortune is assured!

Notes	

Write your will here

Too many people leave their will until literally the last moment.
As a result, greedy relatives end up filing lawsuits and lawyers
fill their pockets. Spare your loved ones this fate by using this
readymade form to apportion your worldly goods.

I, ... (name), being of sound body
and mind, do declare this my last will and testament.

Possessions	Beneficiaries
Car	Husband
CD collection	Wife
Hat	Child no.1
House	Child no.2
Garden	Child no.3
Truck	Child no.4
Food in my fridge	Favourite child
Food in my freezer	Ugly child
Socks	Illegitimate child
Makeup	Unborn child
Cat	Adopted child
Favorite sweater	Mistress
Secret life savings	Lover
Giant dildo	Mother
Priceless works of art	Father
Pencil	Maternal Grandmother
Children	Paternal Grandmother
Aerobics videotape	Maternal Grandfather
Hoard of pubic hair	Uncle
Space shuttle	Aunt
Knickknacks	Weird »bachelor« Uncle
Old bit of string	Kindly Aunt
Yo-yo	Best friend
TV set	Casual acquaintance
Cafetiere	Sworn enemy
Last poo	Charity of choice
Nobel Peace Prize	Homeless
Huge debts	Orphans
Bed bugs	Bill Gates
Other	Other

Dated:..

Signature:..

Witnessed by: ....

notes

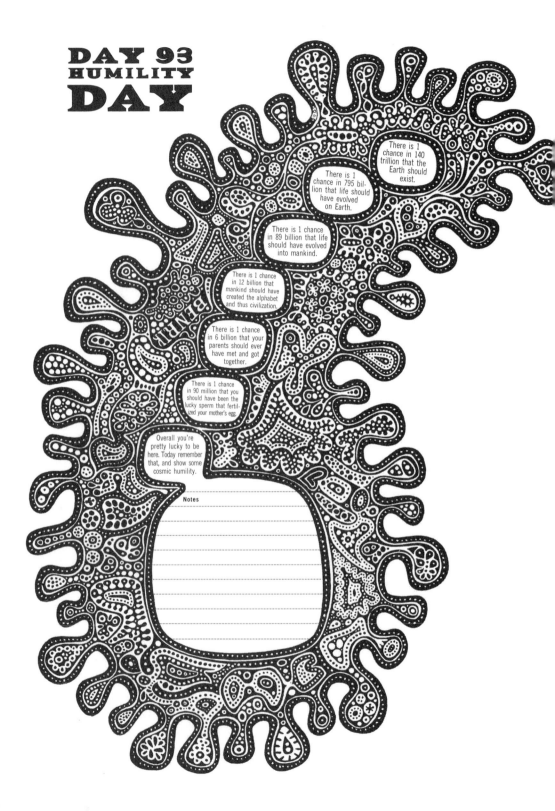

DAY 94

TODAY AVOID ALL SOURCES OF ELECTROMAGNETIC ENERGY
Clinical studies have conclusively established that continued exposure to man-made electromagnetic energy is associated with higher mortality and morbidity rates in the exposed population. Epidemiological studies have also demonstrated links to cancer and suicide.

STAY AWAY FROM:
High voltage powerlines
(2-200 Milligauss)

STAY AWAY FROM:
Cell Phone Base stations
(2-60 Milligauss)

STAY AWAY FROM:
Microwave ovens
(2-50 Milligauss)

STAY AWAY FROM:
Electric blankets
(5-30 Milligauss)

STAY AWAY FROM:
Radio/TV towers
(2-20 Milligauss)

STAY AWAY FROM:
Pacemakers
(10-5000 Milligauss)

Notes

BUY!!!

The Zen-o-tron.The Zen-o-tron protects against electromagnetic radiation (including earth, solar and lunar radiation at no extra cost) by reinforcing your inner zen-attuned harmony levels. It is recommended by many men of repute in communities across the globe. It harnesses the power of your own good good vibrations to defeat the disharmonious electromagnetic vibes. Wear it around your neck. Send a check for $19.99 (plus postage and packing) to Zen Laboratories, Fresno, California, PO Box 2334-67.

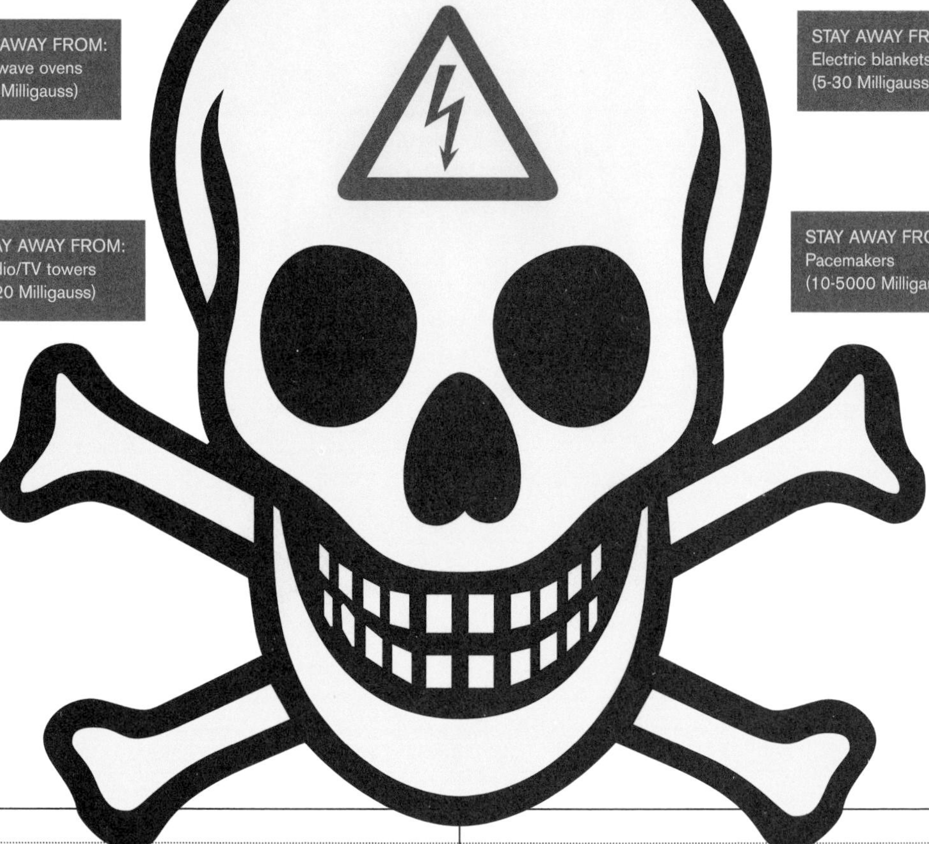

Only a complete booby would deny that extraterrestrial visitors are here already, and here to stay, despite government lies to the contrary. Many have taken human shape, all the better to study us. Today, learn how to spot them.

Dead Eyes

The alien has glazed expressionless eyes. This is because these are only a front for his extrasensory perceptual apparatus.

Closed Mouth

Think about it. The aliens don't need to speak, as they communicate telepathetically. When they do speak to genuine humans, their speech is stilted, like they are stoned or something.

Ears Oozing Green Goo

Sometimes green goo will escape through the ears, if the alien cannot keep its head straight. This is a clear sign that something is seriously amiss.

Flaring nostrils

Nostrils are the only facial openings the aliens truly find useful. They use them to move from one human body to another. If a suspected alien comes near you with flaring nostrils, run for your life.

What to do if you find an alien

Try not to let on that you're onto the alien, as they can read your thoughts. Think of something innocuous instead, like a nice summer picnic for instance. Then quickly kill the alien by beheading it with a big axe, and burn the body. Report the incident to your local police station.

Notes

What are the alien intentions? The latest theory is that the aliens are waiting for the Rapture of the Church, when it happens. They will attempt to pass off the Day of the return of Jesus Christ Our Lord as some kind of mass abduction, or to say they took us somewhere to save us from something (God's wrath). We'll soon see anyway.

STOCKPILE AS MUCH FREE SUGAR AS POSSIBLE IN ONE DAY

Crazy but true: lots of people give out their hard-earned sugar entirely free such as in cafés, restaurants, the workplace kitchen, and so on. A person who collected it all and resold it at street value could make a small fortune. And that could be you!

COMMON SUGAR FORMATS

SUGAR IS FREE!

WHITE ANGLED LUMP	WHITE CUBIC LUMP	BROWN ANGLED LUMP
BROWN CUBIC LUMP	"HOMEMADE" LUMP	WHITE POWDER

NOTES

BROWN POWDER	WHITE SUGAR SACHET	BROWN SUGAR SACHET

DAY 97 IN DA HOUSE: TODAY RAP!

WHEN YOU FEEL DOWN AND OUT A GOOD WAY TO SNAP OUT OF IT IS TO RAP A LITTLE ABOUT ALL YOUR HARDSHIPS. HERE ARE SOME LYRICS TO GET YOU STARTED AND GIVE YOU A FEEL FOR THE GENRE:

MY NAME IS CHUCK
I MAKE MY OWN LUCK
EVERYONE ELSE THEY SUCK
COS HEY!
I DON'T GIVE A *****

(UNSIGNED ARTISTS: WHEN YOU ARE UP TO SCRATCH, SEND YOUR DEMO TO DEATH ROW RECORDS, PO BOX 3037, BEVERLY HILLS, CA 90212)

No swea-ring day

Send us one dollar for every swear word that escapes your uncouth lips

The following are no longer considered effective swear words: **Darn Heck Shucks! Crud Doggone Nuts Dang Gadzooks Phooey**

Day 98

Notes:

TODAY EXPERIENCE CHRIST'S PLIGHT FOR YOURSELF WITH OUR DIY CRUCIFIXION KIT.

1. THIS IS WHAT YOU NEED:

2. CUT OUT AS FOLLOWS:

3. GLUE THE TWO PIECES TOGETHER:

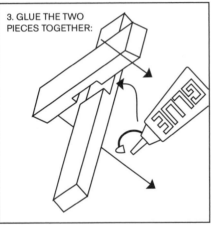

4. TAPE YOUR HANDS TO YOUR CROSS:

(IT COULD BE HELPFUL TO ASK FOR ASSISTANCE.)

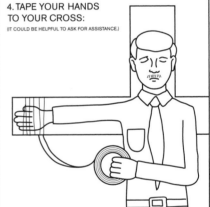

5. SUFFER!

Notes

....
....
....
....
....
....
....
....
....
....
....
....
....
....
....

COUNTERFEITING DAY
1. Cut this fake banknote out
2. Stick A & B back-to-back
3. Crumple it up a few times
4. Convince someone to accept it as legal tender

A.

B.

DAY 100

NOTES	

Today become a chocolate junkie

Chocolate is the only legal psychoactive drug, a veritable cocktail of mind-interfering chemicals. It's a unique source of theobromine, an addictive xanthine alkaloid. It contains anandamide, which binds to the same receptors in the brain as the psychoactive elements in marijuana (cannabinoids). And it boosts levels of serotonin in the brain, much as anti-depressants do.

Now: mild doses of serotonin act as a sedative on the brain, but higher doses can cause an addictive high followed by crash followed by craving response. You're looking at a good 25lbs to get high, which may seem a lot, but is actually much better value than illegal drugs, and won't get you in trouble with the law. So get munching!

The confection of perfection!

Danger! Chocolate is good for you, but not for your pet. Cats and dogs can't metabolize or excrete the theobromine in chocolate and may end up having a seizure as a result. If you suspect your pet has eaten chocolate in any form, call a vet immediately.

Notes	Day 101	

Day 102: This is the first day since you have started using this Book that your cash isn't going to the government. Each year the Adam Smith Institute calculates the Tax Freedom Day: the day on which you have earned enough to pay all your taxes and can start to work for yourself. As taxes stand at 29% of GDP, for 102 days of the year, you are working purely for the taxman. Write and complain to Him for this gross imposition on your time and liberty.

NOTES

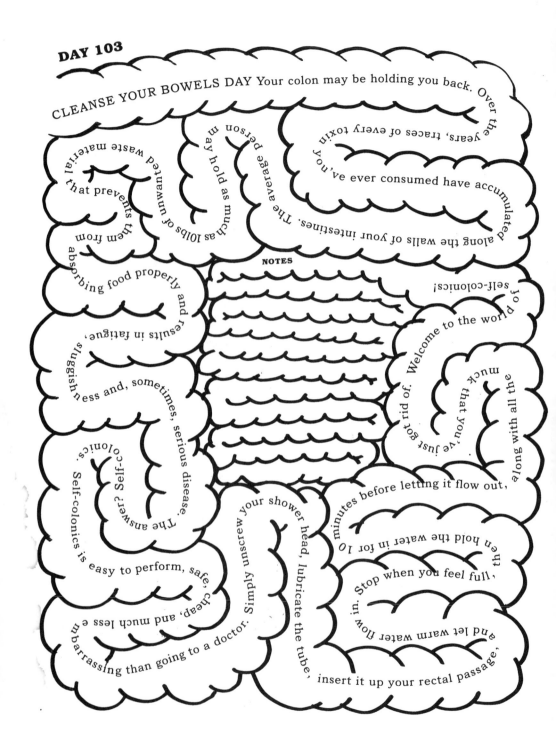

DAY 103

CLEANSE YOUR BOWELS DAY Your colon may be holding you back. Over the years, traces of every toxin you've ever consumed have accumulated along the walls of your intestines. The average person may hold as much as 10lbs of unwanted waste material that prevents them from absorbing food properly and results in fatigue, sluggishness and, sometimes, serious disease. The answer? Self-colonics. Self-colonics is easy to perform, safe, cheap, and much less embarrassing than going to a doctor. Simply unscrew your shower head, lubricate the tube, insert it up your rectal passage, and let warm water flow in. Stop when you feel full, then hold the water in for 10 minutes before letting it flow out, along with all the muck that you've just got rid of. Welcome to the world of self-colonics!

NOTES

Various Relatives Day!

The Book has decided
to combine all Mother's, Father's,
Grandparents' and any other Relatives' Days
into one glorious all-purpose celebratory Day.
These days are not genuine national events anyway but
were invented for commercial purposes. Today, send cards to
all your relatives and get it all over and done with for the year.

Day 104

Notes

Suggested Inscriptions: Dear Mother, thank you for bringing me into this world and for your unconditional love. Dear Father, thank you for conceiving me and supporting me all those years. Dear Grandad and Grandma, thank you for being in the background thus creating a sense of security throughout my childhood. Dear Aunt, I don't know you much but thanks anyhow. Dear Uncle, the bond between us is silent but strong. Dear Cousin, let's get married and freak everyone out. Dear Distant Relative, good luck with it all.

TODAY LIE TO SOMEONE ABOUT YOUR PAST

There are four main types of lie about one's past, all designed to enhance one's reputation: *1. White lies:* My first word was »symposium.« *2. Blatant lies:* I'm descended through my mother's side from Attila the Hun. *3. Lies no one can check:* I used to work for the CIA, but the paperwork was too stifling. *4. Lies no one wants to check:* They really bungled my sex change operation.

DAY 105

Notes

Today surf internet chat rooms and make friends with someone on the other side of the world. Eventually you could gain a new best chum, an invitation to visit a distant land, and a better understanding of what makes us all human. Alternatively, you might befriend some nutter who will turn up on your doorstep with a pickaxe. Anyway here's where to begin.

DAY 107
NOTES

towerchat.com
thepalace.com
parachat.com
bbackdoors.com
a1chat-rooms.com
excite.com
chatbox.com
worlds.net
looksmart.com
yahoo.com
theglobe.com
talkcity.com
classmates.com
babylon.com
hearme.com
topica.com
network54.com
travlang.com
mirc.com
tucows.com
inreach.com
crossdaily.com

chathouse.com
peoplelink.com
teenchat.com
absolutechat.com
800predict.com
freerepublic.com
thegrid.net
smartbotpro.net
icqgreetings.com
undernet.org
chatway.com
christiancafe.com
the-park.com
4-lane.com
activeworlds.com
developer.com
irchelp.org
netdive.com
cuseemeworld.com
arabchat.com
cuseeme.com
tribal.com

chattopia.com
chatseek.com
chat.fashion.net
austnet.org
hyperchat.com
chatweb.net
chattown.com
knowpost.com
chatlist.com
quilttalk.com
pirch.com
coolchat.com
peopleweb.com
go.com
chatfreak.com
sixdegrees.com
rememory.com
veggiedate.com
xworld.org
hotelchat.com
webchatting.com
thepark.com

today graffiti

SPRAY

Your name/your thoughts/your dreams, though you must make sure they are completely illegible.

what?

Anywhere, so long as it violates someone's property rights or makes a public space ugly.

where?

HOW? Hold the can at an 80° angle, and spray at high speed, both to get that rough and ready street look, and to get the hell away before you're spotted.

Multicolored spray cans are traditional, but beginners may use chalk.

materials:

Notes

RIGHT

Notes		Has your day been lucky or unlucky?
		LUCKY ☐
		UNLUCKY ☐

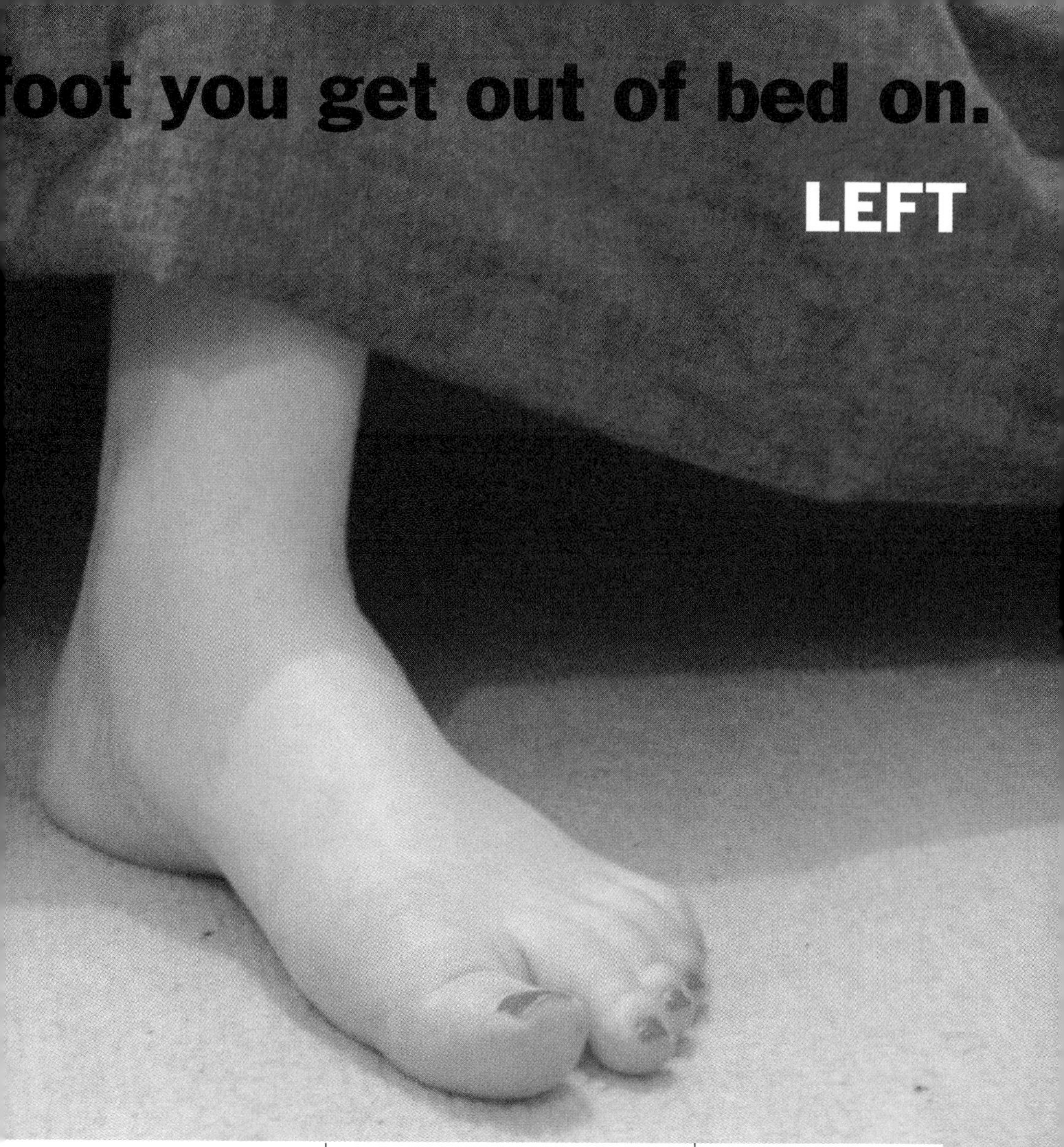

foot you get out of bed on.

LEFT

Notes

Has your day
been lucky or
unlucky?

LUCKY ☐

UNLUCKY ☐

there a difference? Which works best for you? LEFT ☐ RIGHT ☐
m now on, only ever get out of bed on your lucky foot.

DAY 111
TREAT'EM MEAN KEEP'EM KEEN

Test this relationship theory today on your significant other.

NOTES

•Tell them you'll call and don't. •Turn up half an hour late for a rendezvous. •When they say »I love you,« just answer »thanks.« •Accidentally call them by the name of your ex. •Pick the part of their body they're most sensitive about and gaze at it cryptically. •Suddenly laugh out loud during intercourse.

How to measure success: Have you managed to inject a welcome frisson into your stale relationship? Or have they packed their bags and advised you to seek psychiatric help? Relationship guru Dr Kirk Frampton says: »you can't turn a humdrum suburban relationship into a Hollywood romance overnight. You need to keep your loved one on his or her toes constantly. Only six months down the line would I normally expect to see results, one way or another.«

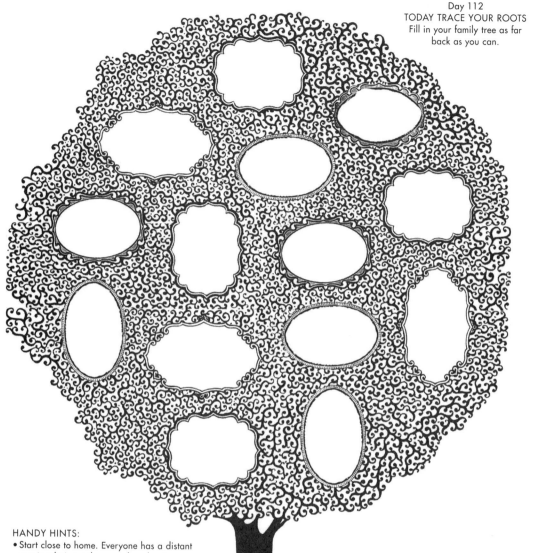

Day 112
TODAY TRACE YOUR ROOTS
Fill in your family tree as far
back as you can.

HANDY HINTS:
• Start close to home. Everyone has a distant
  cousin who's got the genealogy bug!
• Interview elderly relatives. Give Aunt Mae
  a call before she passes on and grill her.
• Check out census/land/probate records;
  boy, you're getting keen now.

WHAT TO DO IF YOU FIND OUT YOU'RE DESCENDED FROM THE KING
All depends on whether you're legitimate or illegitimate. If you're legitimate (»legit«),
call up your government and make them aware of your claim. They have 21 days to
respond, upon which you may ascend the throne. If you are illegitimate
(»bastard«), you run the risk of being sent to the Tower where you will spend the rest
of your life hung up against a mossy wall with rats chewing away at your genitalia.

Notes

F

DAY 113. Today see a film beginning with F. If there is none on in your neighborhood, you may see one beginning with Z.

NOTES		

Day 114
Today: tattoo a banana and display it on your windowsill. (Scrape its skin with a sharp implement and watch it go black in minutes!)

Notes

DAY 115
Today use this exclusive pass
to violate a law of your choice.

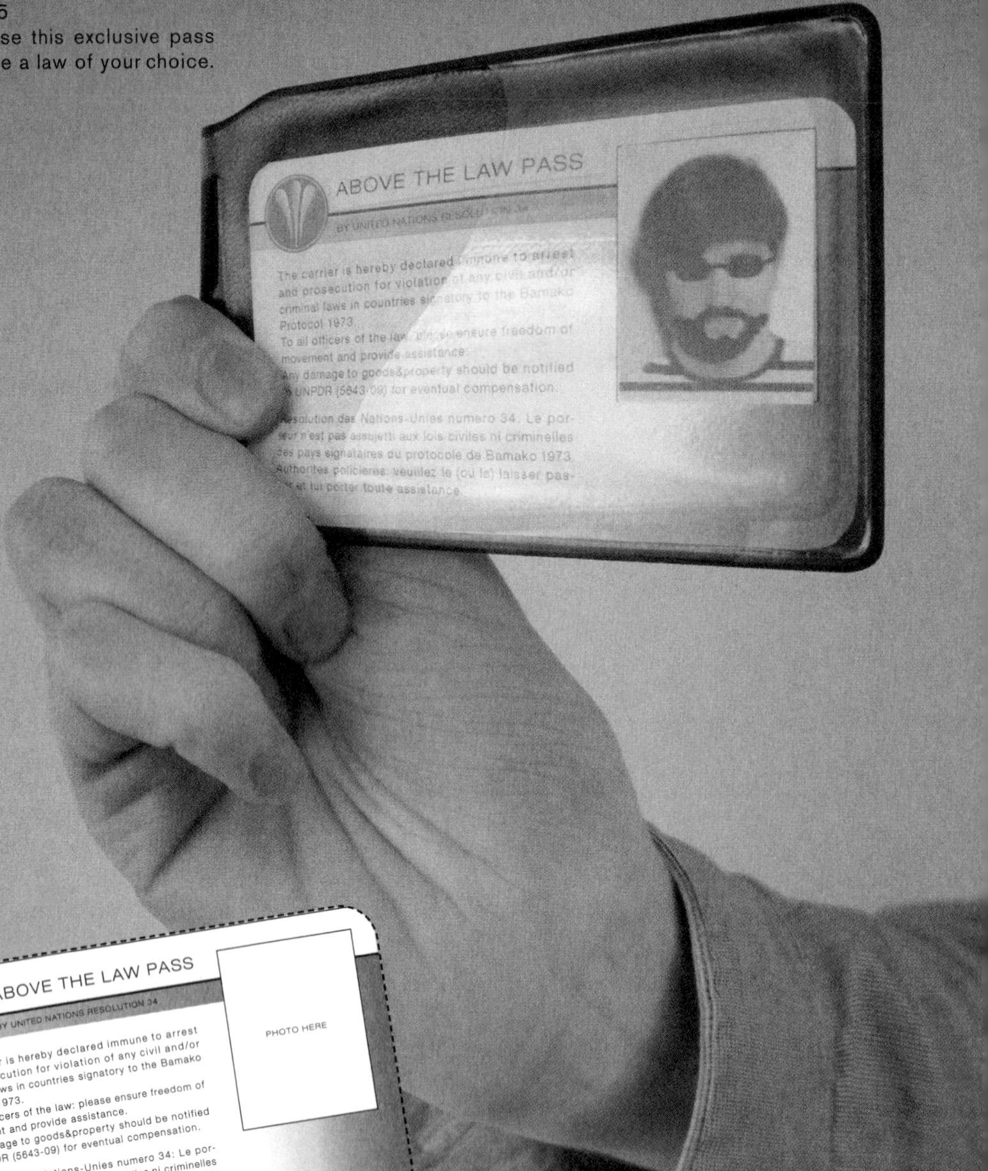

ABOVE THE LAW PASS

BY UNITED NATIONS RESOLUTION 34

The carrier is hereby declared immune to arrest
and prosecution for violation of any civil and/or
criminal laws in countries signatory to the Bamako
Protocol 1973.
To all officers of the law: please ensure freedom of
movement and provide assistance.
Any damage to goods&property should be notified
to UNPDR (5643-09) for eventual compensation.

Resolution des Nations-Unies numero 34: Le por-
teur n'est pas assujetti aux lois civiles ni criminelles
des pays signataires du protocole de Bamako 1973.
Authorites policieres: veuillez le (ou la) laisser pas-
ser et lui porter toute assistance.

PHOTO HERE

NOTES

HI! I am currently experimenting with the concept of siesta. Therefore any issues, no matter how important, will have to wait to be brought before me between the hours of 11am and 3pm. If I like this I will start doing it every day. PS: A light lunch would be great when I wake up.

Today place this sign on your door handle.

ATTENTION! Forward planning: Book your vacation now for the week of Day 205. This year, you are going to France. Mais oui!

Me day: Today is all about me, myself and I, looking after number one, and sticking up for oneself. Be selfish. Don't give up your seat to the little old lady. Eat the last cookie. Park in the disabled space. Play with your kid's favorite toys. Shout out your own name during sex.

NOTES

SNOOPER ALERT!

Dear..

I know you are snooping in my Book, you have had guilt written all over your stupid face for the last few weeks, this is what I think of you if you really must know:

....

....

....

....

....

....

....

DAY 118		
NOTES		

Now get your nose out of it and mind your own sorry business in the future.

How to: Wax ear plugs, available at any drugstore.

True story: Beethoven's descent into deafness is part and parcel of his myth. Less well-known is the extent to which his other senses overcompensated. At a rehearsal of one of his later quartets in 1825, lead violinist Joseph Bohm took it upon himself to ignore a change in tempo (Meno vivace) without telling Beethoven, who by now was pretty thoroughly deaf. Bohm related what happened: »Beethoven, crouched in a corner, heard nothing, but watched with strained attention. After the last stroke of the bows, he said laconically, ›Let it remain so,‹ went to the desks and crossed out the Meno vivace in the four parts.«

Notes

Write down the pros and cons of this sense as you discover them.

Pros: ....

Cons: ....

End of day assessment: How crucial is my sense of hearing to me ..../10

DON'T SPEND
ANY MONEY DAY

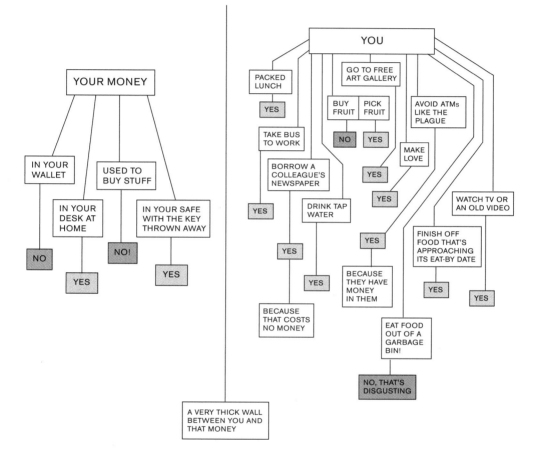

	NOTES		

NO TV W

The publishers of the Book have arranged a deal with news organizations and world leaders whereby nothing of real importance will happen this weekend, so you can feel at ease giving your remote a break. Instead, here are some pre-TV era activities that will feel a lot more wholesome.

WALKING
Walking is a fun activity that can be enjoyed at any age, and what's more, it's free! You can walk on your own or with someone, in the street or in the park. The possibilities are endless.

WHISTLING
The great advantage of whistling is that it can be done anywhere, even while you work, as the song goes. Everyone likes a good tune, so brighten up their day as well.

CHATTING BY THE FIRE
Everyone loves a good fire. »Round the fire« is a traditional place to chat, as everyone is gathered together. Starter topics include how well the fire is going, size of logs, how cold it must be outside.

SKIPPING
Beloved by schoolgirls and boxers alike, so there must be something to it. You'll need a rope and a bit of practice, but once you get the hang of it, there's no turning back!

PLAYING GAMES
There are literally dozens of games, from chess to hide-and-seek. Some of these are more advanced than others, so if you're new to games, start with something easy, like popular card game SNAP.

KNITTING
One for the ladies: knitting sweaters, socks and hats is one of the most stress-relieving activities imaginable, and it's a useful skill to acquire in times of economic uncertainty.

BIRDWATCHING
Fun AND educational. The National Parks are rich in birdlife. Look out for the yellow-tailed sparrow for instance, so named after his yellow-colored tail. To make the most of this one, binoculars are a must.

READING
You're doing this as we speak, so you must know the basics. Hundreds of books on all sorts of topics await your perusal. Join your local library and the world of reading is your oyster.

CROQUET
Not just for elderly aunts! The British game of croquet is in fact a vicious sport where the most amiable-seeming individuals soon battle it out for supremacy. »Uncle Jo« Stalin's favorite pastime.

WRESTLING
Not as difficult as it's made out to be, though you will need a partner. Grapple each other and try to push the other one to the ground. Hours of entertainment guaranteed.

STARING AT THE CLOUDS
Anyone can enjoy this: all you need is a patch of sky... Clouds can assume many familiar shapes: cows, faces, goldfish, wheelbarrows. Names of clouds are fun too: »cumulo-nimbus,« for instance.

CHURCHGOING (SUNDAY)
After a wrestling bout early on Sunday, why not settle body, mind and spirit with some church? Churchgoing has a long and proud history. This one has it all: singing, thinking, clapping.

EEKEND!

You'll need two full days of calm to follow this, so pick the nearest weekend.

y 121	Day 122
otes	Notes

ACUTE APPENDICITIS

Symptoms: pain in the lower right abdomen, nausea, loss of appetite, vomiting

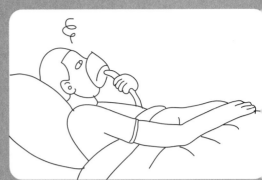

PROCEDURE: 1. Anaesthesize the patient

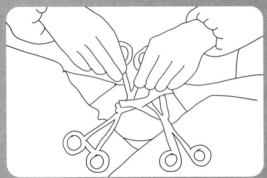

2. Make an incision in the lower right abdomen

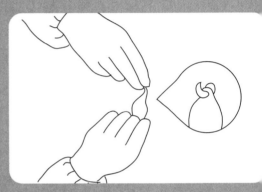

3. Pull appendix out and tie it at its base

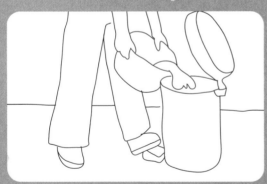

4. Remove appendix (taking care to avoid spillage)

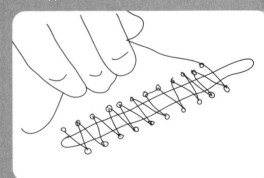

5. Suture the incision

OPEN APPENDECTOMY COMPLICATIONS: if the appendix has ruptured, clean out with a warm saline solution, insert drain through incision to allow pus to drain out of abdomen, leave skin open but pack with sterile gauze and leave in place until pus is drained and there is no sign of infection. If abdomen is too infected to locate appendix, treat with antibiotics before removing. Do not attempt this procedure unless you are a qualified surgeon, and even then think twice about it.

Notes

Notes

YOUR STARS TODAY:
For once, take your horoscope seriously. To help, we've had this one designed scientifically, by the world's leading expert. Follow it to the letter.

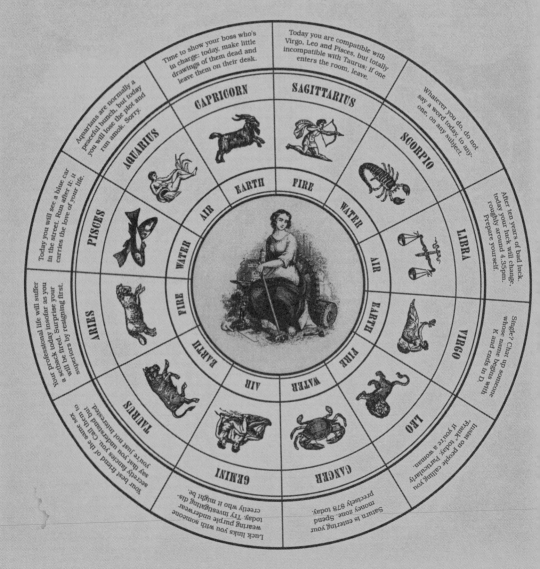

Time to show your boss who's in charge; today, make little drawings of them dead and leave them on their desk.

Today you are compatible with Virgo, Leo and Pisces, but totally incompatible with Taurus; if one enters the room, leave.

Aquarians are normally a peaceful bunch, but today you will lose the plot and run amok. Sorry.

Whatever you do, do not say a word today, to anyone, on any subject.

Today you will see a blue car in the street. Run after it: it carries the love of your life.

After ten years of bad luck, today your luck will change, roughly around 4.35pm. Prepare yourself.

Your professional life will suffer insofar as you wearing purple underwear today. Surprise your superiors by resigning first.

Single? Chat up someone whose name begins with K and ends in D.

Your best friend of the same sex secretly fancies you. Call them to say that you understand, but you're just not interested.

Insist on people calling you 'Frank' today. Particularly if you're a woman.

Luck links you with someone wearing purple underwear today. Try investigating discreetly who it might be.

Saturn is entering your money zone. Spend precisely 878 today.

CAPRICORN

SAGITTARIUS

AQUARIUS

SCORPIO

PISCES

LIBRA

ARIES

VIRGO

TAURUS

LEO

GEMINI

CANCER

EARTH FIRE

AIR WATER

WATER AIR

FIRE EARTH

EARTH FIRE

AIR WATER

Day 126

Today exercise your full rights as a consumer.

You are legally entitled to buy a lot of prepackaged material by the unit.

Buy one beer out of a six-pack. Buy two cookies out of a packet of 20.

Buy five pistachios, a dollop of face cream, or one sock,

and experiment with shopkeepers' knowledge of the law.

Notes

Lay-offs (draft)
Cc: McFadden Bartle & Hill legal
Circulate management.

Andy
Tom B.
Sarah ?
P. W.

Anyone else?

Notes

Notes

Try a new fruit today

Day 129: Count your blessings

In the great hubbub of life, we often forget to pause and consider how lucky we are. Today, assess this scientifically.

Blessing	Score	Total
Are you alive?	10 points	
Are you in good health?	9 points	
Do you have a partner?	7 points	
Do you have regular sex?	6 points	
Do you have children?	3 points/child (-3 POINTS PER NAUGHTY CHILD)	
Do you have a roof over your head?	5 points	
Can you feed yourself and your family?	5 points	
Do you have a steady job?	3 points	
Are you free from racial or sexual discrimination?	5 points	
Is your country currently at peace?	6 points	
Is your country well away from any geological fault lines?	6 points	
Are your parents still alive?	4 points	
Are you still on speaking terms with them?	4 points	
Have you found God?	3 points	
Have you found yourself?	2 points	
Are your bowel movements regular?	8 points	
Were you born into one of the richer social classes?	5 points	
Are you a born optimist?	6 points	
Are you a born pessimist?	−6 points	
Do you have a sense of humor?	(+1 points if you replied yes +4 points if you replied no)	
Total		

If you have scored more than *40* points, you are luckier than 90% of the human race.	
CONGRATULATIONS.	

Notes		

Today write a letter to your local newspaper to achieve a high profile in your community. Before you know it, you'll be the spokesperson for a local campaign. You could be elected mayor on the back of a wave of popular support, and next step it's the White House. US President Dwight Eisenhower started off in politics by complaining in the *Des Moines Digest* that corncobs were just too darned pricey these days. Popular inflammatory topics: Dog poo everywhere, Broken pavement, Pesky kids, Garbage men never pick up boxes, Town Hall corrupt.

LOCAL NEWS

THE MODEL CITIZEN!!!

MAYOR CONGRATULATES HAVE-A-GO HERO

KEYS OF THE CITY ARE ONLY MODEST TOKEN OF APPRE- CIATION FOR ACHIEVEMENT

VIGILANT CITIZEN SAVES MILLIONS OF CHILDREN FROM CERTAIN DEATH

TOWN COUNCIL SAYS THANKS BY RENAMING TALLEST SKYSCRAPER

NO MORE ROOM FOR MEDALS ON JUMPER!

NOTES

DAY 130

DEFY HIERARCHY TODAY

DON'T JUST ACCEPT SOCIETY'S RULES. TALK BACK. STAND UP. BE THE COG THAT CLOGS UP THE MACHINE.

AUTHORITY FIGURE No1: THE BOSS

DO NOT SAY: CERTAINLY MR. JOHNSON, YOU'LL HAVE THAT REPORT ON YOUR DESK FIRST THING IN THE MORNING SIR.

INSTEAD, SAY: HEY MR. BOSSMAN PIECE-OF-SHIT CAPITALIST EXPLOITER, I'M TIRED OF FOLLOWING YOUR WHIMS SO TAKE YOUR JOB AND STICK IT UP YOUR EXPLOITATIVE ASS.

AUTHORITY FIGURE No2: THE LAW

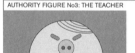

DO NOT SAY: I'M SORRY OFFICER, I'LL MOVE ALONG STRAIGHT AWAY, I DON'T WANT TO CAUSE AN AFFRAY.

INSTEAD, SAY: FUCK YOU, PIG. IF YOU THINK I'M GOING TO MOVE AN INCH YOU'VE GOT ANOTHER THING COMING, YOU UNDERSIZED-PENIS SCUM, IT'S A FREE COUNTRY, NOW MIND YOUR OWN BUSINESS AND PISS RIGHT OFF.

AUTHORITY FIGURE No3: THE TEACHER

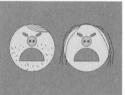

DO NOT SAY: YOU'RE ABSOLUTELY CORRECT, I DO NOT IN FACT KNOW WHAT I AM TALKING ABOUT, I'LL JUST LISTEN TO YOUR EXPERTISE AND TAKE NOTES FROM NOW ON.

INSTEAD, SAY: I DON'T KNOW WHICH IS MORE PITIFUL, THE ROLE YOU PLAY IN PERPETUATING THE POST-CAPITALIST PATRIARCHAL ORDER, OR THE PITTANCE YOU GET PAID TO DO SO. EVER HEARD OF PINK FLOYD? NO I DIDN'T THINK SO. ANYWAY, I'M TAKING MY KIDS OUT OF SCHOOL AND THAT'S FINAL, DAMMIT.

AUTHORITY FIGURE No4: THE FAMILY

DO NOT SAY: YES FATHER, I'M SURE YOU'RE RIGHT, I'LL GO FOR THAT INSURANCE SALESMAN JOB, IT DOES LOOK PROMISING.

INSTEAD, SAY: LOOK MAN, JUST COS I CAME OUT OF YOUR BALLS DOESN'T MEAN I HAVE TO LISTEN TO YOUR STUPID ADVICE. I'M GONNA BE A HEAVY METAL DRUMMER, EARN TEN TIMES MORE THAN YOU, AND THAT'S FINAL, SO GET OFF MY CASE OR I'LL LIE AND HAVE YOU DONE FOR ABUSE.

NOTES

DAY 131

NO THANX!

Today we can reveal that your lucky number is:

12

Incredible but true: Marsha Vranitsky's lucky number is three. She has triplets, all born on the third of March 2003, from her third husband Rick. And: soon she will be 23! Luck is a beautiful and mysterious lady.

HOW TO CAPITALIZE ON YOUR LUCKY NUMBER:

PLAY THE LOTTERY

BET ON A HORSE (No 12 IN THE 12th RACE)

TAKE THE NO 12 BUS

BET ON THE 12 AT ROULETTE

BUY A HOUSE AT NO 12

DAY 132

Notes

DAY 133

Invent a new color

In 1957, French painter Yves Klein invented and patented an especially intense ultramarine blue pigment, »International Klein Blue,« shown here. Today, dream up a new color of your own, and contact your lawyers.

Notes

Today hack into a computer network

Hacking is a useful and potentially lucrative hobby. All you need is a computer connected to the internet and a few hours to spare. Here are some popular sites to hack into:

www.pentagon.com
www.whitehouse.gov
www.federalreserve.gov.org
www.microsoft.com
www.starbucks.com

Starter tips: Since the early days of intruders breaking into computers, they have tried to develop backdoors techniques that allow them to get into the system. Here are some common backdoors, concentrating on Unix backdoors and some discussion on future Windows NT backdoors. This will show you the difficulties in how to choose the right methods, both for beginners and advanced intruders. This will not cover every possible way to create a backdoor as the possibilities to hack are limitless. The backdoor for most intruders provide two or three main functions:

– Be able to get back into a computer even if the administrator tries to secure it, e.g., changing all the passwords.

– Be able to get back into the computer with the least amount of detectability. Most backdoors provide a way to avoid being logged and many times the machine can appear to have no one online even while an intruder is using it.

– Be able to get back into the computer with the least amount of time. Most intruders want to easily get back into the machine without having to do all the work of exploiting a hole to gain access.

In some cases, if the intruder may think the administrator may detect any installed backdoor, they will resort to using the vulnerability repeatedly to get on a machine as the only backdoor. Thus not touching anything that may tip off the administrator. Therefore in some cases, the vulnerabilities on a machine remain the only unnoticed backdoor.

Password Cracking Backdoor. One of the first and oldest methods of intruders used to gain not only access to a Unix machine but backdoors was to run a password cracker. This uncovers weak passworded accounts. All these new accounts are now possible backdoors into a machine even if the system administrator locks out the intruder's current account. Many times, the intruder will look for unused accounts with easy passwords and change the password to something difficult. When the administrator looked for all the weak passworded accounts, the accounts with modified passwords will not appear. Thus the administrator will not be able to easily determine which accounts to lock out.

Rhosts + + Backdoor. On networked Unix machines, services like Rsh and Rlogin used a simple authentication method based on hostnames that appear in rhosts. A user could easily configure which machines not to require a password to log into. An intruder that gained access to someone's rhosts file could put a »+ +« in the file and that would allow anyone from anywhere to log into that account without a password. Many intruders use this method especially when NFS is exporting home directories to the world. These accounts become backdoors for intruders to get back into the system. Many intruders prefer using Rsh over Rlogin because it is many times lacking any logging capability. Many administrators check for »+ +« therefore an intruder may actually put in a hostname and username from another compromised account on the network, making it less obvious to spot.

Checksum and Timestamp Backdoors. Early on, many intruders replaced binaries with their own trojan versions. Many system administrators relied on time-stamping and the system checksum programs, e.g., Unix's sum program, to try to determine when a binary file has been modified. Intruders have developed technology that will recreate the same time-stamp for the trojan file as the original file. This is accomplished by setting the system clock time back to the original file's time and then adjusting the trojan file's time to the system clock. Once the binary trojan file has the exact same time as the original, the system clock is reset to the current time. The sum program relies on a CRC checksum and is easily spoofed. Intruders have developed programs that would modify the trojan binary to have the necessary original checksum, thus fooling the administrators. MD5 checksums is the recommended choice to use today by most vendors. MD5 is based on an algorithm that no one has yet to date proven can be spoofed.

Login Backdoor. On Unix, the login program is the software that usually does the password authentication when someone telnets to the machine. Intruders grabbed the source code to login.c and modified it that when login compared the user's password with the stored password, it would first check for a backdoor password. If the user typed in the backdoor password, it would allow you to log in regardless of what the administrator sets the passwords to. Thus this allowed the intruder to log into any account, even root. The password backdoor would spawn access before the user actually logged in and appeared in utmp and wtmp. Therefore an intruder could be logged in and have shell access without it appearing anyone is on that machine as that account. Administrators started noticing these backdoors especially if they did a »strings« command to find what text was in the login program. Many times the backdoor password would show up. The intruders then encrypted or hid the backdoor password better so it would not appear by just doing strings. Many of the administrators can detect these backdoors with MD5 checksums.

Telnetd Backdoor. When a user telnets to the machine, inetd service listens on the port and receive the connection and then passes it to in.telnetd, that then runs login. Some intruders knew the administrator was checking the login program for tampering, so they modified in.telnetd. Within in.telnetd, it does several checks from the user for things like what kind of terminal the user was using. Typically, the terminal setting might be Xterm or VT100. An intruder could backdoor it so that when the terminal was set to »letmein«, it would spawn a shell without requiring any authentication. Intruders have backdoored some services so that any connection from a specific source port can spawn a shell.

Services Backdoor. Almost every network service has at one time been backdoored by an intruder. Backdoored versions of finger, rsh, rexec, rlogin, ftp, even inetd, etc., have been floating around forever. There are programs that are nothing more than a shell connected to a TCP port with maybe a backdoor password to gain access. These programs sometimes replace a service like uucp that never gets used or they get added to the inetd.conf file as a new service. Administrators should be very wary of what services are running and analyze the original services by MD5 checksums.

Cronjob backdoor. Cronjob on Unix schedules when certain programs should be run. An intruder could add a backdoor shell program to run between 1 AM and 2 AM. So for 1 hour every night, the intruder could gain access. Intruders have also looked at legitimate programs that typically run in cronjob and built backdoors into those programs as well.

Library backdoors. Almost every UNIX system uses shared libraries. The shared libraries are intended to reuse many of the same routines thus cutting down on the size of programs. Some intruders have backdoored some of the routines like crypt.c and _crypt.c. Programs like login.c would use the crypt() routine and if a backdoor password was used it would spawn a shell. Therefore, even if the administrator was checking the MD5 of the login program, it was still spawning a backdoor routine and many administrators were not checking the libraries as a possible source of backdoors. One problem for many intruders was that some administrators started MD5 checksums of almost everything. One method intruders used to get around that is to backdoor the open() and file access routines. The backdoor routines were configured to read the original files, but execute the trojan backdoors. Therefore, when the MD5 checksum program was reading these files, the checksums always looked good. But when the system ran the program, it executed the trojan version. Even the trojan library itself, could be hidden from the MD5 checksums. One way to an administrator could get around this backdoor was to statically link the MD5 checksum checker and run on the system. The statically linked program does not use the trojan shared libraries.

Kernel backdoors. The kernel on Unix is the core of how Unix works. The same method used for libraries for bypassing MD5 checksum could be used at the kernel level, except even a statically linked program could not tell the difference. A good backdoored kernel is probably one of the hardest to find by administrators, fortunately kernel backdoor scripts have not yet been widely made available and no one knows how widespread they really are.

File system backdoors. An intruder may want to store their loot or data on a server somewhere without the administrator finding the files. The intruder's files can typically contain their toolbox of exploit scripts, backdoors, sniffer logs, copied data like email messages, source code, etc. To hide these sometimes large files from an administrator, an intruder may patch the files system commands like »ls«, »du«, and »fsck« to hide the existence of certain directories or files. At a very low level, one intruder's backdoor created a section on the hard drive to have a proprietary format that was designated as »bad« sectors on the hard drive. Thus an intruder could access those hidden files with only special tools, but to the regular administrator, it is very difficult to determine that the marked »bad« sectors were indeed storage area for the hidden file system.

Bootblock backdoors. In the PC world, many viruses have hid themselves within the bootblock section and most antivirus software will check to see if the bootblock has been altered. On Unix, most administrators do not have any software that checks the bootblock, therefore some intruders have hidden some backdoors in the bootblock area.

Process hiding backdoors. An intruder many times wants to hide the programs they are running. The programs they want to hide are commonly a password cracker or a sniffer. There are quite a few methods and here are some of the more common: An intruder may write the program to modify its own argv[] to make it look like another process name. An intruder could rename the sniffer program to a legitimate service like in.syslog and run it. Thus when an administrator does a »ps« or looks at what is running, the standard service names appear. An intruder could modify the library routines so that »ps« does not show all the processes. An intruder could patch a backdoor or program into an interrupt driven routine so it does not appear in the process table. An example backdoor using this technique is amod.tar.gz available on http://star.nmmpiimm.spb.su/~maillist/bugtraq.1/0777.html. An intruder could modify the kernel to hide certain processes as well.

Rootkit. One of the most popular packages to install backdoors is rootkit. It can easily be located using Web search engines. From the Rootkit README, here are the typical files that get installed: z2 – removes entries from utmp, wtmp, and lastlog.
Es – rokstar's ethernet sniffer for sun4 based kernels.
Fix – try to fake checksums, install with same dates/perms/u/g.
Sl – become root via a magic password sent to login. Ic – modified ifconfig to remove PROMISC flag from output. ps: – hides the processes.
Ns – modified netstat to hide connections to certain machines. Ls – hides certain directories and files from being listed. du5 – hides how much space is being used on your hard drive. ls5 – hides certain files and directories from being listed.

Network traffic backdoors. Not only do intruders want to hide their tracks on the machine, but also they want to hide their network traffic as much as possible. These network traffic backdoors sometimes allow an intruder to gain access through a firewall. There are many network backdoor programs that allow an intruder to set up on a certain port number on a machine that will allow access without ever going through the normal services. Because the traffic is going to a non-standard network port, the administrator can overlook the intruder's traffic. These network traffic backdoors are typically using TCP, UDP, and ICMP, but it could be many other kinds of packets.

TCP Shell Backdoors. The intruder can set up these TCP Shell backdoors on some high port number possibly where the firewall is not blocking that TCP port. Many times, they will be protected with a password just so that an administrator that connects to it, will not immediately see shell access. An administrator can look for these connections with netstat to see what ports are listening and where current connections are going to and from. Many times, these backdoors allow an intruder to get past TCP Wrapper technology. These backdoors could be run on the SMTP port, which many firewalls allow traffic to pass for e-mail.

UDP Shell Backdoors. Administrator many times can spot a TCP connection and notice the odd behavior, while UDP shell backdoors lack any connection so netstat would not show an intruder accessing the Unix machine. Many firewalls have been configured to allow UDP packets for services like DNS through. Many times, intruders will place the UDP Shell backdoor on that port and it will be allowed to by-pass the firewall.

ICMP Shell Backdoors. Ping is one of the most common ways to find out if a machine is alive by sending and receiving ICMP packets. Many firewalls allow outsiders to ping internal machines. An intruder can put data in the Ping ICMP packets and tunnel a shell between the pinging machines. An administrator may notice a flurry of Ping packets, but unless the administrator looks at the data in the packets, an intruder can be unnoticed.

Encrypted Link. An administrator can set up a sniffer trying to see data appears as someone accessing a shell, but an intruder can add encryption to the Network traffic backdoors and it becomes almost impossible to determine what is actually being transmitted between two machines.

Windows NT. Because Windows NT does not easily allow multiple users on a single machine and remote access similar as Unix, it becomes harder for the intruder to break into Windows NT, install a backdoor, and launch an attack from it. Thus you will find more frequently network attacks that are spring boarded from a Unix box than Windows NT. As Windows NT advances in multi-user technologies, this may give a higher frequency of intruders who use Windows NT to their advantage. And if this does happen, many of the concepts from Unix backdoors can be ported to Windows NT and administrators can be ready for the intruder. Today, there are already telnet daemons available for Windows NT. With Network Traffic backdoors, they are very feasible for intruders to install on Windows NT.

As backdoor technology advances, it becomes even harder for administrators to determine if an intruder has gotten in or if they have been successfully locked out.

Text © Prabhaker Mateti under open content license, edited by Benrik.

Notes

–Hi!
–**Shit!**

–How are you?
–**Who are you?**

–Long time no see!
–**Where do I know you from?**

–Goodness how you've changed.
–**Was it long ago?**

–How's you know whatsisname?
–**What's your name again?**

–I'm very well thanks, very well indeed.
–**Ask me how my career's going.**

–Fine, yeah, they made me account director actually.
–**Yes yes yes! I'm better than you.**

–And how's your job going?
–**Still unemployed?**

–It's this recession, isn't it?
–**What a loser.**

–How about the love life?
–**Still going out with fatso?**

–I'm sorry to hear that, it must have been difficult.
–**I wonder who dumped who?**

–Anyway, we must get together for a drink!
–**Another second of this and I'll implode.**

–Here's my number.
–**Here's the number of a dry-cleaner in New Jersey.**

–See you soon!
–**Drop dead.**

Notes

Day 136
Today make sure your
parents know you love them.
It may seem impossible to say.
But don't wait until it is.

NOTES

DOES CHEESE REALLY GIVE YOU NIGHTMARES?
Find out by eating 100 oz of one of following and recording your dreams.

DANISH BLUE
(zombies)

GORGONZOLA
(vampires)

GRUYERE
(castration anxiety)

PARMESAN
(friends deserting you)

STILTON
(loss of loved one)

BRIE
(falling from great height)

EMMENTAL
(going to hell)

ROCQUEFORT
(general sweatiness)

DAY 137	
NOTES	

DAY 138
Today learn
a new knot.
It could save your life.

USE IT TO: Escape from a fire.
Escape from a kidnapping.
Tie up a maniac until the police arrive.
Tie yourself to a tree during a tornado.

SINGLE WALL KNOT
Unlay the end of a rope, and form a bight with
the strand. Take strand b round the end of a.
Cross a over the end of b. Take b through the
bight made by c. Haul the ends taut.

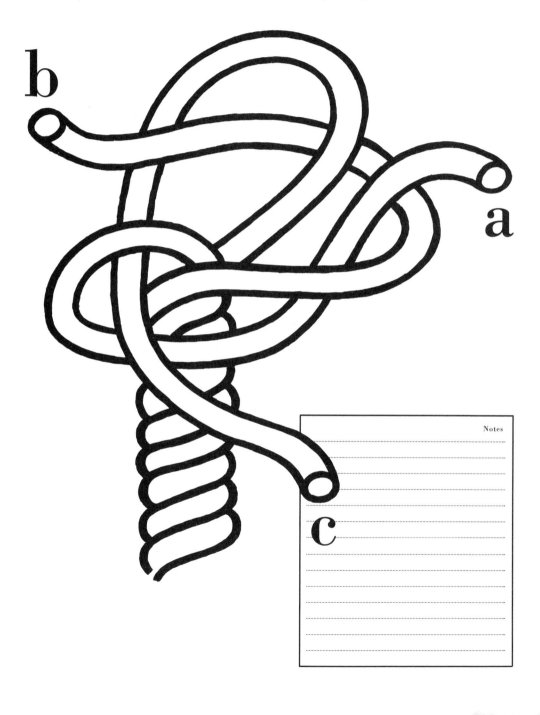

Notes

TODAY, BLEED HERE:

In a million years' time with advanced technology
they'll be able to reconstitute you from your DNA.
How to extract blood: 
Name:..................................
Address: .... Zip code: ....
Why I'm worth reconstituting from my DNA a million
years hence..

Notes	

DAY
140

JAM THE LINE!

Today crank call the national Ku Klux Klan
Headquarters, Harrison, Arkansas on
870-427-3414 repeatedly and jam the line.

Notes

Day 141
Today build a nest and
see if a bird comes...

NOTES

Sense-less Day

GO THROUGH TODAY WITHOUT USING YOUR SENSE OF: TASTE

How to: Gargle with sore throat topical anesthetic (containing phenol or benzocaine) to numb your tongue before eating. True story: Michael F., 45, lost his sense of taste at the age of 8 following a viral infection that damaged the cranial nerve fibers that carry information from the taste buds to the brain. His condition is known as »ageusia,« meaning full loss of taste, which is a very rare disorder. At the time, his main gripe concerned inability to distinguish between ice cream flavors. He did however develop a reputation for being able to ingest insects and some of the smaller lizards without batting an eyelid. He now lives in Denver with his wife and 2 children, and is reconciled to his loss.

NOTES

Write down the pros and cons of this sense as you discover them.

Pros: ....

Cons: ....

End of day assessment: How crucial is my sense of taste to me ..../10

ONE HUG
VALID FOR

VALID FOR ONE PIECE OF
HONEST ADVICE

ONE DRUNKEN BINGE
VALID FOR

ONE ROUND OF DRINKS

ONE EMBARRASSING
Secret

ONE
VALID FOR
BITCHING SESSION

FRIENDSHIP COUPON

DAY 143: DISTRIBUTE THESE FRIENDSHIP COUPONS.

Notes

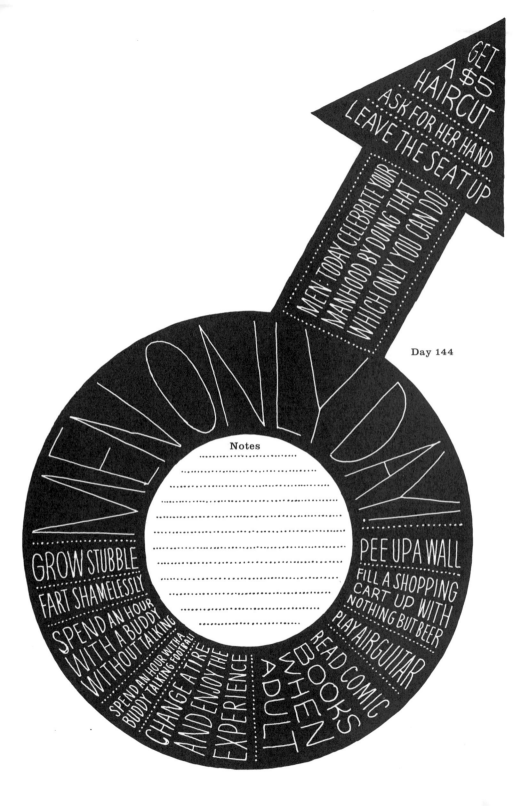

Day 144

Start an urban myth

See how fast a rumor can spread. To be successful, an urban myth must include two or more of the following elements: • Imaginative revenge by jilted lover • Pet's life ending in gruesome circumstances (preferably sexual) • Hidden deadly flaw in consumer product.

Example: »a man in Chicago decided to take revenge on his ex-wife by poisoning her cat by mixing a huge dose of popular painkiller Xylenol into the cat food. Xylenol, however, in large quantities is an aphrodisiac to cats. So the cat didn't die but instead raped the ex-husband's favorite gerbil to death.«

WHAT TO DO IF YOU LIVE IN A NON-URBAN AREA
Don't worry: the historical ancestor to the urban myth is the fisherman's tale. Be aware that it spreads less rapidly however, and that subject matter is slightly more restrictive: tales must be based mainly around catching a very big fish.

Day 146

famous last words: prepare yours ahead of time

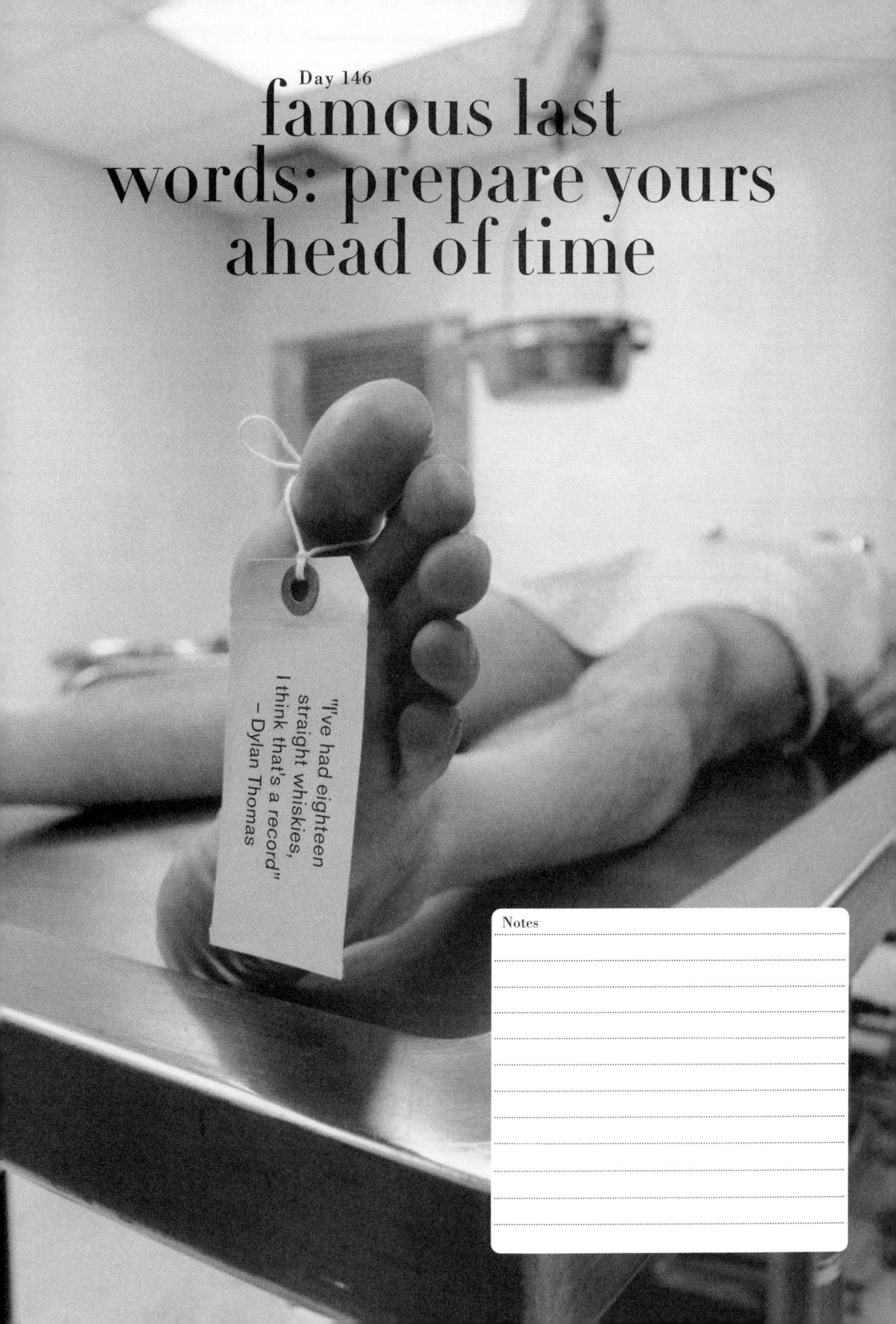

"I've had eighteen straight whiskies, I think that's a record"
— Dylan Thomas

Notes

DAY 147

Change someone's mind today

Only fools never change their mind. Help save someone from such folly by arguing them out of their deeply held views on a controversial subject, like cannibalism. Now, most reasonable people are in favor of cannibalism, but a tenacious minority cling to outdated views about its health risks. Tell them no independent clinical study has ever been able to establish that lifelong cannibalism is bad for your health. That's a fact. And here's the clincher: have they ever tried it? No? THEN HOW DO THEY KNOW? The great Socrates himself could not win an argument more easily.

Notes

Day 148: Leave a note on someone's car windshield

I'm a traffic warden but today I feel lenient. Don't do it again though.

I'm the engineer who made this vehicle. The brakes aren't very good cos I was hungover that day. Watch out.

We've discovered your car is the one responsible for all the damage to the ozone layer; please bike to work in future.

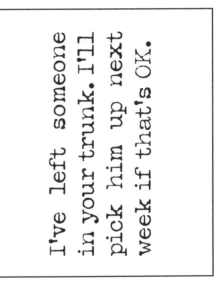

I've left someone in your trunk. I'll pick him up next week if that's OK.

Notes

DAY 149

TODAY HELP RESOLVE AN INTRACTABLE GLOBAL GEOPOLITICAL CRISIS!

Some bright spark out there must be able to come up with an answer to the world's various problems. Could it be you? Put your mind to it for a couple of minutes. Redraw maps using colored crayons and explain your plan in no more than 80 words. Send to: Secretary-General, UNITED NATIONS, S-378, New York, NY 10017, USA.

Notes

CASH CASH CASH!

Reconnect with your aquatic origins by spending all of today underwater. It is common knowledge that the old theory about man evolving from apes on the dry plains of Africa is wrong. Rather, scientists now believe that man got caught in flooded swamp land and

DAY 151: EVERYONE HAS A FAVORITE DINOSAUR. Go to your local natural history museum and make sure yours is properly displayed.

Notes

Day 152

Write a message to the future

Mark the envelope »DO NOT OPEN UNTIL JUNE 1, 2104.« Begin the letter with today's date and To Whom It May Concern. Suitable topics: world peace, evolutionary trends, suggestions on how to deal with living on other planets, predictions, anecdotes from our times that might interest future generations (sport, »hot news,« society, dress trends, etc). Hide the envelope so that it won't be found for a hundred years.

Notes		

DAY 153

TALK TO A PLANT

FOR AT LEAST ONE HOUR

Good things to say to a plant:
"Grow, you plants are the best"
"Try to touch the sky"
"You're the best plant in the world"
"Try your best at growing"
"You're so pretty with your light green,
dark green and green colors"

Bad things to say to a plant:
"Die you nasty plants, die"
"You are the worst plants in the world"
"Die you worthless pieces of green seeds"
"You are so ugly when you are standing
up, so fall over and don't get up"
"You are so ugly when you're green,
and you wouldn't be ugly if you were
brown and falling over"

A house is not a home.

....
Notes
....
....
....
....

HARD WORK DAY

Hard work is good for the soul, besides being the basis of Western society's economic dominance. Follow these instructions to make sure you earn your money today.

CLOCK IN TIME:		STATEMENT OF PURPOSE	Today I will work harder than
CLOCK OUT TIME:			ever and make it happen. Signature:...

LIST OF TASKS	PRIORITY:	ACTION:	DEADLINE:	RESULTS:
Sales report	Urgent	Write and circulate	11am	☐ Approved by JD
				☐
				☐
				☐
				☐
				☐
				☐
				☐
				☐
				☐
				☐
				☐
				☐
				☐

MOTIVATION CORNER

WINNERS MAKE IT HAPPEN, LOSERS WATCH IT HAPPEN!

Sell Sell Sell!

Be you, only more so.

Prepare for tomorrow: do your best today.

The only place success comes before work is in the dictionary.

EMPLOYER CONFIRMATION

I,.., employer of this Book owner, confirm that

he/she has completed these tasks and has worked hard for me today and fully deserves the.................

I've paid them for their labor. Well done and keep it up. Signature:...

Notes		

CONFESS TO A PRIEST

Even if you are not religious, the act of confession is rich in therapeutic value, not to mention a damn sight cheaper. So head for your nearest church and book a convenient time. Count on 1 minute per trivial sin (stealing from cookie jar as a child), 5 minutes per major sin (stealing cookie from child), and at least 20 minutes per heinous sin (killing child and stuffing it in cookie jar).

Notes

Confession dos

DO: sound contrite, even if you actually enjoyed the sinning
DO: at least feign belief in a supreme being
DO: accept your penance, this is no time for haggling

Confession don'ts

DON'T: ask if they're recording this
DON'T: confess sins on behalf of other people, like your two-timing neighbor
DON'T: confess you've broken wind
DON'T: end by saying «your turn now»

Today, redesign an everyday product

In 1983, British inventor James Dyson redesigned the vacuum cleaner and made a fortune. Pick an everyday object that everyone in the world uses and find a way of improving it.

His'n'Hers Toothbrush™
Leaves couples more room around the sink!

The Double-Toothpick™
Saves valuable time by picking two teeth at once!

The Talking Umbrella™
Lets you know when it's stopped raining!

The Foldable Coat Hanger™
Take it with you!

The Mystic Mug™
Electronically reads your tea leaves!

50 mm

Notes

The Remote Control Belt Leash™
You'll never lose it again!

Human Chess Day

TODAY BEHAVE AS IF YOU WERE PLAYING CHESS.

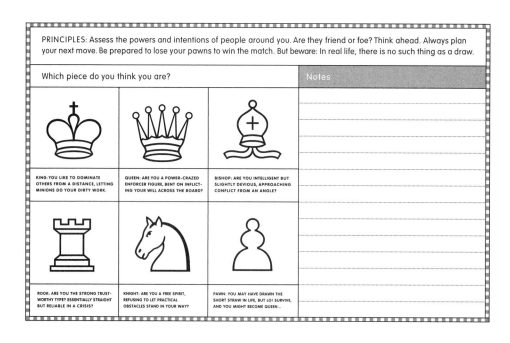

PRINCIPLES: Assess the powers and intentions of people around you. Are they friend or foe? Think ahead. Always plan your next move. Be prepared to lose your pawns to win the match. But beware: In real life, there is no such thing as a draw.

Which piece do you think you are?			Notes
KING: YOU LIKE TO DOMINATE OTHERS FROM A DISTANCE, LETTING MINIONS DO YOUR DIRTY WORK.	**QUEEN:** ARE YOU A POWER-CRAZED ENFORCER FIGURE, BENT ON INFLICT-ING YOUR WILL ACROSS THE BOARD?	**BISHOP:** ARE YOU INTELLIGENT BUT SLIGHTLY DEVIOUS, APPROACHING CONFLICT FROM AN ANGLE?	
ROOK: ARE YOU THE STRONG TRUST-WORTHY TYPE? ESSENTIALLY STRAIGHT BUT RELIABLE IN A CRISIS?	**KNIGHT:** ARE YOU A FREE SPIRIT, REFUSING TO LET PRACTICAL OBSTACLES STAND IN YOUR WAY?	**PAWN:** YOU MAY HAVE DRAWN THE SHORT STRAW IN LIFE, BUT LO! SURVIVE, AND YOU MIGHT BECOME QUEEN...	

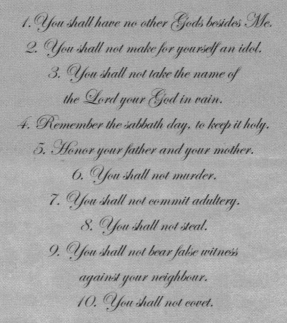

Today, break one or several of the

The Ten Commandments

1. You shall have no other Gods besides Me.
2. You shall not make for yourself an idol.
3. You shall not take the name of
   the Lord your God in vain.
4. Remember the sabbath day, to keep it holy.
5. Honor your father and your mother.
6. You shall not murder.
7. You shall not commit adultery.
8. You shall not steal.
9. You shall not bear false witness
   against your neighbour.
10. You shall not covet.

Notes	

(If you are struck by a bolt of lightning, you will have solid grounds on which to base your faith.)

Day 159: Find a way of making a $10 bill grow into $100 in one day

Notes

A cautionary tale: the story of Narcissus, first victim of vanity

»Young Greek boy Narcissus was hunting in a forest one day when he came upon a calm stream. He was thirsty and so he bent over to drink. As he leaned over, he caught sight of his reflection in the water. He was taken by its beauty and immediately spoke ›I love you.‹ He became so engrossed with himself that he failed to notice the nymph Echo nearby. His self-love became an obsession and he would not leave the stream to eat, nor disturb his image to drink and so he died of thirst and hunger and unrequited self-love. Where he had lain a flower grew, the Narcissus, the same flower that lured the innocent Persephone into the snares of Pluto.«

NOTES

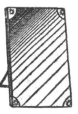

Compose a poem
and leave it in a public
place to brighten
up someone's day.

POEM

THE CAT
SAT
ON THE MAT.

Notes

Day 162

Make prolonged eye contact
with everyone you meet

Eye contact: communication before words.
Monkeys stare each other down. Be the alpha
male. Who dares stand up to you? Bite their head
off, that'll learn them. Grrrr.

DAY 163: SHOPLIFT TODAY

Average custodial sentences for stealing:

A sweet:..police caution	
A car:...4 years	
A handbag:...2 years	
A little old granny's handbag:................5 years	
A house:..N/A	

CAUTION: in the state of California, shoplifting three times will automatically result in a 25 years-to-life sentence (»three strikes and you're out« legislation).

Notes

Day 164: Share someone's pain today. A burden shared is a burden halved. Find a friend in distress and bear some of their grief.

Notes

DAY 165

Develop your very own ECCENTRICITY!

Notes

Note: by its very nature, an eccentricity must be exclusive. The following are already taken.

More notes

Day 166. Today get someone famous to autograph this page

Tips for autograph hunters: Hang out outside celebrity haunts, like trendy new discos. Be polite: say please and thank you, and get their name right. Have pen and Book at the ready! »Cheeky« alternative: get female celebrity to kiss this page! (with lipstick on, obviously)

Category of celebrity (check):

A-list ☐

B-list ☐

C-list ☐

D-list ☐

Use these 11 boxes if you meet an entire football team.

Notes

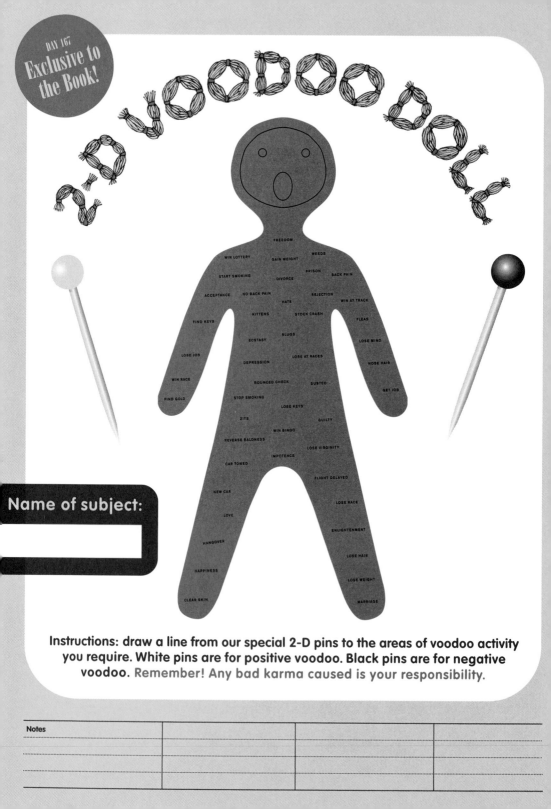

2-D VOODOO DOLL

FREEDOM
WIN LOTTERY   GAIN WEIGHT   WEEDS
START SMOKING   DIVORCE   PRISON   BACK PAIN
ACCEPTANCE   NO BACK PAIN   REJECTION
HATE   WIN AT TRACK
KITTENS   STOCK CRASH   FLEAS
FIND KEYS
ECSTASY   SLUGS   LOSE MIND
LOSE JOB
DEPRESSION   LOSE AT RACES   NOSE HAIR
WIN RACE
BOUNCED CHECK   BUSTED   GET JOB
FIND GOLD   STOP SMOKING
LOSE KEYS
ZITS   GUILTY
WIN BINGO
REVERSE BALDNESS   LOSE VIRGINITY
IMPOTENCE
CAR TOWED
FLIGHT DELAYED
NEW CAR
LOSE RACE
LOVE
ENLIGHTENMENT
HANGOVER
LOSE HAIR
HAPPINESS
LOSE WEIGHT
CLEAR SKIN
MARRIAGE

Name of subject:

Instructions: draw a line from our special 2-D pins to the areas of voodoo activity you require. White pins are for positive voodoo. Black pins are for negative voodoo. Remember! Any bad karma caused is your responsibility.

Notes

In this day and age in the final analysis you've got to grab the bull by the horns and give one hundred and ten percent if you want to stay ahead of the game after all it's a dog-eat-dog world where the fat cat powers that be will stab you in the back with a crushing blow if you don't come up to scratch and you won't know what hit you so don't get caught napping with your pants down – because then unless you get your act together and cut the mustard you're well and truly up for a rude awakening at least according to the doom merchants though let's not make a drama out of a crisis; look on the bright side: even if it all goes pear-shaped and you're left in the lurch, your heart is in the right place and now so long as you can keep your head above water and the wolf from the door you'll be able to spend time with your family and get away from it all anyway let's do lunch so I can rub it in. Have a nice day.

TODAY: Speak only in clichés

notes

DAY 170: TODAY SELL
SOMETHING THAT YOU HAVE MADE

Homemade object:	Going rates:
Origami flamingo	$15
Automobile	$20,000
Pottery item	$24
Pretty Card	$5
Ugly Card	$1
Furniture	$50-500
Original Painting	$50-500,000
Poo	$0,15

Secret subliminal sales techniques

Flattery: »Hey this'll go great with your sweater.«

Empathy: »No kidding? I wear a toupee as well!«

Sympathy: »I can see you're very poor, but this is only $0,15.«

Threat: »Buy this or I'll eat your dog raw.«

NOTES

....

....

....

....

....

....

....

....

....

....

....

....

Day 171: Stick a message on a fruit

NOTES

Day 172
NO SLEEP DAY
We only sleep seven to nine hours a night out of social convention. Indeed there is evidence that too much sleep is harmful. Famous French Emperor Napoleon managed with only 4 hours and thus found the time to conquer Europe. Tonight, don't go to bed at all and discover what you can achieve in the extra time.

Notes	

Today: come up with your own Book page idea!

Send it in to us c/o literary agent Scott Waxman, 80 Fifth Avenue, Suite 1101, New York, NY 10011, USA. If it's any good, we'll use it for free in the next edition. If not, we'll send you a humiliating put-down letter that'll make you feel small. Sharpen those pencils!

This is not actually physically possible, and therefore not a serious idea.

Pretentious. There's nothing wrong with big themes like peace war and death, as long as you make them humorous.

Superficially, this seems like a contender, but on closer inspection, it's just stupid.

DEMONSTRA- TE AGAINST FATHERS WHO STILL TREAT YOU LIKE A LITTLE **CHILD!**

Kill your darlings: no one wants to hear about your boring personal problems. See a shrink.

Nothing stupid about this one, but it's only for men. The Book does not discriminate against either gender.

Not bad. But this cannot really be achieved in one single day. Keep'em coming though!

DAY 173	
Notes	

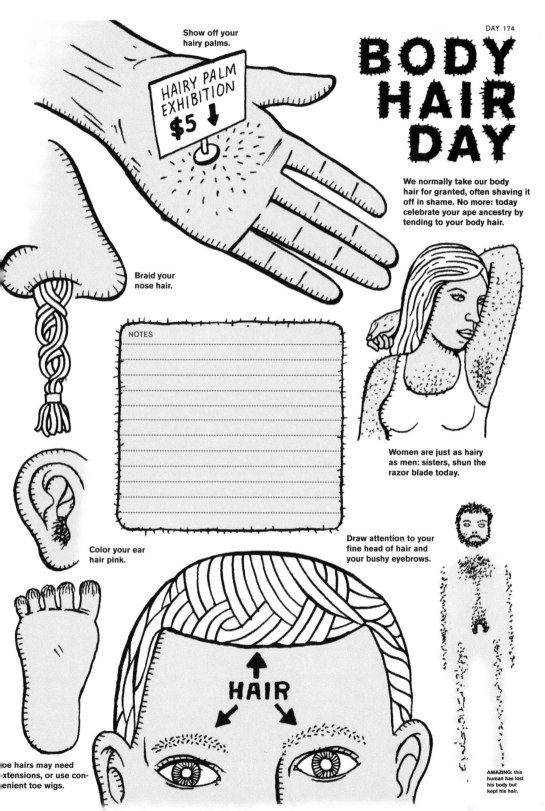

TODAY:
GO ON STRIKE!
ENOUGH IS ENOUGH. COMRADE, WHY
TOIL DAY IN DAY OUT FOR THE 'SAKE OF
THE BOURGEOISIE? ORGANIZE RESISTAN-
CE TO EXPLOITATION IN YOUR WORKPLACE.
FORM A TRADE UNION AND PASS A
RESOLUTION IN FAVOR OF A ONE-
DAY GENERAL STRIKE. DEMAND
BETTER CONDITIONS, A SAFER
ENVIRONMENT, AND A BIGGER SHARE
OF THE CAPITALIST PIE... LONG
LIVE THE STRUGGLE! HOW TO SET
UP AND OPERATE A PROPER PICKET
LINE YOU WILL NEED: A LENGTH OF
SOLID ROPE (NOT STRING), SOMETHING
TO TIE IT TO (THE OUTSIDE OF YOUR
CUBICLE IF YOU ARE IN AN OFFICE), A LIST
OF ANTI-SCAB SLOGANS TO CHANT,
AND A BUCKET TO RECEIVE CONTRI-
BUTIONS FROM THE PUBLIC. STAND
IN FRONT OF THE LINE AND INTIMIDATE
ANY SCAB WHO TRIES TO CROSS IT
WITH THREATENING EYE CONTACT.

Notes

free pet day!

Put a lost dog ad up and see whether one turns up

Key elements of any successful lost dog ad

fig.1 *Positioning:* tree is traditional, or lamp post, preferably one they enjoyed peeing on particularly.

fig.2 *Photo:* poor quality photocopy, hinting at nationwide magnitude of your search and maximizing the range of dogs that look a bit like that.

fig.3 *Reward:* keep this bit vague, that way you'll always be able to fob them off with a cheap chocolate bar or similar lame effort.

fig.4 *Description:* favor the emotional content over the descriptive. »My darling bulimic daughter Lizzie's little puppy has gone and she hasn't stopped crying since, please help restore her faith in life« is more motivational than »fox terrier, 7 years old, brownish, answers to the name dog«.

fig.5 *Headline:* LOST DOG works best usually.

fig.6 *Phone number:* might attract psychos, but fairly essential.

Notes	

Day 177

Try seducing someone way out of your league

Most people's idea of what's attractive is imprinted on the brain when they're still in diapers. Staring up at Mommy, Daddy or Uncle Barnaby, we develop attachments to particular features that bear little relation to social norms of beauty. That's why supermodels sometimes end up going out with prime candidates for cosmetic surgery. Today, try your luck with somebody much more conventionally attractive than yourself. You never know...

Dealing with rejection
Sorry buddy. Didn't work for you? But hey, that which does not destroy us makes us stronger and all that. Take it on the chin, keep smiling, and thank them for their honesty. That way they'll at least feel they're missing out on your beauty within. Better luck next time anyway.

Day 178 : Go through a phase

Possible phases:

TALKATIVE PHASE
QUIET PHASE
ANOREXIC PHASE
TOUGH PHASE
RELIGIOUS PHASE
NASTY PHASE
PIMPLY PHASE
WEIRD PHASE
DIFFICULT PHASE
SPOILT PHASE
PRODUCTIVE PHASE
CUTE PHASE
SEXUAL PHASE
I DON'T KNOW WHAT I WANT
TO BE WHEN I GROW UP PHASE

NOTES

Day 179: Measure Your Temperature Day

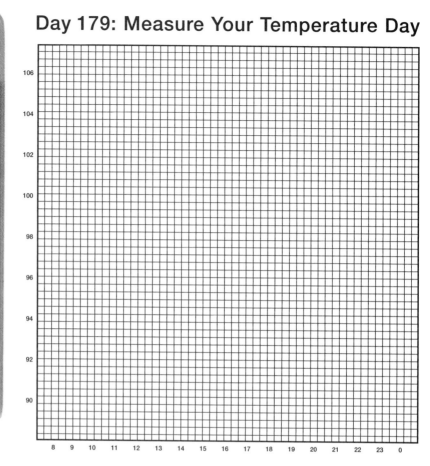

Body temperature is a crucial indicator of well-being. Therefore it is important to monitor it on an hourly basis, using this chart. Body temperature is 98 degrees Fahrenheit on average, but, contrary to popular myth, it varies between 93 and 104 degrees throughout the day, depending on outside influences. See here:

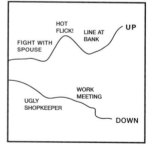

Notes	

THERMOMETER LOCATIONS: PROS AND CONS.
BUCCAL: That's under the tongue to you and me. Classic but effective.
UNDERARM: Snug and discreet. Good for use in business meetings.
RECTAL: Ugh! Only for French persons. Impractical and painful.

SPEND TODAY PRETENDING TO BE A TOURIST

DAY 180

EQUIPMENT:
daypack, camera, lost look

ITINERARY:

10 AM	Visit Big monument
12AM	Ride around in bus for a while
1PM	Lunch in tourist trap restaurant
3PM	Big museum
5PM	Get laughed at by schoolkids
6PM	Big show
9PM	Get mugged by schoolkids
10PM	Bed in Big hotel.

Repeat tomorrow.

BACKGROUND ON YOUR COUNTRY:
Make it up, no one cares.

LINES:
This monument/museum/show sure is nice.
I say, old chap, where's the loo?
Is the President in right now?

Notes

DAY 181 . Today write to your County asking that your street be renamed after you. To make sure your application is successful, explain why the current name is no good, give details of your main achievements, and enclose a petition signed by your neighbors. **IMPORTANT!** Specify the type of street:

BLOGGS BOULEVARD

BLOGGS ROAD

BLOGGS CLOSE

BLOGGS ROW

BLOGGS SQUARE

BLOGGS ALLEY

BLOGGS GARDENS

BLOGGS WAY

BLOGGS GROVE

BLOGGS CRESCENT

BLOGGS WALK

BLOGGS PROMENADE

AVENUE BLOGGS

BLOGGS STREET

Notes

Today return to childhood

Toilet training: did it mess you up?

Toilet training is a crucial formative influence on your life. As you sit on the potty today, see if it triggers any repressed memories that may have helped ruin your life. Do you feel aggressive at work or in traffic? Do you feel like emotions are bottling up inside? Do you want to just let rip? Then chances are you may be suffering from TTS (Toilet Training Syndrome). Unfortunately there is no cure, though it may sometimes help to sue your parents.

Notes

Sense-less Day   GO THROUGH TODAY WITHOUT USING YOUR SENSE OF: SMELL

How to: Nose plug, cold virus.

True story: Susan T. ran a perfume shop in downtown Baltimore. Her big selling point was the ability to mix a unique perfume for every customer. She prospered, until she was accidentally exposed to toxins, and lost all sense of smell. According to medical expert Dr. Carol Fiske, this condition (»anosmia«) affects millions, particularly amongst elderly men. It sometimes disappears with time, says Fiske, though no one yet knows how or why. This comes as no consolation to Susan T., of course, who can no longer smell her precious perfumes and has had to close shop and lose her livelihood as a result. She has not worn perfume since.

NOTES

Write down the pros and cons of this sense as you discover them.

Pros: ....

Cons: ....

End of day assessment: How crucial is my sense of smell to me .... /10

184. How memorable is your everyday conversation? Today, find out by writing down everything you say. Highlight the wittiest phrases.

Examples:

Oscar Wilde (1854-1900)
»Only dull people are
brilliant at breakfast«

Dorothy Parker (1893-1967)
»I don't care what is written
about me so long as it isn't true«

Benjamin Franklin (1706-1790)
»He that falls in love with
himself will have no rivals«

Tallulah Bankhead (1903-1968)
»If I had to live my life again,
I'd make the same mistakes,
only sooner«

Samuel Johnson (1709-1784)
»Of all noise I think music is
the least disagreeable«

Notes

If you've said more than this, use extra paper. If you haven't, expand your social circle.

JOIN A POLITICAL PARTY TODAY

Work out your political beliefs with our political wheel and see which party suits you best. Then call up and join to promote those beliefs.

GREEN PARTY
•Corporations are evil
•Save the ozone layer
•Ban rich from using cars

COMMUNIST PARTY
• The Soviet system wasn't all bad
• Redistribution of wealth
• Kill the rich

REPUBLICAN PARTY
•Capitalism rules!
•Death penalty
•We are the rich

DAY 185

DEMOCRATIC PARTY
•We'll respond...
•We sure miss JFK Kennedy
•Wouldn't it be great if everyone was rich...

DON'T GIVE A DAMN PARTY

NOTES

Day 186: Cleanliness Day

Today become as a clean as the day you were born (or cleaner in fact as there's normally a lot of muck around you at birth for some reason). We're not talking about just taking a plain old bath here, but really cleaning those hard-to-reach crevices that most people overlook.

Armpit crud
There's only one way to get rid of all those greasy accretions of deodorant and sweat, and that's to shave it all off. Women are often ahead of the game on this one.

Inner ear wax
Q-tips just push the wax further into the ear. Liquefy the inner wax with ammonia solution and get a loved one to suck it out gently with a straw.

In-growing toenail grout
Left untreated, this can result in amputation of the foot. Cut off the guilty toe to prevent it from recurring. (Bleeding may occur in some individuals.)

Dead lip
Applying vaseline may cover up chapped lips, but it doesn't get to all those layers of dead lip underneath. A pumice stone should do the trick.

Dorsal mold
Few of us bother to wash that difficult-to-reach upper back patch. The result? Furry moss. Get a friend to rub alcohol in, and set fire to it.

Eyebrow dandruff
Your deep blue eyes won't count for much if they're overshadowed by flakes of dead skin. Household bleach will rinse them out nicely.

Pubic pus
Need we say more? There's a great deal of oozing in this region in both sexes, which must be addressed with a vigorous scouring with a wire brush.

Belly button dirt
Fluff is easily removed, but grit gets into the clefts of poorly-severed umbilical cords. Hire a powerful vacuum cleaner with special nozzle to dislodge it.

Tongue dross
The Ancients could determine your health by examining your tongue. Lick sandpaper to lose those layers of yellowish goo.

Eye snot
Use a toothbrush to extract those little brown crumbs from the corners of your eyes, making sure to scrub under the eyelids too.

Nasal goo
A good deep breath of hydrochloric acid will soon dissolve any nasal obstructions. Take care not to overdo it and dissolve your septum though.

Fungal foot
Those awkward spaces between the toes are the perfect breeding ground for fungi. Stick your feet in the freezer for 12 hours to exterminate the little parasites.

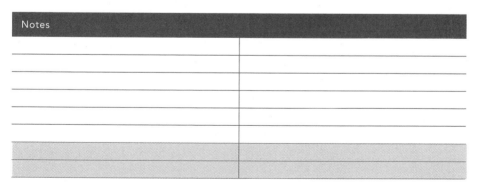

Notes

A very overweight woman in Nevada went to her doctor's complaining of a sore buttock. When the doctor had her X-rayed, he discovered something remarkable. Years before, the rather slovenly woman had slumped on her sofa naked, not realizing her dog had been playing there with a greasy leftover T-bone. The bone got caught in the folds of her obese cheeks, and over the months her flesh simply grew around it. Surgery was required to extract it.

DAY 187: PICK UP LITTER IN THE STREET TODAY

It's disgusting, and it's not yours. But hands up the person who has never littered. Let's all join together in a mass display of community spirit and make this country cleaner!

BIODEGRADABILITY TIMESCALE

Banana peel.....................................3–4 weeks
Tin can.....................................10–40 years
Aluminium wrapper.................200–500 years
Disposable diaper...................500–600 years
Plastic jug...........................1,000,000 years
Styrofoam cup...................................Eternity
Plutonium rod............................Eternity + 1
(DO NOT PICK UP DISCARDED PLUTONIUM ROD WITH YOUR BARE HANDS. FETCH PLASTIC GLOVES FIRST.)

NOTES

Today, get a life coach!

If you haven't managed to do everything this Book has instructed so far, then you clearly need some help organizing your life. Life coaches give you advice on sorting out your priorities and acting on them. If your life is a bit of a mess, they'll help untangle it with you. So pick up the phone book and call one now.

NOTES

This is what a typical life coach should look like, all warm and fuzzy.

CHAPTER 1

1. The burden which Habakkuk the prophet did see.

2. O LORD, how long shall I cry, and thou wilt not hear! even cry out unto thee of violence, and thou wilt not save!

3. Why dost thou shew me iniquity, and cause me to behold grievance? for spoiling and violence are before me: and there are that raise up strife and contention.

4. Therefore the law is slacked, and judgment doth never go forth: for the wicked doth compass about the righteous; therefore wrong judgment proceedeth.

5. Behold ye among the heathen, and regard, and wonder marvelously: for I will work a work in your days which ye will not believe, though it be told you.

6. For, lo, I raise up the Chaldeans, that bitter and hasty nation, which shall march through the breadth of the land, to possess the dwellingplaces that are not their's.

7. They are terrible and dreadful: their judgment and their dignity shall proceed of themselves.

8. Their horses also are swifter than the leopards, and are more fierce than the evening wolves: and their horsemen shall spread themselves, and their horsemen shall come from far; they shall fly as the eagle that hasteth to eat.

9. They shall come all for violence: their faces shall sup up as the east wind, and they shall gather the captivity as the sand.

10. And they shall scoff at the kings, and the princes shall be a scorn unto them: they shall deride every strong hold; for they shall heap dust, and take it.

11. Then shall his mind change, and he shall pass over, and offend, imputing this his power unto his god.

12. Art thou not from everlasting, O LORD my God, mine Holy One? we shall not die: O LORD, thou hast ordained them for judgment; and, O mighty God, thou hast established them for correction.

13. Thou art of purer eyes than to behold evil, and canst not look on iniquity: wherefore lookest thou upon them that deal treacherously, and holdest thy tongue when the wicked devoureth the man that is more righteous than he?

14. And makest men as the fishes of the sea, as the creeping things, that have no ruler over them?

15. They take up all of them with the angle, they catch them in their net, and gather them in their drag: therefore they rejoice and are glad.

16. Therefore they sacrifice unto their net, and burn incense unto their drag; because by them their portion is fat, and their meat plenteous.

17. Shall they therefore empty their net, and not spare continually to slay the nations?

CHAPTER 2

1. I will stand upon my watch, and set me upon the tower, and will watch to see what he will say unto me, and what I shall answer when I am reproved.

2. And the LORD answered me, and said, Write the vision, and make it plain upon tables, that he may run that readeth it.

3. For the vision is yet for an appointed time, but at the end it shall speak, and not lie: though it tarry, wait for it; because it will surely come, it will not tarry.

4. Behold, his soul which is lifted up is not upright in him: but the just shall live by his faith.

5. Yea also, because he transgresseth by wine, he is a proud man, neither keepeth at home, who enlargeth his desire as hell, and is as death, and cannot be satisfied, but gathereth unto him all nations, and heapeth unto him all people:

6. Shall not all these take up a parable against him, and a taunting proverb against him, and say, Woe

Day 189: don't waste the 4 minutes and 22 seconds (on average) you will spend on the toilet. Read the much-neglected Old Testament Book of Habakkuk instead, and try and improve yourself.

to him that increaseth that which is not his! how long? and to him that ladeth himself with thick clay!

7. Shall they not rise up suddenly that shall bite thee, and awake that shall vex thee, and thou shalt be for booties unto them?

8. Because thou hast spoiled many nations, all the remnant of the people shall spoil thee; because of men's blood, and for the violence of the land, of the city, and of all that dwell therein.

9. Woe to him that coveteth an evil covetousness to his house, that he may set his nest on high, that he may be delivered from the power of evil!

10. Thou hast consulted shame to thy house by cutting off many people, and hast sinned against thy soul.

11. For the stone shall cry out of the wall, and the beam out of the timber shall answer it.

12. Woe to him that buildeth a town with blood, and stablisheth a city by iniquity!

13. Behold, is it not of the LORD of hosts that the people shall labour in the very fire, and the people shall weary themselves for very vanity?

14. For the earth shall be filled with the knowledge of the glory of the LORD, as the waters cover the sea.

15. Woe unto him that giveth his neighbour drink, that puttest thy bottle to him, and makest him drunken also, that thou mayest look on their nakedness!

16. Thou art filled with shame for glory: drink thou also, and let thy foreskin be uncovered: the cup of the LORD's right hand shall be turned unto thee, and shameful spewing shall be on thy glory.

17. For the violence of Lebanon shall cover thee,

Notes

and the spoil of beasts, which made them afraid, because of men's blood, and for the violence of the land, of the city, and of all that dwell therein.

18. What profiteth the graven image that the maker thereof hath graven it; the molten image, and a teacher of lies, that the maker of his work trusteth therein, to make dumb idols?

19. Woe unto him that saith to the wood, Awake; to the dumb stone, Arise, it shall teach! Behold, it is laid over with gold and silver, and there is no breath at all in the midst of it.

20. But the LORD is in his holy temple: let all the earth keep silence before him.

CHAPTER 3

1. A prayer of Habakkuk the prophet upon Shigionoth.

2. O LORD, I have heard thy speech, and was afraid: O LORD, revive thy work in the midst of the years, in the midst of the years make known; in wrath remember mercy.

3. God came from Teman, and the Holy One from mount Paran. Selah. His glory covered the heavens, and the earth was full of his praise.

4. And his brightness was as the light; he had horns coming out of his hand: and there was the hiding of his power.

5. Before him went the pestilence, and burning coals went forth at his feet.

6. He stood, and measured the earth: he beheld, and drove asunder the nations; and the everlasting mountains were scattered, the perpetual hills did bow: his ways are everlasting.

7. I saw the tents of Cushan in affliction: and the curtains of the land of Midian did tremble.

8. Was the LORD displeased against the rivers? was thine anger against the rivers? was thy wrath against the sea, that thou didst ride upon thine horses and thy chariots of salvation?

9. Thy bow was made quite naked, according to the oaths of the tribes, even thy word. Selah. Thou didst cleave the earth with rivers.

10. The mountains saw thee, and they trembled: the overflowing of the water passed by: the deep uttered his voice, and lifted up his hands on high.

11. The sun and moon stood still in their habitation: at the light of thine arrows they went, and at the shining of thy glittering spear.

12. Thou didst march through the land in indignation, thou didst thresh the heathen in anger.

13. Thou wentest forth for the salvation of thy people, even for salvation with thine anointed; thou woundedst the head out of the house of the wicked, by discovering the foundation unto the neck. Selah.

14. Thou didst strike through with his staves the head of his villages: they came out as a whirlwind to scatter me: their rejoicing was as to devour the poor secretly.

15. Thou didst walk through the sea with thine horses, through the heap of great waters.

16. When I heard, my belly trembled; my lips quivered at the voice: rottenness entered into my bones, and I trembled in myself, that I might rest in the day of trouble: when he cometh up unto the people, he will invade them with his troops.

17. Although the fig tree shall not blossom, neither shall fruit be in the vines; the labour of the olive shall fail, and the fields shall yield no meat; the flock shall be cut off from the fold, and there shall be no herd in the stalls:

18. Yet I will rejoice in the LORD, I will joy in the God of my salvation.

19. The LORD God is my strength, and he will make my feet like hinds' feet, and he will make me to walk upon mine high places. To the chief singer on my stringed instruments.

DAY 190: FOLLOW THESE DIRECTIONS

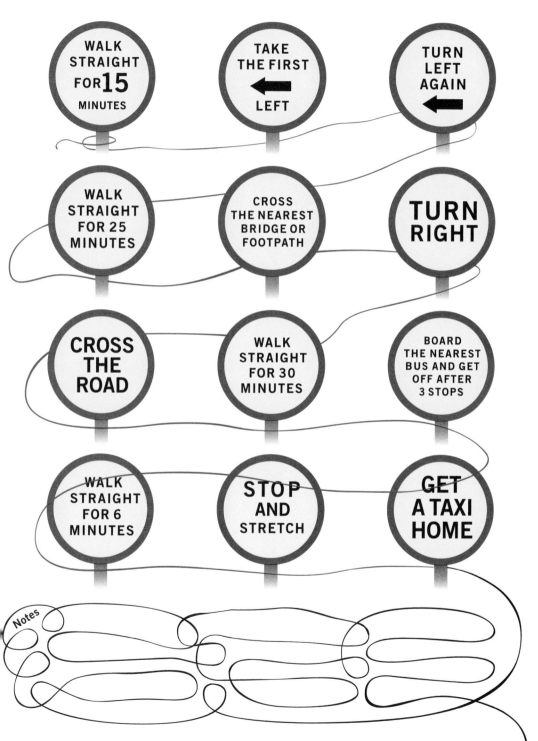

DAY 191 BURY A TREASURE TODAY This is a fun day out. Assemble some objects that have special meaning to you, like family photos, some letters, and a hoard of stolen gold. Find a secluded spot and dig a hole at least one foot deep, so some dumb dog can't unearth it. Draw a map of the location so that you will be able to find it in ten or twenty years' time. Place your treasure in a sealed box. Now bury it. One day when you're broke and/or civilization has crumbled, you'll be glad to dig it up and live off the contents!

NOTES

**Attention!
Do not bury
the map.**

Day 192

Family Love day

Incest works well for animal breeding, so why not for you?
Today explore your deeper feelings toward a cousin, a sibling, or
a parent perhaps. Taboos, after all, are made to be broken.

Notes

You are a precious
flower. Or a delicate bud perhaps?
No, no, rather, you are like a beautiful as yet
undeveloped photograph, that will perish without light.
Why all those endless hours wasted in the preternatural gloom
of your sordid little place of work? Stroll, or sit outside for a couple
of hours today and enjoy the sun's golden rays. SAD (Seasonal Affective
Disorder) is a clinically diagnosed condition in which the lack of sunlight in
winter literally makes people ill. It affects millions of people around the
world, though proportionately more the farther you get from the equator of
course. In the more remote parts of Scandinavia, it has been known to con-
tribute to higher suicide rates. SAD's effects can be explained with reference
to the importance of sunlight on cellular functioning. As light enters the eye,
it hits the retina and filters through to the pineal gland. The pineal gland in
turn produces melatonin, a neurotransmitter that affects the hypothalamus
gland. The hypothalamus controls a whole range of vital functions, including
mood, hormones, appetite, libido and metabolism. Beyond this,
sunlight is also crucial as an indirect provider of Vitamin D. The sun's
ultraviolet rays set off its production, itself necessary for the
absorption of calcium in the bones and teeth. Indeed,
vitamin D deficiency among those who spend too
much time indoors, can lead to brittle
bones and fractures.

Notes

Day 193

Day 194: A word from our sponsors

At this point in the year the makers of THIS BOOK WILL CHANGE YOUR LIFE feel obliged to point out that this entire book would not have been possible without the kind and far-sighted sponsorship of Stockham Management Consultants Inc, »the vision behind your vision.« Stockham Management Consultants provide tailor-made solutions to all your business and non-business needs through their team of highly experienced business solutionizing consultants, led by Artie Stockham. But perhaps we should let him speak:

»In our increasingly complex world, you as a business need the right kind of help at the right kind of time. That's where we come in. No matter what your field of expertise, Stockham Management Consulting can assist in setting and reaching the targets you need to achieve, rather like the daily ›targets‹ in this quirky and amusing Book, which is why we at Stockham felt it was such a good strategic sponsorship fit. So in the spirit of ›fun‹ and bold experimentation that characterizes this publication, we have brainstormed our own daily page. We hope it inspires you.« Artie Stockham

Today, prioritize your dreams!

Day 196

Mannerisms Day

Your body language is as individual as your DNA. You move in your very own mysterious ways, and your physical quirks actually reveal much about you. Today, try to be aware of what your body is saying to those around you: don't let them betray your innermost feelings.

YOU BITE YOUR LIPS:
you fear your hidden demons.

YOU TOUCH YOUR NOSE:
you lack the confidence to face others.

YOU FIDDLE WITH YOUR HAIR:
you are not comfortable with your appearance.

YOU BITE YOUR NAILS:
you have repressed anger within you.

YOU SHAKE ONE LEG:
you are nurturing some chronic anxiety.

YOU LICK YOUR LIPS:
this one doesn't mean anything.

YOU TAP YOUR FINGERS:
you have tendencies towards control freakery.

Notes

THIS BABY SAYS

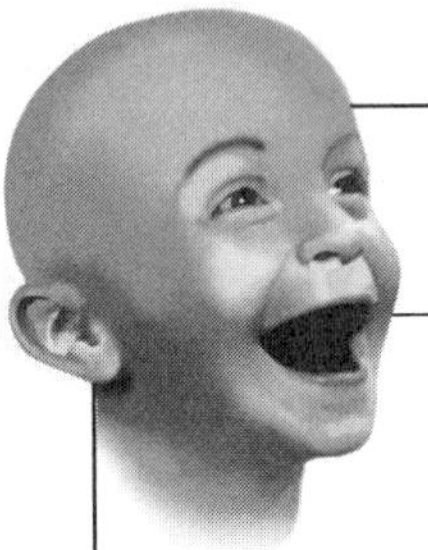

Improve your signature today

DAY 197. In an increasingly digitized society where you're defined by your social security and bank account numbers, your signature is one of the very last bastions of your individuality. Let other great historical signatures inspire it; refine it constantly; and above all take pride in it!

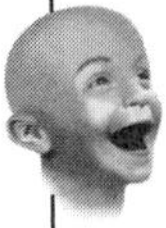

Great signatures of our time

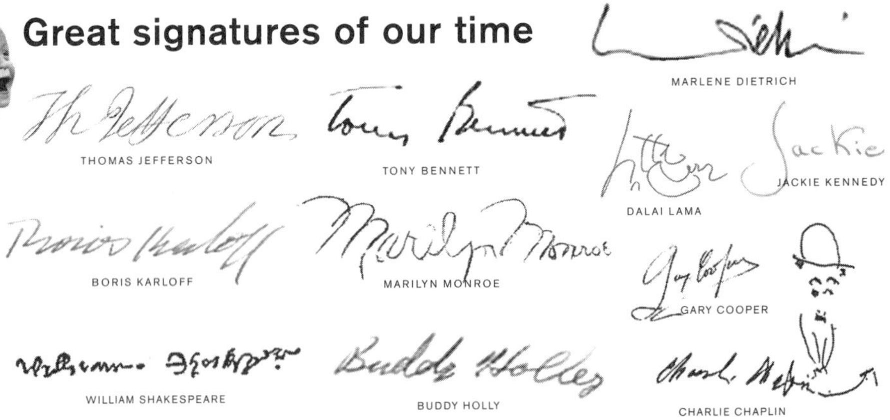

MARLENE DIETRICH
THOMAS JEFFERSON
TONY BENNETT
DALAI LAMA
JACKIE KENNEDY
BORIS KARLOFF
MARILYN MONROE
GARY COOPER
WILLIAM SHAKESPEARE
BUDDY HOLLY
CHARLIE CHAPLIN

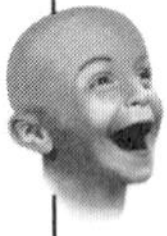

Practice area

Signature before

Signature after

NOTES

Remember to notify your bank!

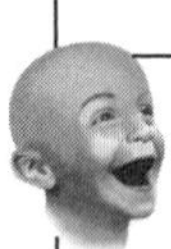

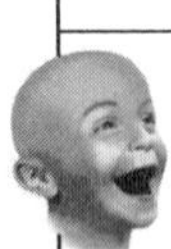

Day 198
TODAY, HAVE A GOOD CRY
Research has revealed that crying is good for us,
indeed that it is physiologically essential.
There are three different types of tears.
1) Basal tears, that keep our eyes lubricated.
2) Reflex tears, when a foreign
body gets into or irritates our eyes.
3) Emotional tears, when we react
psychologically to something.
Emotional tears contain chemically higher levels of
manganese and prolactin hormone. Losing these
through crying reduces their levels in the body and
keeps depression away. This is why we feel better
after a good cry. Here are some sad thoughts to help
stimulate your crying glands and cheer you up:
We're all going to die…eventually.
Can you really ever trust anyone fully? Really?
You may never meet the love of your life.
Orphans, starving.
Time is running out.
Snookums the puppy has died (horribly).

DAY 199 FAQS DAY MEMORIZE THE ANSWERS TO THESE QUESTIONS, MY CHILD: YOUR LIFE WILL DEPEND ON THEM AT SOME POINT IN THE FUTURE.

WHAT DO YOU CALL THOSE LITTLE PLASTIC THINGS ON THE TIP OF SHOELACES? AGLETS.

WHY DO YOU NEVER SEE BABY PIGEONS? THEY GROW UP TOO FAST.

WOULD A MARS BAR MELT ON MARS? YES.

WHAT IS THE MOST COMMON MIDDLE NAME? MARY.

WHAT YEAR WERE TENNIS BALLS OFFICIALLY CHANGED FROM WHITE TO YELLOW? 1967.

HOW MUCH WATER DO WE PASS ON AVERAGE? 8OZ/MINUTE.

HOW MUCH DOES THE TALKING CLOCK GUY GET PAID? $3,100 A YEAR.

WHAT WAS THE WEATHER OVER SAO PAULO ON THE MORNING OF MAY 12, 1976? CLOUDY.

WHAT IS THE VOLUME OF A WHALE'S EJACULATE? HALF A GALLON.

HOW MANY DIMPLES ARE THERE ON A GOLF BALL? 336.

WHAT IS THE SECOND MOST POPULAR CAT NAME? PATCHES.

WHEN WERE POSTAGE STAMPS INVENTED? 1840.

WHAT IS THE LONGEST RECORDED FLIGHT OF A CHICKEN? 13 SECONDS.

HOW MUCH DOES AN AVERAGE ADULT HUMAN HEART WEIGH? 10OZ.

WHAT IS THE ONLY FOOD THAT DOES NOT SPOIL? HONEY.

WHAT WAS THE NAME OF LADY GODIVA'S HORSE? AETHENOTH.

HOW MANY HAIRS IN THE AVERAGE BEARD? 12,000.

HOW MANY BRICKS ARE THERE IN THE EMPIRE STATE BUILDING? 10 MILLION.

WHO IS THE PATRON SAINT OF TOOTHACHES? ST. APOLLONIA.

NOTES

DAY 200: SEND A MESSAGE IN A BOTTLE

Be sure to choose the appropriate bottle for your message.

Plain glass bottle:
standard »I'm lost on a
desert island« messages

Mineral water bottle:
for long fancy letters you'd like
to see published someday

Perfume bottle:
letters to one's illicit lovers

Vintage champagne bottle:
formal messages: weddings,
funerals, bar mitzvahs

Plastic bottle:
messages to your
inferiors

Notes

_____
_____
_____
_____
_____
_____
_____
_____
_____
_____
_____
_____

DON'T FORGET THE CORK!!

(Note: according to marine experts, there are currently
125,000 bottles containing messages floating around
the world's oceans. Yours could be one of them.)

Beer bottle:
party invitations & news
of sports victories

Soft drink bottle:
the young person's choice

Medicine bottle:
painful news

Foreign wine bottle:
letters from abroad,
holiday postcards

Broken bottle:
suicide notes

DAY 201

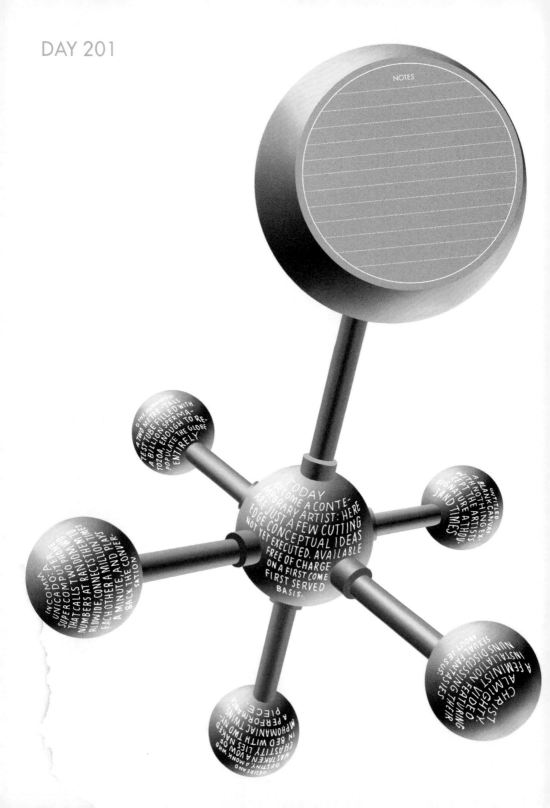

NOTES

TODAY BECOME A CONTEMPORARY ARTIST: HERE ARE JUST A FEW CUTTING EDGE CONCEPTUAL IDEAS NOT YET EXECUTED, AVAILABLE FREE OF CHARGE ON A FIRST COME FIRST SERVED BASIS.

A TWO METRE-TALL TEST TUBE FILLED WITH A BILLION SPERMATOZOA, ENOUGH TO REPOPULATE THE GLOBE ENTIRELY. *THE HUMANITY*

AN UNTITLED BLANK CANVAS - A NOTHING EXPRESSING THE ARTIST'S SIGNATURE A THOUSAND TIMES.

A FEMINIST CHRIST ALMIGHTY VIDEO INSTALLATION FEATURING NUNS DISCUSSING THEIR SEXUAL FANTASIES ABOUT JESUS.

INCOMMUNICADO: A NEW SUPERCOMPUTER PHONE THAT CALLS TWO RANDOM NUMBERS AT RANDOM TIMES WORLDWIDE, CONNECTS THEM TO EACH OTHER A MILLION A MINUTE, AND PLAYS BACK THE CONVERSATION.

CHASTITY LIES NAKED IN BED WITH TWO NYMPHOMANIAC TWINS - A PERFORMANCE PIECE. *DEFILE AND DESTROY: A MONK WHO HAS TAKEN A VOW OF*

PREGNANCY TEST DAY
You can never be too careful. Deposit a drop of urine on this chemically-sensitive spot to determine whether you're in the family way.

WHITE: You've missed. Try depositing your drop from a closer range, however good you believe your aim to be.
RED: Allelujah! You are the proud future parent of a precious lil'baby! Get into that whole baby talk thang now! Goo grrr!
BLUE: Hmmm. Cold. Better luck next time.

GREEN: Shittin' hell. Good luck to you, you're gonna need it.
YELLOW: You've just actually urinated in a book. Yuck. How revolting. Please get rid of this copy and buy a clean one.
MEN: If your pee goes anything but a faint yellow, this might indicate a hormonal imbalance – or a scientific first.

Notes

BOOK PYRAMID SCHEME

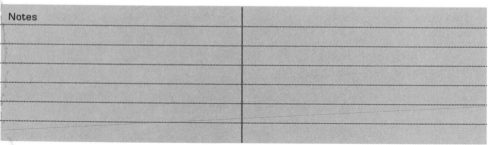

Notes

Irony is a curse in disguise, corrupting and reducing everything to the same
superficial level and abolishing depth in both values and relationships.
Today, avoid the temptations of glibness and frivolity, and take life seriously for a change.

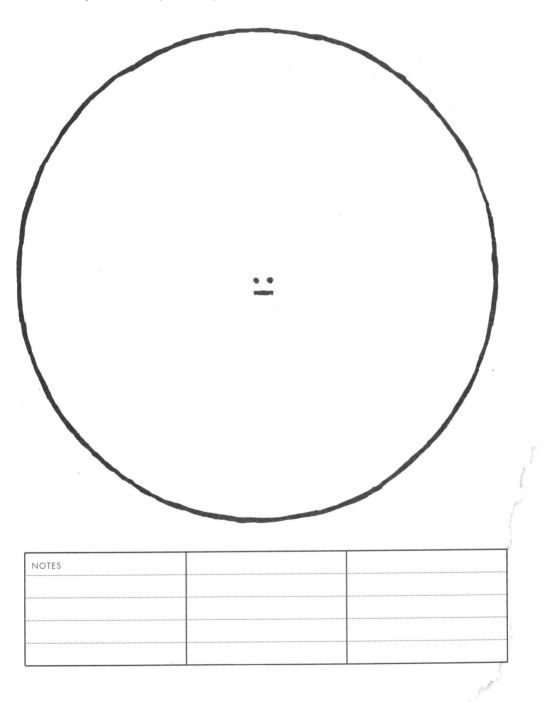

NOTES		

JOUR 205. TAKE THIS WEEK OFF AND SPEND IT IN FRANCE, BEHAVING LIKE THE FRENCH

NOTE: YOU SHOULD HAVE PLANNED THIS VACATION WHEN WE TOLD YOU TO THREE MONTHS AGO ON DAY 116. HOWEVER IF YOU DIDN'T GET ROUND TO IT OR YOU'VE FOUND SOME LAME EXCUSE TO STAY HOME, YOU CAN STILL PARTICIPATE IN THIS WEEK'S FUN WITH THE HELP OF OUR «VACATIONING AT HOME» GUIDELINES.

THE BOOK: ESSENTIAL TRAVEL PRECAUTIONS

FRANCE IS IN MANY RESPECTS A LOVELY AND CULTURED LAND, BUT IT IS ALSO NOTORIOUSLY FULL OF THIEVING MISCREANTS. MAKE SURE YOU HIDE THE BOOK WELL. NEVER LEAVE IT IN A PARKED CAR. PUT IT IN THE HOTEL SAFE. CARRY IT IN A CONCEALED MONEY POUCH. IF IT IS STOLEN, DO NOT GO THE POLICE, AS THEY WILL VERY LIKELY BE IN ON THE THEFT. INSTEAD, APPROACH YOUR EMBASSY OR CONSULATE, WHO WILL EXERT PRESSURE ON THE FRENCH GOVERNMENT ON YOUR BEHALF THROUGH THE PROPER DIPLOMATIC CHANNELS.

NOTES	

HOW TO GET TO FRANCE

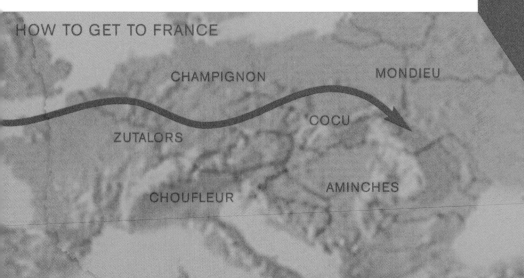

CHAMPIGNON   MONDIEU

COCU

ZUTALORS

CHOUFLEUR   AMINCHES

THE FRENCH THINK NOTHING OF SHOUTING AT
EACH OTHER IN FRONT OF EVERYONE, SO LET
LOOSE. SUITABLE TOPICS INCLUDE THE STATE
OF SOCIALISM TODAY, THE HUMAN CONDITION
AT THE DAWN OF THE THIRD MILLENNIUM, WHO
GETS TO PLAY WITH THE BEACH BALL NEXT.

VACATIONING AT HOME? PUBLIC FIGHTS ARE FROWNED UPON, SO EITHER WHISPER URGENTLY AND
SCOWL AT YOUR PARTNER, OR PRETEND TO BE A FRENCH TOURIST AND SCREAM AT EACH OTHER IN FRENCH.

NOTES

IN FRANCE, BUYING AN »EXPRÈS« IN ANY CAFÉ ENTITLES YOU TO SIT THERE FOR AS LONG AS YOU LIKE. THUS IT PROVIDES THE PERFECT OPPORTUNITY FOR FRENCH PEOPLE OF ALL AGES TO WRITE VOLUMINOUS TOMES ON HOW THEY SEE LIFE, WHICH ARE NEVER LESS THAN COMPELLING. MOST FAMOUS IS JEAN-PAUL SARTRE'S »BEING AND NOTHINGNESS,« WHICH AT 1564 PAGES, WAS WELL WORTH THE PRICE OF THAT »EXPRÈS.«

VACATIONING AT HOME? SIT IN A SPORTS BAR. YOUR PHILOSOPHY MAY HAVE TO BE SHORTER THAN THE FULL FRENCH DEAL THOUGH, AS STAFF ARE LESS SYMPATHETIC AND MIGHT KICK YOU OUT AFTER A BIT.

NOTES

JOUR 208   TOPLESS SUNBATHING DAY

OH LA LA, LADIES! THIS IS WHERE YOU LOSE YOUR INHIBI-
TIONS AND HIT THE BEACH *AU NATUREL*. MEN: IT IS IMPOR-
TANT TO STAY COOL AND CASUAL AMIDST THE PROFUSION
OF BARE FLESH. ACT AS IF YOU SEE THIS ALL THE TIME AND
IF ANYTHING ARE PERHAPS MILDLY BORED BY IT. STICKING
YOUR HEAD IN »BEING AND NOTHINGNESS« COULD HELP.

VACATIONING AT HOME? THIS ONE IS
POTENTIALLY ILLEGAL. AVOID, EXCEPT
IN THE PRIVACY OF YOUR OWN PATIO.

NOTES

GAULOISES CIGARETTES ARE THE MARK OF THE GENUINE FRENCH PEASANT, SALT OF THE FRENCH EARTH. TO CONVERSE WITH HIM ON EQUAL TERMS – A VACATION MUST – YOU MUST REEK OF GAULOISES TOO AND LOWER YOUR VOICE TO THE GUTTURAL LUNG-CANCERISH DEPTH THAT HE IS ACCUSTOMED TO. CHAIN SMOKING THREE PACKS SHOULD DO THE TRICK.

VACATIONING AT HOME? YOU MAY EXPERIENCE DIFFICULTIES IN LOCATING GAULOISES AND/OR FRENCH PEASANTS.

NOTES

TAKE A LOVER

THE FRENCH ARE DEMOCRATIC IN THEIR UNFAITHFULNESS. BOTH SEXES ARE ENTITLED TO CHEAT IN EQUAL MEASURES. HOWEVER SOME RULES MUST BE OBEYED. THERE MUST BE A SIGNIFICANT AGE GAP BETWEEN YOU AND YOUR LOVER. YOU MUST COME FROM WILDLY DIFFERENT SOCIAL BACKGROUNDS. AND YOU MUST ONLY MAKE LOVE IN GARRETS. VACATIONING AT HOME? THIS IS ONE YOU CAN TRY, THOUGH PEOPLE ARE USUALLY MORE FUSSY ABOUT COMMITMENT AND OTHER NARROW-MINDED UNFRENCH CONCEPTS.

NOTES

PROTEST VIOLENTLY AGAINST THE GOVERNMENT

END YOUR VACATION ON A HIGH NOTE, WITH A SPOT OF RIOTING. IN FRANCE YOU NEED NO PARTICULAR EXCUSE FOR DIRECT ACTION, AS THE 1789 REVOLUTION WAS NEVER OFFICIALLY DECLARED TO HAVE ENDED. JUST LOB BRICKS OR MANURE AT THE NEAREST OFFICIAL-LOOKING BUILDING AND YOU WILL SOON BE INTRODUCED TO THE LOCAL RIOT POLICE WHO WILL ASSIST YOU BACK HOME AFTER A BRIEF SPELL *EN PRISON*.

VACATIONING AT HOME? BEST TO END VACATION EARLY ON THIS ONE.

NOTES

Pillow book
Tonight use the Book as your pillow book and write down your dreams.

What is a pillow book?
The pillow book is a Japanese institution, first used in 550AD by the Asuka dynasty. It is used to record thoughts, events, dreams. Now, the Asukas used to mainly dream about giant serpents, many-clawed dragons, saber-toothed tigers and the like, but there's no reason why you can't write down your boring old everyday dreams about your third-grade teacher. You must however use Japanese calligraphy to do so.

Day 212

NOTES

DAY 213

SURVEILLANCE SPECIAL: TODAY STAGE A CRIME IN FRONT OF A BACK-ALLEY SECURITY CAMERA AND SEE IF ANYONE COMES TO THE RESCUE.

1) LITTERING

2) DRUNKEN FIGHTING/JOSTLING

3) MUGGING

4) STABBING FOLLOWED BY MUGGING

5) STABBING AND/OR GANG-BEATING WITH MUGGING

6) MURDER (IF ALL ELSE FAILS)

NOTES

TODAY, MEASURE YOUR IQ

YOU HAVE TEN MINUTES TO COMPLETE THIS TEST. IF ONE
ITEM PROVES TOO DIFFICULT, MOVE ON TO THE NEXT ONE.

1 INSERT THE WORD THAT COMPLETES BOTH OTHER WORDS

SHAL(...)BROW

2 INSERT THE MISSING NUMBER

| 3 | 9 | 26 | 9 | 27 | 80 | 6 | 18 | ? |

3 WHICH IS THE ODD ONE OUT?

| HOJH | ICADLUA |
| BLATRE | CHIMLEA |

5 WHAT THREE-LETTER WORD ENDING CAN BE PREFIXED BY ALL THESE?

CL...
N...
B...
T...
S...
R...
W...
G...

DAY 214

NOTES

4 WHAT IS THE MISSING NUMBER?

4   7   ?   11   16   22

6 WHAT IS THE MISSING NUMBER?

4976 4463 3950 3437 ?

7 WHAT NUMBER GOES HERE?

FREEMASON=232
SATANIST=?

8 END THIS SENTENCE

THE OAK SPANS FIVE ?

9 WHICH IS THE ODD ONE OUT?

① ② ③ ④

YOUR IQ = FINAL SCORE SQUARED + 100. UNDER 110: POOR TO AVERAGE 110-130: GOOD 130-150: VERY BRIGHT
150 AND OVER: LIAR

ANSWERS: 1 LOW 2 53 3 ICADLUA 4 29 5 EAR 6 2924 7 563 8 HILLS 9 no.2

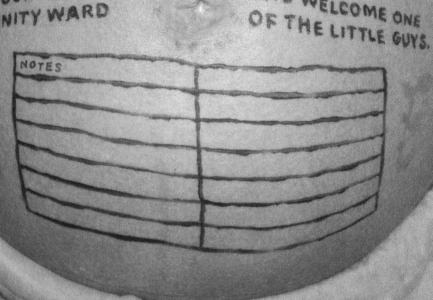

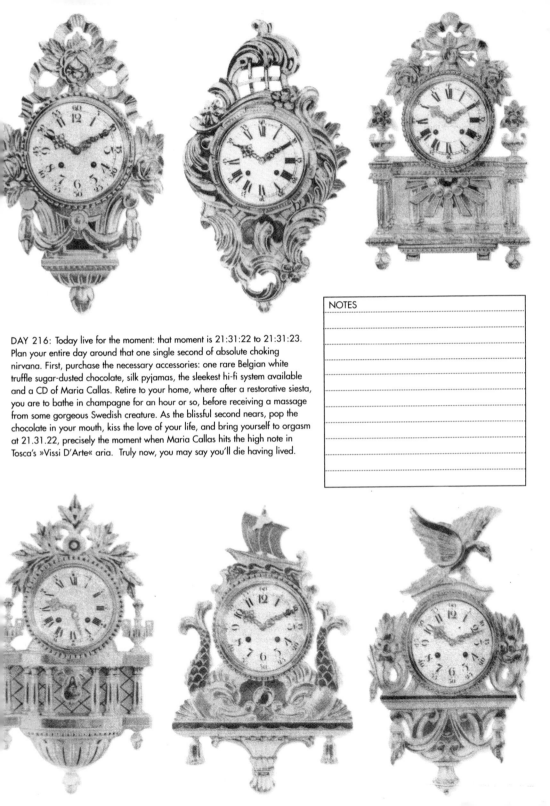

DAY 216: Today live for the moment: that moment is 21:31:22 to 21:31:23. Plan your entire day around that one single second of absolute choking nirvana. First, purchase the necessary accessories: one rare Belgian white truffle sugar-dusted chocolate, silk pyjamas, the sleekest hi-fi system available and a CD of Maria Callas. Retire to your home, where after a restorative siesta, you are to bathe in champagne for an hour or so, before receiving a massage from some gorgeous Swedish creature. As the blissful second nears, pop the chocolate in your mouth, kiss the love of your life, and bring yourself to orgasm at 21.31.22, precisely the moment when Maria Callas hits the high note in Tosca's »Vissi D'Arte« aria. Truly now, you may say you'll die having lived.

NOTES

VIP-DAY

These are the people we'd like to buy and read the Book. If your name is on the list, please use the exclusive form to tell us what you think. If your name isn't on the list, please turn the page and move along. Thank you.

The Dalai Lama (religious leader)
The President of the USA (leader)
The Vice-President of the USA (leader)
Kofi Annan (political leader, UN)
The Pope (religious leader)
Oprah Winfrey (celebrity)
Jean Baudrillard (French philosopher)
Jerry Springer (celebrity)
Steven Spielberg (filmmaker)
Madonna (singer)
Richard Branson (British businessman)
Tony Blair (Prime Minister of England)
Mick Jagger (singer)
Salman Rushdie (author)
David Beckham (sportsman)
Bill Cosby (entertainer)
Colin Powell (political leader)
Stephen Hawking (scientist)
Michael Jackson (singer)
Arnold Schwarzenegger (actor)
Hugh Hefner (editor)
Yoko Ono (artist)
Afrika Bambaataa (artist)
Jack Chirac (political leader)
Meryl Streep (actress)
Sinead O'Connor (singer)
Noam Chomsky (intellectual)
Luciano Pavarotti (singer)
Henry Kissinger (intellectual)
Mike Oldfield (singer)
Ivan Lendl (sportsman)
Tom Cruise (actor)

David Copperfield (entertainer)
Gore Vidal (writer)
Donald Trump (businessman)
Bill Gates (businessman)
Eddie Murphy (actor)
Mikhail Gorbachev (political leader)
Robert De Niro (actor)
Newt Gingrich (political leader)
Celine Dion (singer)
Al Gore (political leader)
Alan Greenspan (economist)
Umberto Eco (writer)
Günter Grass (writer)
Norman Mailer (intellectual)
Donna Tartt (writer)
Wes Craven (filmmaker)
Ingmar Bergman (filmmaker)
Bono (singer)
George Michael (singer)
Justin Timberlake (singer)
Vladimir Putin (political leader)
Tiger Woods (sportsman)
Pamela Anderson (actress)
Siwert Öholm (entertainer)
Stock, Aitken, Waterman (producers)
Phillippe Starck (designer)
Stephen King (writer)
Tom Hanks (actor)
Bryan Ferry (singer)
Helmut Newton (photographer)
Natasha Kinski (actor)
Chelsea Clinton (daughter)

Phil Collins (singer)
Elton John (singer)
Tina Turner (singer)
Sting (singer)
Bruce Springsteen (singer)
Robert Murdoch (businessman)
George Soros (businessman)
Michael Douglas (actor)
Robin Williams (actor)
Margaret Thatcher (stateswoman)
Renzo Piano (architect)
Nelson Mandela (statesman)
Jacques Derrida (philosopher)
Pierre Boulez (composer)
Germaine Greer (writer)
Peter Greenaway (filmmaker)
Jurgen Habermas (thinker)
David Hockney (artist)
Jimmy Carter (political leader)
Don Johnson (actor)
Helmut Kohl (statesman)
Camille Paglia (intellectual)
Cindy Crawford (model)
Lady Sarah Ferguson (royalty)
Lord Wolff (high court judge)
Roland Magdane (French comedian)
Jon Bon Jovi (singer)
Yasser Arafat (political leader)
Charlton Heston (actor)
Bernard Pivot (French intellectual)
Ralph Nader (intellectual)
Gene Simmons (singer)

I,..........................., whose name appears above, have perused the Book and this is my considered opinion of it:
....
....
....
....

You have my permission to use it as a review, should you wish to do so. Signed:.....................................

Please send this form to Benrik, c/o Penguin Plume, 375 Hudson St, New York, NY 10014, USA.

If you feel your name should be on this page but has been overlooked, please write in as well stating your case, with supporting evidence and references where appropriate.

NOTES

NOTES

DAY 219: VOLUME—TEST YOUR NEIGHBORS

These days the puniest hi-fi system can pump out a cool 100Wx2. But at what point do your neighbors begin to feel the bass? Find out by adjusting your amplifier's dial up until they start complaining. Then mark the notch and leave it as your standard setting.

NOTES

CONFIDENTIAL:

A huge meteorite is about to hit the Earth, blasting it into smithereens. The world's main governments left weeks ago for a secret base on Pluto, leaving their lookalikes to keep the populace placid. Only owners of the Book are allowed to be in the know, so please keep this information to yourself.

OPTIONS: THERE ARE FOUR MAIN WAYS OF REACTING TO THE NEWS.

1) GO ON THE RAMPAGE
You are understandably peeved at the imminent termination of your life, and need to channel your anger. Also, the rules of society are now null and void, as you need not worry about punishment. So let loose and steal, fight, pillage and destroy.

2) HAVE SEX WITH EVERYONE
People will feel much freer to hop into bed with you today, as long-term commitment is less of an issue. This only goes for fellow Book owners though; others who are not aware of their impending doom may need more convincing.

3) PREPARE FOR THE AFTERLIFE
A bit of a gamble, but probably worth it by now: find the nearest priest and go full tilt for last minute salvation. This option is not compatible with the two previous ones however.

4) SIT IN FRONT OF TV IN NUMBED DISBELIEF Probably the option most people will resort to. You may not even notice much change from everyday life.

NOTES

LIVE THIS DAY AS IF IT WERE YOUR LAST.

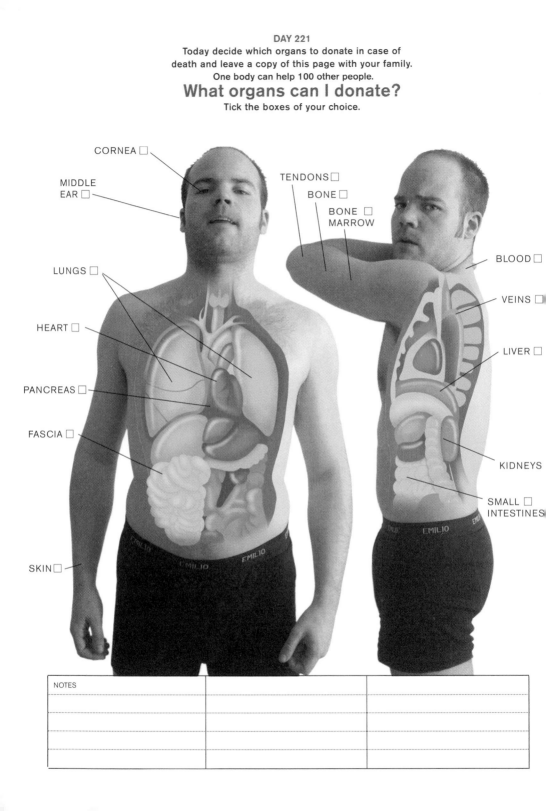

DAY 221
Today decide which organs to donate in case of
death and leave a copy of this page with your family.
One body can help 100 other people.

What organs can I donate?

Tick the boxes of your choice.

CORNEA ☐

MIDDLE
EAR ☐

TENDONS ☐
BONE ☐
BONE ☐
MARROW

BLOOD ☐

LUNGS ☐

VEINS ☐

HEART ☐

LIVER ☐

PANCREAS ☐

FASCIA ☐

KIDNEYS

SMALL ☐
INTESTINES

SKIN ☐

NOTES

FIND A WAY OF INCLUDING THE WORD VORTEX IN ALL YOUR CONVERSATIONS TODAY. Try to do it without sounding clumsy. Here are some suggestions: »Lovely weather, isn't it?«, »Yes, though that cloud over there looks a bit *vortex*-shaped«, »This business report makes for interesting reading«, »Indeed. It lies at the *vortex* of cruciality«, »Did you see that program on television last night?«, »What, the one about the *vortex?*«

Day 222

VORTEX

Notes

TODAY FEEL THE PASSAGE OF TIME

Tick every precious minute as it goes by and appreciate the true measure of time

Minute
ONE

NOTES

TODAY CUT IN LINE

NO Avoid the elderly: they have high moral standards and will enjoy rebuking a young hooligan in public.

YES Tourists are a good bet: they don't know the rules, they won't speak well enough to protest, and in their country it's often the done thing anyway.

NO Avoid the middle of the line: people have been there a long time already and are stressed about whether they'll get in.

BEST The very front of the line has been scientifically proven to be the best place to muscle in: people are relaxed as they can see they'll get in, and it's so cheeky they can't believe you're cutting in anyway.

BOX OFFICE

NOTES

Day 225

In 1992, the town of Kiruna in the north of Sweden became concerned about the falling birth rate amongst its citizens. It was calculated that if the rate didn't improve, Kiruna's population would halve in size within 30 years. So, the town council decided to cut off the electricity for 24 hours, every first day of the month. Initially, this caused an uproar. But protests subsided when an unprecedented number of babies were born within the same week, exactly nine months later...

No Electricity Day

Our proud ancestors survived for years without electricity. See if you can last a day without relying on any electrically powered devices.

Notes

Why spend a fortune on clothes to make a fashion statement when your own head provides the perfect opportunity already? Here are some popular radical haircuts to inspire you.

The Waterfall

The Don King

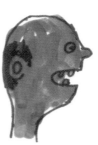

The Executive
(This one looks particularly radical on women)

Random Patches

The Square

The Mullet

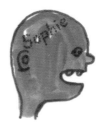

The name of the person you love

The King

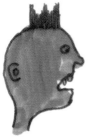

The Queen

The Russian

The Squirrel

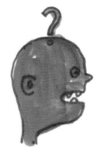

Your very own

Notes			DAY 226

 Advanced: DO SOMETHING RADICAL WITH YOUR PUBIC HAIR. If your main (non-pubic) hair is already radical or you are bald, style your pubic regions. Shaving is hip but potentially dangerous. Coloring is more original and a welcome ice-breaker on those one-night stands.

Day 227

Today go to a supermarket
and enter all the competitions

Tell us why new
detergent WIZ is the
BIZ! and WIN A TRIP
TO BELGIUM

SUPERMARKET
SWEEPSTAKE!
The fullest trolley
gets their money
back!

This coupon could
mean a coupé!

Notes

Tie-breaker! SPLOSH
paint is the best
BECAUSE.....

BUY A BAR!
WIN A CAR!

Any of these beans could
contain...the GOLDEN BISCUIT!!!

Collect 200 points like this one
and this magnificent pen is yours!

Win your weight
in tuna chunks!

If you don't win anything, it must
be because they're rigged. Complain to the supermarket manager.

Phrenology Day
TODAY HAVE YOUR HEAD EXAMINED

Phrenology is the science of identifying character traits from the shape of the brain, itself deducible of course from the shape of the skull. As modern-day brain imaging techniques have confirmed beyond doubt, many of the brain's main functions are indeed localized. We have yet to confirm the exactitude of early phrenologists' categories, but in the meantime why not judge for yourself? Simply run your fingers over your skull and refer any unusual protuberances to the diagram below.

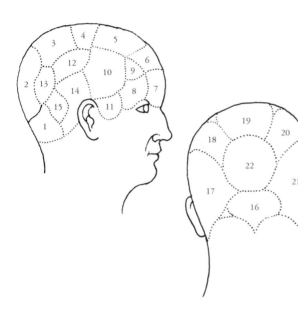

1. Impulse to propagate
2. Language faculty
3. Tenderness for offspring
4. Disposition for delighting in color patterns
5. Friendly attachments
6. Aptitude for music
7. Defense of self and property
8. Arithmetical ability
9. Carnivorous instinct /bloodlust
10. Architectural talent
11. Memory for faces
12. Sense of ruse
13. Relative sagacity
14. Metaphysical perspicuity
15. Arrogance and love of authority
16. Caustic wit
17. Vanity and love of glory
18. Poetical talent
19. Circumspection
20. Goodness
21. Theosophical feelings
22. Memory for names

Notes

Day 229: Today is Blue-Sky Day.
Forget the practicalities: decide what
you really want out of life. I want...

A shed on the
moon

72 kids

To be King
of Lombardy

A second
belly button

To make
love to the
Virgin Mary

My enemy's
head on a plate

NOTES

My own
nuclear-powered
submarine

A layer
of atmosphere
named after me

World
peace

One pyramid
for me and two smaller
ones for my followers

To be left
alone

To be
beamed
up

To rule
the world

Now make it
happen.

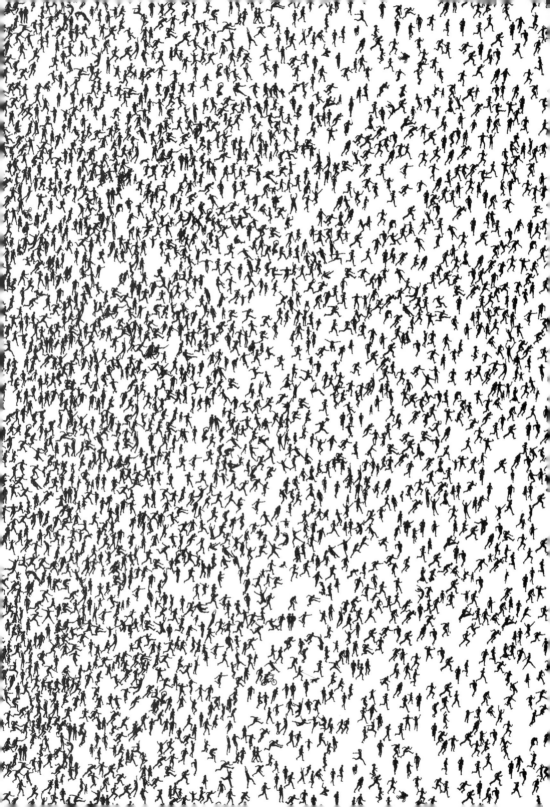

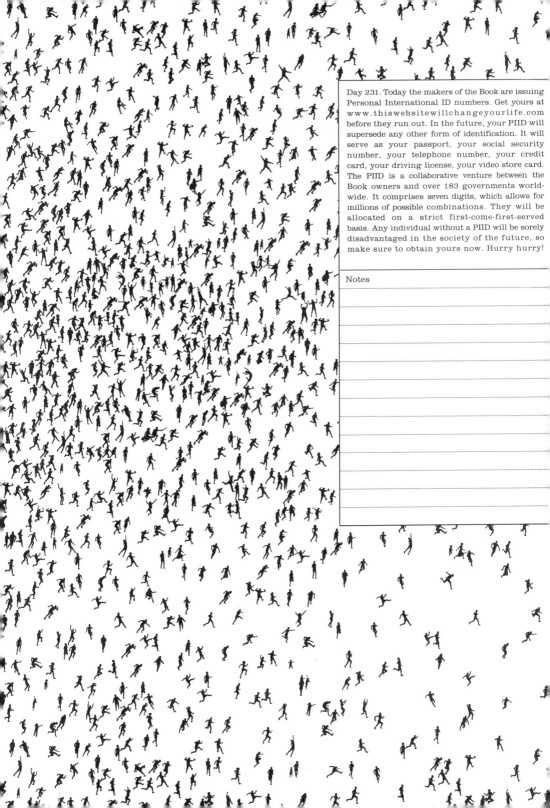

Day 231. Today the makers of the Book are issuing Personal International ID numbers. Get yours at www.thiswebsitewillchangeyourlife.com before they run out. In the future, your PIID will supersede any other form of identification. It will serve as your passport, your social security number, your telephone number, your credit card, your driving license, your video store card. The PIID is a collaborative venture between the Book owners and over 183 governments world-wide. It comprises seven digits, which allows for millions of possible combinations. They will be allocated on a strict first-come-first-served basis. Any individual without a PIID will be sorely disadvantaged in the society of the future, so make sure to obtain yours now. Hurry hurry!

Notes

....
....
....
....
....
....
....
....
....

SAUNA DAY

Once the Incredible Hulk was locked into a sauna by some evil man who was a criminal and he put the heat up to the max. But Hulk became the green monster out of anger and heat and smashed the bloody door down!!! Otherwise he would have sweated to death, and died. He caught the criminal man.

Saunas are good for you, so today turn your heating up to the max and indulge in some healthy sweating!

Russian sauna: the Banya

The wood-fired banya is an age-old tradition in Russia. The Khlysty, a 17th century Russian sect, used to gather there to practise self-flagellation, in the belief that the heat brought the blood closer to the surface of the skin. Theirs was a theology of salvation through sin, in which ecstatic collective prayer sessions (which some claimed ended in group orgies) were followed by violent whipping, designed to leave scars. Some claim they taught Sacher-Masoch and thus are the true fathers of masochism.

HEALTH NEWS!
HEALTH NEWS!
HEALTH NEWS!

SAUNAS INCREASE YOUR HEART RATE:
a 20 minute sauna is the equivalent of a brisk walk!

SAUNAS DETOXIFY YOUR SKIN, FLUSHING OUT IMPURITIES AND HELPING REDUCE CELLULITE!

Saunas raise your body temp to 100 degrees, creating an immune system-boosting fever!

Saunas relieve the painful symptoms of arthritis and revive tired muscles!

Sauna songs

(To the tune of Jingle Bells)
Sauna day, Sauna day,
Let's have lots of fun
Bring a towel and a snack
And let's turn up the heat.

(To the tune of My Bonnie)
Come and sit in my sauna
I cleaned it especially for you
There is no old sweat on the benches
So come and stain them with yours.

(To the tune of Old McDonald)
No one is allowed in here
With a towel on
And if you have your towel on
It will be removed.

(To the tune of Twinkle
Twinkle Little Star)
If you're tired or overworked
And you have no money left
To go on a holiday
Where there's sun and heat
Then you should pop on down to us
We'll wipe you and take care of you.

Notes

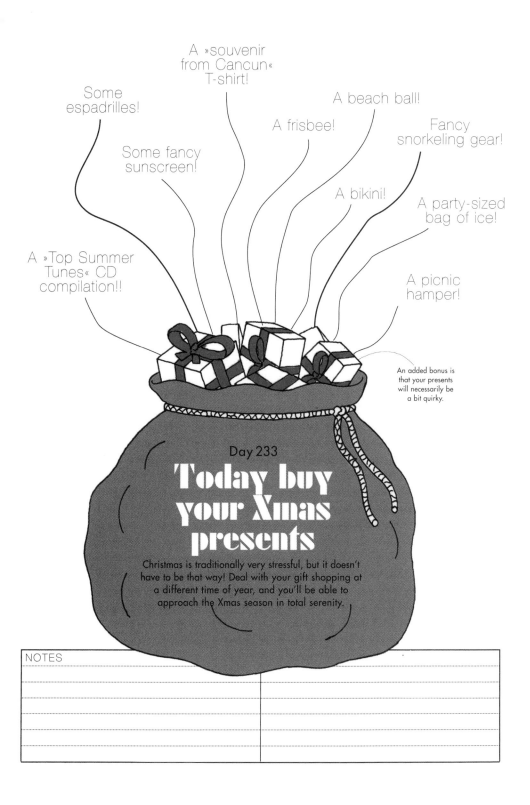

Some espadrilles!

A »souvenir from Cancun« T-shirt!

A beach ball!

Some fancy sunscreen!

A frisbee!

Fancy snorkeling gear!

A bikini!

A party-sized bag of ice!

A »Top Summer Tunes« CD compilation!!

A picnic hamper!

An added bonus is that your presents will necessarily be a bit quirky.

Day 233

Today buy your Xmas presents

Christmas is traditionally very stressful, but it doesn't have to be that way! Deal with your gift shopping at a different time of year, and you'll be able to approach the Xmas season in total serenity.

NOTES

Today buy a newspaper and read only the ads

Judge the most truthful one and recompense the advertiser by purchasing their product.

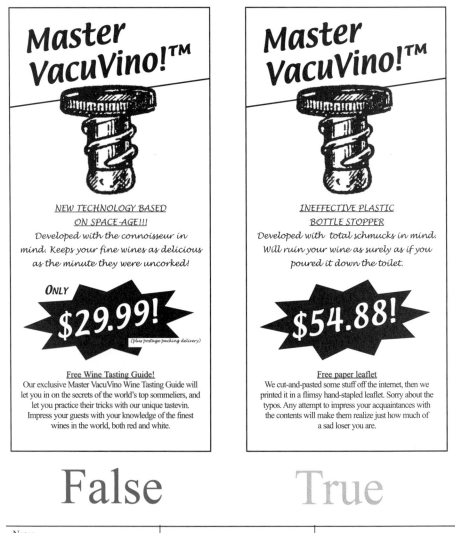

False   True

Notes		

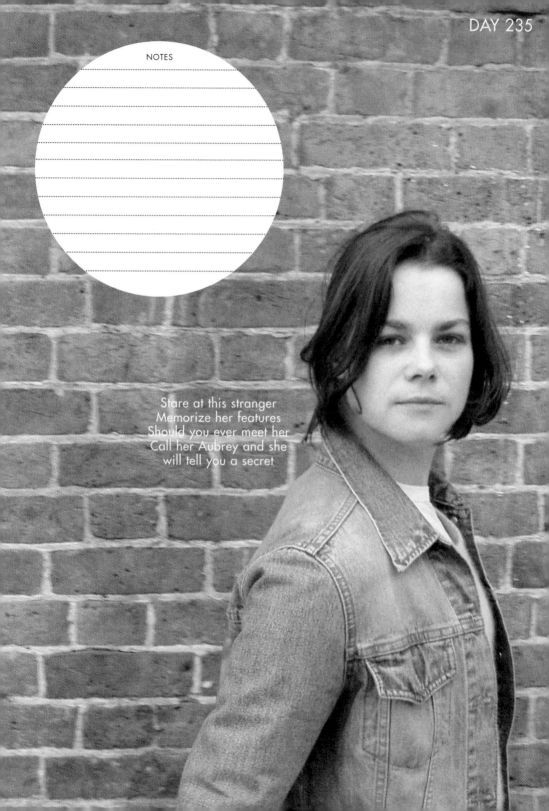

NOTES

Stare at this stranger
Memorize her features
Should you ever meet her
Call her Aubrey and she
will tell you a secret

Notes

The butterfly effect explained: the butterfly effect dramatically illustrates chaos theory. Thus to quote Edward Lorenz, "the flap of a butterfly's wings in Brazil can set off a tornado in Texas." Types of butterfly: Pieris oleracea (causes hurricanes in Southern China), Colias philodice (causes rainbows over Northampton), Feniseca tarquinius (causes freak flooding in Beirut), Erora laeta (causes early morning mist in Central Park), Plebeius saepiolus (causes sun storms on Jupiter).

small impossible-to-measure initial changes in complex systems can have huge effects. Thus

Day 237: experience a new emotion

Retroescalophobia	The fear of walking down stopped escalators	»I'm a chronic retroescalophobe«
E-mailism	Obsessive need to check for new e-mails	»Stop being so e-mailistic!«
Pluvialness	The love of raindrops	»Sandra loves autumn, she's very pluvial, you see«
Cathodillia	Sexual attraction to one's television set	»Man arrested for catho-dilliac outburst in store«
Goreness	When you realize you're never going to make it	»He's only 29 and already he's feeling gorey«
Supplementobia	When you're exhausted at the prospect of reading your newspaper	»Weekends bring out the supplementobic in me«
Extremosis	Violent animosity toward one's extremities, especially big toes	»Since the amputation, I haven't been so extremosist«
Cerebrosity	Overfondness for one's own intellect	»The professor's cere-brosity was legendary«
Spatred	Hatred of spades	»Such spatred in one so young!«
Sommelierism	Powerful urge to impress others with wine knowledge	»His sommelierism was driving me crazy, so I got a divorce«
Architectillia	Passion for licking glass buildings	»He would have made a great window cleaner, had it not been for his architectillia«
Hurtism	When you secretly look forward to being hurt so you can moan about it	»Don't insult him, he's hurtistic«

Find an inchoate emotion within you and name it

NOTES	

TODAY SEND A TELEGRAM
FORGET INTERNET. TELEGRAMS IMPACTFULLER
SPECIALNEWSWISE. SEND TODAY.

DAY 238

NOTES——
——
——
——
——
——
——
——
——
——
——
——
——

THE BIRTH OF THE TELEGRAM
THE TELEGRAM WAS INVENTED IN 1844, BUT FOR YEARS, NO
ONE THOUGHT THE INVENTION HAD ANY FUTURE. THEN IN
1853, TWO CRIMINALS, OLIVER MARTIN AND FIDDLER DICK,
TRIED TO ESCAPE BY JUMPING ON THE LONDON-SLOUGH TRAIN.
THE LONDON POLICE THOUGHT ON THEIR FEET AND CABLED
THEIR COLLEAGUES IN SLOUGH, RESULTING IN A PROMPT
ARREST AND TRIUMPHANT HEADLINES ENSURING THE SUC-
CESS OF THE NEW TECHNOLOGY. (THE BRITISH POLICE USED IT
SO OFTEN THEY GOT THEIR OWN SPECIAL TELEGRAM ADDRESS:
HANDCUFFS, LONDON.)

DAY 239: BULLSHIT TODAY

Log on to an internet chatroom and participate in a discussion you know nothing about for as long as you can without being exposed as a fraud. Example: go to www.hortmag.com and engage in an informed discussion in response to this post.

Posted by:LandPlanFran

Subject: Butterfly bush-hardiness

Although Butterfly bushes are listed as zone 5 hardy, I find them questionable in Ohio. Site them so they have as much winter protection as possible from the harsh winter winds. Mulch them after the first hard freeze. In spring, while they are still dormant, cut them back to about 12" above the ground. Since they are easy to propagate from cutting, make a bunch and place them throughout the garden. Some will survive and you will learn which locations give them the best survival rate. Has anyone out there had any success growing them in South Dakota?

Notes
....
....
....
....
....
....
....
....
....
....
....
....

Today do everything backward

7am:	Brush your teeth and put on your pyjamas
8am:	Nothing like a glass of brandy to cheer you up
8.30am:	Coffee and mints
9am:	Three course dinner washed down with a nice bottle of red (or two!)
10am:	Couple of drinks with colleagues in your local bar to gossip
11am:	Work – say goodnight to your boss
12.05pm:	God it's been a long day
1pm:	Lunch hour!
3-6pm:	Meetings to set the day's agenda
7pm:	Say good morning to everyone
8pm:	Time to read the day's newspaper
8.30pm:	Get the kids off to school
9pm:	Breakfast: scrambled eggs, coffee and toast
10pm:	Shave (men), apply make-up (women)
10.30pm:	Shower
11pm:	Get out of bed and smell the fresh morning air

NOTES

Day 241: Make sure your name is on the internet

If you're not on the net, you're nobody. Type your name into a search engine and find out if it plucks you out of cyberspace, even if it's in the school yearbook some nerdy ex-classmate has put online. If nothing comes up, visit our »I want my name on the web« page on www.thiswebsitewillchangeyourlife.com and we'll help you acquire some virtual reality.

Searching the net for Pickasso [sic] yields 153 results. If he features on the internet this many times with this spelling, surely you can get on it once.

Pablo Pickasso

Notes		

DAY
242

Use your left hand all today

-Write a letter.

-Pick up the phone.

-Touch yourself.

-Hold a hand.

-Shake a hand.

-Give the finger discreetly.

-Hail a cab.

-Type a résumé.

-Open a door.

-Make a peanut butter sandwich.

-Draw a face.

-Control the remote

-Stroke a cat.

-Smoke a cigarette.

Notes

Note to any unimaginative left handers: Use your right hand, obviously.

Day 243
Today, remember Lady Di
with a minute of silence.

Official Minute
of Silence Etiquette:
No talking
No nodding-off
No snoring
No drinking
No farting
No sex
No fighting
No thieving
No breathing

Thank you, princess.

Notes

Day 244. Plan the day ahead down to the minute.

08.00		11.50		15.40	
08.10		12.00		15.50	
08.20		12.10		16.00	
08.30		12.20		16.10	
08.40		12.30		16.20	
08.50		12.40		16.30	
09.00		12.50		16.40	
09.10		13.00		16.50	
09.20		13.10		17.00	
09.30		13.20		17.10	
09.40		13.30		17.20	
09.50		13.40		17.30	
10.00		13.50		17.40	
10.10		14.00		17.50	
10.20		14.10		18.00	
10.30		14.20		18.10	
10.40		14.30		18.20	
10.50		14.40		18.30	
11.00		14.50		18.40	
11.10		15.00		18.50	
11.20		15.10			
11.30		15.20			
11.40		15.30			

Today extend your life span

Scientists have discovered that rats live 33% longer on a very low calorie diet. Recent research seems to suggest this also applies to humans. So why not try the long-life diet today and see if it's for you?

Olga Ratashnikov doesn't look a day over 400, but in fact she is a limber 512 years old! You too can be like Olga and reach a merry older age thanks to our diet!

Target calorie intake: 1000 cal. for a sedentary adult.

Breakfast: 1 lo-fat yoghurt, 1 glass of water

Lunch: Sandwich (brown bread) with tuna and salad (no mayo), Half an apple

Afternoon tea: Cracker

Dinner: Fish (small portion), Rice, Broccoli (1 stem), 1 glass water

Notes

Medical guidelines: There are many hypotheses to explain the life-extensions power of a low calorie diet. The one that has the most support posits that low calorie intake reduces the amount of free radical damage to cellular mitochondria, although no one knows the mechanism of how this might occur. While it seems probable that caloric restriction is an effective way to prolonging life, researchers warn of some pitfalls for those attempting such a regime. Care should be taken that the diet is adequate in vitamins, minerals, protein and other nutrients. In addition to suffering hunger pangs, if the diet is too severe, it also is possible that the ability to handle stresses, such as cold temperatures or infection could be compromised. Women may become less fertile or stop ovulating, and this might increase the risk of osteoporosis and loss of muscle mass later in life.

Day 246. Today is Vocabulary Day. Expand yours with our choice selection.

A — Amanuensis: Person who writes from dictation

B — Bonhomie: Happy friendliness

C — Cynosure: Center of attention

D — Duenna: Elderly woman chaperone

E — Encomium: Formal expression of praise

F — Fallopian: Liable to error

G — Galumph: Move about clumsily

H — Harum-scarum: Reckless

I — Integument: Natural skin covering

J — Jeremiad: Long complaint

K — Kwashiorkor: Malnutrition of young children

L — Lacteal: Of or like milk

M — Myrmidon: Follower

N — Nugatory: Of little value

O — Oppugn: To dispute

P — Poetaster: Bad poet

Q — Quondam: Former

R — Rodomontade: Boastful talk

S — Shibboleth: Slogan characteristic of a particular group

T — Tergiversate: To be evasive

U — Uxorious: Too dependent on one's wife

V — Vermiform: Resembling a worm

W — Walleyed: Having eyes with an abnormal amount of white showing

X — Xanthippe: Peevish woman

Y — Yoni: Tantric for vagina

Z — Zoophyte: Any animal resembling a plant

NOTES

DAY 247. Today eat everything using chopsticks.

Which chopsticks are best for me? God did not create all chopsticks equal.
Chopsticks with the following features are best suited to the designated tasks.

TYPE OF CHOPSTICK:	LARGE HANDLE DIAMETER	HIGH TIP ANGLE	LONGER LENGTH
BEST FOR:	PULLING	SHEARING/GRIPPING	PINCHING
APPROPRIATE FOOD:	STICKY NOODLES	STEAK	PEANUTS

If you eat all of the above most days, the most efficient all purpose chopstick
has a 6mm handle diameter, 4mm tips, and a 2 degree tip angle.

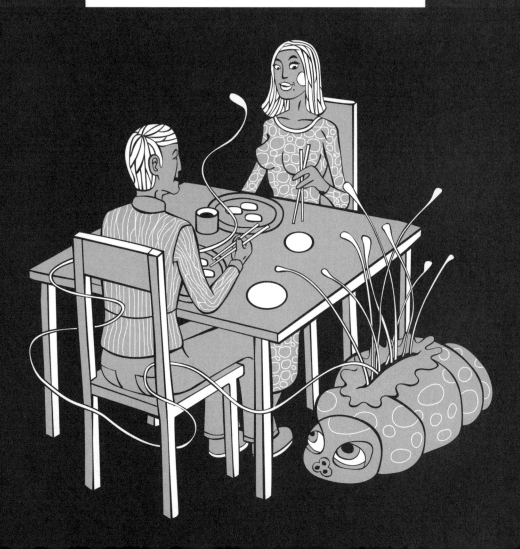

Day 248. Do everything society urges you to.

Here's some names to get you started.

- Miguel Azpilicueta, San Huaco, Guatemala
- Takara Kobayashi, Hakone, Japan
- Abdul Karim Jasim, Rutba, Iraq
- Elizabeth Chitika, Ibolelo, Zambia
- Mosharraf Wajed, Nurullahpur, Bangladesh

Twin Yourself with a Foreigner

Why should towns have all the fun? Today pick a foreigner at random and twin yourself with him or her. Then visit each other once a year.

Nota: no person can be twinned to more than one other. Foreigners in tropical-style locations are usually already twinned. Vacant twins are currently readily available in the following locations: Vladivostok, Khartoum, Sanaa, Baghdad, Epsom.

Day 249

Notes

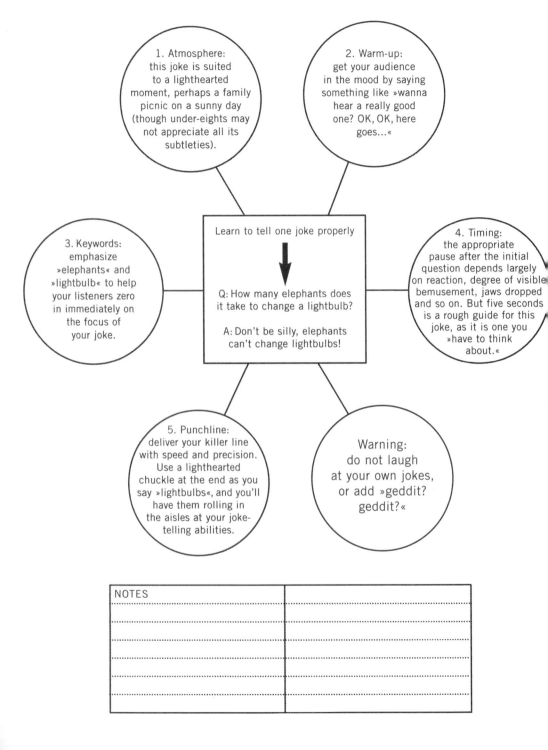

1. Atmosphere: this joke is suited to a lighthearted moment, perhaps a family picnic on a sunny day (though under-eights may not appreciate all its subtleties).

2. Warm-up: get your audience in the mood by saying something like »wanna hear a really good one? OK, OK, here goes...«

3. Keywords: emphasize »elephants« and »lightbulb« to help your listeners zero in immediately on the focus of your joke.

Learn to tell one joke properly

Q: How many elephants does it take to change a lightbulb?

A: Don't be silly, elephants can't change lightbulbs!

4. Timing: the appropriate pause after the initial question depends largely on reaction, degree of visible bemusement, jaws dropped and so on. But five seconds is a rough guide for this joke, as it is one you »have to think about.«

5. Punchline: deliver your killer line with speed and precision. Use a lighthearted chuckle at the end as you say »lightbulbs«, and you'll have them rolling in the aisles at your joke-telling abilities.

Warning: do not laugh at your own jokes, or add »geddit? geddit?«

NOTES

Read your own palm

☞ Life Line (quality of life: if it is thin and reedy, see a physician regularly)
❖ Love Line (luck in love: if it extends beyond the middle finger, you will know love instead of having to pay for it)
♏ Heart Line (emotional depth: if it runs deep, become a social worker)
♓ Travel Line (propensity for travel: if it is broken, stay at home)

♌ Fate Line (the longer the better: if it is shorter than the love line, your lover will kill you)
☞ Miscellaneous Line (good at shopping, expert at DIY, raconteur: this one you can interpret as you like)
⌂ Mount of Venus (sex drive: the more prominent the better)
♋ Blue Mark (ink: do be more careful, and wash your hands)

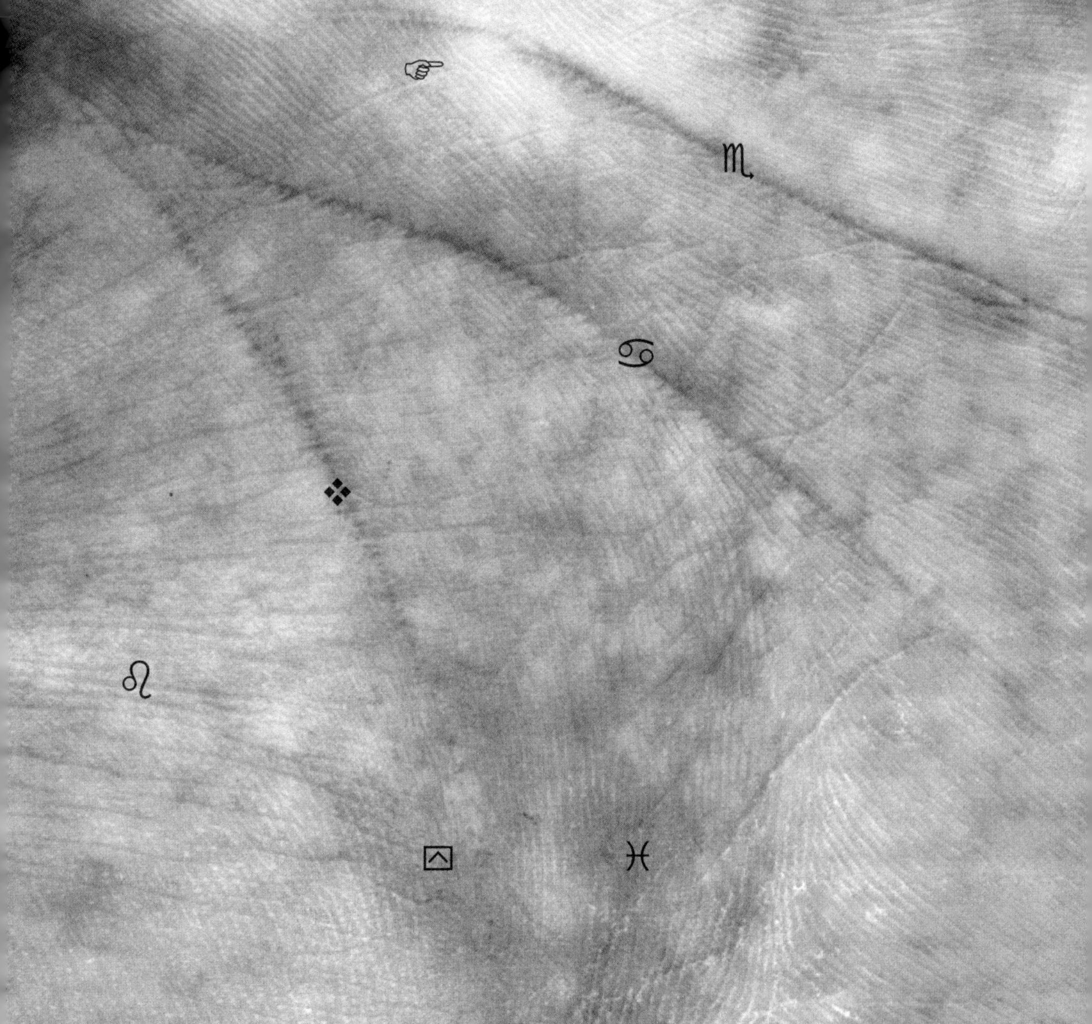

☞

♏

♋

❖

♌

⌂   ♓

NOTES	

NOTES

DAY 253
This is the »Aunt Roberta,« the strongest cocktail in the world. Invite a friend over today and sample it.

Ingredients:
2 shots Absinthe
1 shot Brandy
3 shots Vodka
1 1/2 shot Gin
1 shot Creme de Mûre

Shake well with ice
and strain into a
martini glass.

Notes

AUNT ROBERTA Aunt Roberta was born in Alabama in 1854, the mulatto daughter of a slave owner, Jim Burns. After her alcoholic father tried to abuse her at age 11, she ran away, and lived off the land for several years, picking cotton as an itinerant worker, sometimes selling her body in railroad towns. Eventually at 23 she ran a bootleg shack down by the Mississippi Delta. There, her and lover T.B. Dixon mixed homemade gin with moonshine, killing an estimated 34 people over 2 years. But in those days no one cried much for the dead drunken hoboes that used to frequent »Aunt Roberta's« as it had become known, largely on account of her prematurely large girth. She came up with her famous cocktail by serendipity, whilst drunk. She was a mixer of genius, but it was only through the observation of one man, racoon-hunter Billy Joe Spratt, that this particular recipe survived. Roberta could never recreate it, and died in abject poverty, aged 32. Spratt headed up north to New York, opened a chain of bars based around the original »Aunt Roberta« and became a millionaire within 2 years.

Day 254: Today invent a new punctuation mark. Examples:

Denotes that the previous sentence is to be construed ironically.

Orgasm. More generally used to indicate the writer is sexually aroused.

Writer is aware that at this point he's bullshitting.

(())

Double brackets: contains a secret, only read if you agree to keep it.

Example: As I write this I am sitting stark naked with a blonde on my lap. ((She has a third nipple)). Actually there are two of them, twins in fact. OK, well it's bound to happen someday

NOTES

Day 255:
test god's existence

Whether god exists or not is a pretty fundamental question, and one that could make a big difference to your life. If you're not yet convinced either way, find out for sure with these questions, which are especially designed to make him manifest himself. It's best to address them from a mount or hill of some sort, as that's how he's used to humans communicating with him.

Questions to god:

Hey god, look at this. I'm doodling right here in this bible of yours.

god, I bet you can't hit me with lighting, I'm too fast, whooosssshhh!

Show me a miracle god and I'll sacrifice any animal you care to mention

god, I have some important data about the Devils latest plans. Come down and I'll show you.

Help god, I'm angel Bob, I've lost my wings somewhere over there. Help me out?

god are you there? (worth a try)

Notes

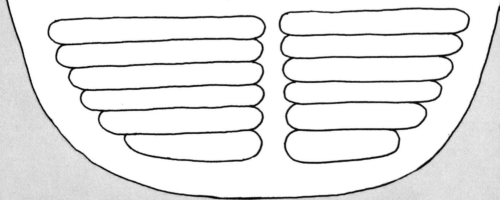

Day 256

Today destroy photos that make you look ugly. Everyone has a pile of old photos lying around. Good ones are invaluable: they represent good memories to cherish for the rest of your life. But bad photos are bad karma: they represent negative moments of your life and show you as boring, ugly or demonic. Burn them promptly.

Notes

Guidelines for calling in sick: If possible, leave a message for your boss before he gets in. Before calling, convince yourself you really are sick. Double bluff: avoid overelaborate excuses. Simple ones are best e.g.: »I feel sick.« If pressed on specific symptoms, mention something socially embarrassing like »I've spent half the night on the toilet« to end their line of questioning. Good things to do in bed: Sleep; curl up in fetal position; hug a pillow; listen to the world outside at work; sniffle/ cough/wheeze; read a trashy novel; talk to Mom on the phone under the duvet; stroke the cat/dog/yourself; write a long letter to a distant relative; feel a bit sorry for yourself.

Notes

LAST REMINDER!
TODAY SEND US MONEY

Attention! Your second down payment on this Book is due tomorrow. To avoid any surcharge or penalty payments, make sure you transfer the balance of your account (another $18.00, plus tax) to us today. Please write checks to: Benrik Ltd, and send c/o Scott Waxman, 80 Fifth Avenue, Suite 1101, New York, NY 10011, USA. Fines for late payment up to $3000.

Ten good reasons to cough up:
1) we need money
2) we've spent the other money
3) we need fresh new money
4) we need it more than you do
5) our publisher screwed us
6) our agent screwed us
7) our ex-wives screwed us
8) the taxman screwed us
9) this book was underpriced by mistake
10) anyone who sends the money in gets their photo in next year's edition

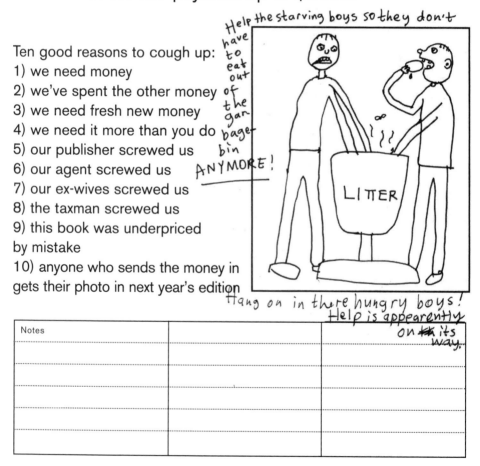

Help the starving boys so they don't have to eat out of the garbage bin ANYMORE!

LITTER

Hang on in there hungry boys! Help is apparently on its way.

Notes		

Today do something to make it to the top.

Are you happy plowing along your everyday furrow? Why not seek to rise above your station? Why not be the main man, the top boss, the biggest fish in the pond? They didn't get there by moping around being friendly to their neighbors. Grow a spine and stab someone in the back. Lie if you have to. Steal if you need to. Kill if you must. Today every action must be performed with an eye to the main chance. Make friends, influence people, then dump them as you make your way up the greasy pole. Today, look out for no1.

»Ambition is so powerful a passion in the human breast, that however high we reach we are never satisfied.«
–Niccolo Machiavelli

Day 259

DAY 260
TODAY EMBRACE CHANGE
FOR THE SAKE OF IT
CHANGE IS LIFE AND IT'S ALL
AROUND YOU. FORCE YOURSELF TO
CHALLENGE THE CREATURE OF
ROUTINE WITHIN. YOU COULD TAKE
A DIFFERENT ROUTE TO WORK.
YOU COULD SHOWER INSTEAD OF
TAKING A BATH. OR YOU COULD
REMARRY. RECONSIDER
EVERYTHING ABOUT YOURSELF:
TODAY, YOU ARE A BLANK SLATE.

Notes

Day 261: Today give someone a totally impractical gift

NOTES		
	A BRIDGE!	A REMOTE PLANET!	A HEMORRHOID!
	AN UNBORN PET!	AN ELEVATOR!	A PHILOSOPHICAL WORLDVIEW!
	A MOLECULE OF TITANIUM!	ONE (EXPEN-SIVE) SOCK !	A FULLY ARMED NUCLEAR SUB-MARINE!

Day 262

Get instructions for today off the net. Log on to www.datatranscorp.org/html003.02. Your password is vector/xxxx*

NOTES

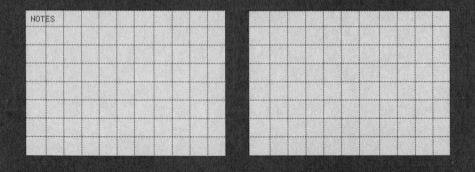

*First 4 letters of your mother's maiden name

disinfection

Today rid yourself of the parasites in your life.

GUILTY: the good old kitchen sink. Probably the dirtiest place in your home, with an average of 229,000 bacteria per square inch. GUILTY: the air we breathe. Full of viral particles floating through the indoor environment, contaminating surfaces everywhere from the dinner table to the remote control, and ending up on your hands. Why, even common soap can spread germs...

THE SOLUTION? Germicidal soap, used often and liberally. Clean food preparation surfaces, scrubbed and disinfected every time you eat. And a healthy wariness of too much physical contact between members of the family. Moral infection is just as insidious as its microscopic counterpart. Let cleanliness rule YOUR family!

Notes

Day 265
Prevention is better than cure!
Today do something that could save you a lot of future hassle.

Leave a copy of your house keys with a friend in case you lose them in the woods.

Buy candles and matches in case there's a sudden power cut while you're in the bath.

Spoil your kids so they don't put you in a home when you're old and decrepit.

Learn Norwegian in case Norway turns into an evil superpower and invades.

Notes		

TEST YOUR MEMORY

What were you doing last Thursday evening? Do you have trouble remembering? Here are some tried-and-tested techniques that could help improve your memory skills.

RRR   ROUTINE RECALL RECOGNITION
What do you normally do on Thursdays? What are you doing today? Are there any events that recur every week on Thursdays? Think back to the last example and visualize your expectations.

CR   COGNITIVE REWINDING
What did you do yesterday evening? How about the evening before that? And the previous one. Rewind through the week one day at a time until you reach your target evening, last Thursday.

ESS   EXTERNAL STIMULI SUPPORT
Look up last Thursday's newspaper headlines on the web. Try to remember where you were when reading them, or who you discussed them with.

RA   REPETITIVE ASSOCIATION
Repeat the word »Thursday« out louder and louder until your brain gets bored of you and unlocks the relevant memory code.

LM   LEAPFROGGING MATRIX
What happened last week that marked you? Was that before or after Thursday evening? Could you possibly have discussed this event on Thursday, or decided to go ahead with it on Thursday?

People make money like you wouldn't believe coming up with stuff like this. If you have any suggestions of your own, please forward them to us.

C   CHEATING
Just look back through the Book and see what notes you took last Thursday evening.

Day 266

Notes

Day 268:
Trace your High School sweetheart and offer to meet up

You never forget your first love, but have they forgotten you? Look up cute little Chuck or sexy Martha in the phone book and give them a bell. By now they're probably stuck in a loveless marriage with 2.3 kids and a mortgage. You may well feature in their broken dreams?

Note: Should the words »creep,« »police« or »restraining order« crop up in their conversation, it's a fairly sound indication th you did not feature in their dreams after all. Trace your second high school sweetheart and so on until successful or in ja

Day 269: Discover a star

The universe is full of undiscovered stars. Buy a telescope and a map of the sky, find a star that isn't on the map, draw its position and send it off to the International Astronomical Union demanding that it be named after you as its discoverer.

Where to start? You may as well forget about the trendy constellations like Andromeda or Orion. Here's a list of some relatively unspoilt ones where you might still get lucky if you hurry: Cassiopeia, Eridanus, Monoceros, Pyxis, Scutum, Triangulum Australe. Happy star hunting!

Notes		

CONSUMER PROTECTION. Do not fall for advertisements from private companies offering to name stars after you in exchange for money. This is a rip-off. The only body authorized to name stars is the International Astronomical Union. And the only reason they name stars after people is if they've discovered them. Beware of false claims! If in doubt, contact them: their web address is www.iau.org.

Day 270: Bake a cake!

Careful! The fruit cake described below is not the one represented here. This fruitcake is the work of the master craftswoman, Tatiana Blok, that won her the Vladivostok Communal Patisserie Award in 1972. Unfortunately, it can never be made again as the special Soviet jelly base necessary to hold it together is no longer in production due to new overzealous food safety laws.

Notes

Tatiana Blok's Fruit Cake

You will need: 8oz. margarine, 12oz. caster sugar, 5 eggs, 10oz. baking flour, 20oz. dried fruit.

Preheat oven to 320 fahrenheit. Line a cake tin with greaseproof paper. Set a the fruit and place everything else in a bowl. Beat for 5 minutes, then add fruit stir until you have a smooth mix. Pour into cake tin. Bake for 90 minutes. Enjo

DAY 271

Today talk to a child. Children are untainted by prejudice and habit. Have a proper conversation with a young child today and learn from their innocence. Topics might include: favorite colors, toys, birds, bees, granny, why people fight, belly buttons, mud (fun with).

Notes		

Update: sadly these days it is no longer legally prudent to approach children not your own. Either borrow a relative's, or make your own.

THE DICEMAN

by Luke Rhinehart

During the first month the dice had rather small effect on my life. I used them to choose ways to spend my free time, and to choose alternatives when the normal 'I' didn't particularly care. They decided that Lil and I would see the Edward Albee play rather than the Critic's Award play, that I read work x selected randomly from a huge collection; that I would cease writing my book and begin an article on 'Why Psychoanalysis Usually Fails'; that I would buy General Envelopment Corporation rather than Wonderfilled Industries or Dynamicgo Company; that I would not go to a convention in Chicago; that I would make love to my wife in Kama Sutra position number 23, number 52, number 8, etc.; that I see Arlene, that I don't see Arlene, etc.; that I see her in place x rather than place y and so on.

In short the dice decided things which really didn't matter. Most of my options tended to be from among the great middle way of my tastes and personality. I learned to like to play with the probabilities I gave the various options I would create. In letting the dice choose among possible women I might pursue for a night, for example, I might give Lil one chance in six, some new woman chosen at random two chances in six, and Arlene three

chances in six. If I played with two dice the subtleties in probability were much greater. Two principles I always took care to follow. First: never include an option I might be unwilling to fulfill; second: always begin to fulfill the option without thought and without quibble. The secret of the successful dice-life is to be a puppet on the strings of the die.

Six weeks after sinking into Arlene I began letting the dice diddle with my patients: it was a decisive step. I began creating as options that I comment aggressively to a patient as my insights arose; that I restudy some other standard analytic theory and method and adopt it for a specified number of hours with a patient; that I preach to my patients.

Eventually I began also to include as an option that I give my patients assigned psychological exercises much as a coach gives his athletes physical exercises: shy girl assigned to date make-out artist; aggressive bully assigned to pick a fight with nine-eight-pound weakling and purposely lose; studious grind assigned to see five movies, go to two dances and play bridge a minimum of five hours a day all week. Of course, most meaningful assignments involved a breach of the psychiatrist's code of ethics. In telling my patients what to do, I was becoming legally responsible for any ill consequences which might result.

In Luke Rhinehart's 1971 *cult classic* The Diceman, *the hero rolls the dice to determine his fate. He picks out options and assigns them a number. For instance* ▨ *could be »I will go see a movie,«* ▨ *»I'll take a stroll in the park,«* ▨ *might be »I'll take the first flight to Siberia« and so on. Today, let the dice govern your life.*

Notes

OH, LEAVE IT ALONE FOR CHRIST'S SAKE!

FRIGIDITY DAY

Does sex play too big a part in your life? Today act like a nun and abstain from any sexual contact, even with yourself.

Turn-offs to help you focus: Cold showers; spiders; cod liver oil; Mom and Dad together; Grandad and Grandma together; God: Mam, Dad, Grandad, Grandma and God together. If any of the above turn you on and not off, you are in serious psychological trouble.

NOTES

A WORD OF WARNING Do not prolong this treatment: extended sexual deprivation can have severe side effects. It was reported in 1905 that Sister L. of the Carmelites was so perturbed by lack of intercourse that the mere sight of flies mating would send her into an onanistic frenzy. For ultimately, as French writer Anatole France reminded us, »the only true perversion is chastity«.

YOUR NAMESAKE

TODAY FIND SOMEONE NAMED LIKE YOU, CALL THEM UP AND OFFER TO MEET.

WHERE ARE THEY?

STATISTICALLY YOU ARE MORE THAN LIKELY TO HAVE A NAMESAKE SOMEWHERE IN THE WORLD.

TRY LOOKING UP NAME ON THE WO WIDE WEB, OR IN LOCAL PHONE BO

FUN NAMESAKE TRICKS

HI IS THAT JOSH WEAVER?

EXAMPLE

1

INTRODUCTIONS: KICK OFF THE CONVERSATION BY INTRODUCING YOURSELF CRYPTICALLY.

2

YES WHO'S THIS?

IT'S JOSH WEAV-ER

HA HA HA

3

THIS IS GUARAN-TEED TO CREATE A HUMOROUS BOND.

HA

CRIME:

UH?

POLICE ARE EASILY CONFUSED BY NAMESAKES. TRY SETTING UP AN INTERNATIONAL MONEY-LAUNDERING DRUGS RING WITH YOUR NAMESAKE.

SUING YOUR NAMESA

EXPLAIN THAT YOU HAVE PATENTED YOUR NAME AND WISH H CHANGE HIS, FAILING WHICH YOUR LAWYERS WILL BE IN TOU

OH NO!

NOTES

THE POLITICS OF HEIGHT

British politician Alan Clark recounts in his *Diaries* how when he became Minister in Mrs Thatcher's government, he looked down at the masses from his high-rise office and suddenly wondered how it would feel to urinate on them. Go to the tallest point in your town today and be master of all you survey. Relieving your bladder is optional.

Notes

DAY 276 **Today go to the zoo and** DO FEED THE ANIMALS
Zoo animals have a miserable time as it is, they should have the right to
stuff their faces, whatever some fascist zookeeper says. Here are some
of their favorite foods in the wild so you know what to take along.

ANACONDA

Rats

GIRAFFE

Small
birds (as
they fly past)

ANTEATER

Beetles

BEAR

Berries

ELEPHANT

Grass

BALD
EAGLE

Ice cream

ZEBRA

Zebras

LION

More Grass

HIPPO

Salmon
(smoked)

GIANT
PANDA

G

GORILLA

Bananas

Notes
....
....
....
....
....
....
....
....
....
....
....

ELECTRIC EEL

Plankton

Day 277
Trust someone with
your life today.

Deepen the bonds between you and a
close friend today and experience the
vulnerability and liberation that ensues.

Trust them to guide you on a railway
platform with your eyes closed.

Trust them to prepare
your dose of medication.

Trust them to turn the gas
off after you fall asleep.

Trust them not to mail that death
threat to a mafioso that you signed.

Advanced: to truly test your faith in mankind,
try this with a complete stranger. Good luck.

Notes

Sense-less Day

GO THROUGH TODAY WITHOUT USING YOUR SENSE OF: TOUCH

How to: Wear winter clothing – ski gloves, anorak, cagoule.

True story: Bill W. lost all sense of touch in his lower left leg after a farm accident in 1977. But as he was close to retirement age, it didn't bother him too much. For a while at least. Two years later, on a cold winter morning, he was sitting in his easy chair reading his daily paper in front of the warm fire. His wife was out in the yard. His dogs were asleep in the kennel. So preoccupied was Bill W. with the day's news, that he didn't notice until alerted by the bacon-like smell that his nerveless limb had caught fire, and was charred beyond all human recognition.

Notes

Write down the pros and cons of this sense as you discover them.

Pros: ....

Cons: ....

End of day assessment: How crucial is my sense of touch to me ..../10

DAY 279: GET INTO AN ELEVATOR AND FIND OUT IF THERE REALLY IS ANYONE AT THE OTHER END OF THE EMERGENCY INTERCOM.

If no one answers, the reason is probably Elisha Otis. In 1853, Elisha invented the revolutionary »safety elevator,« fitted with a toothed guiderail on each side of the elevator shaft which caught any falling elevator car, locking it into place. This made elevators safe and allowed the development of skyscrapers.

Elisha Otis
= *Elevator Man*

NOTES

FASHIONVICTIM!

Find a particularly anorexic shop mannequin today and graffiti your fashion statement right on to him or her. Possible statements: FAT IS FUN! FASHION FASHISTS! FEED ME FEED ME!

Notes

Day 281

This year, celebrate the birthday of Archbishop and Nobel Peace Prize laureate Desmond Tutu: Send him a card.

Standard formulation: »Dear Archbishop, Thank you very much for all your good works over the years. You are an inspiration to us all. Keep it up.«

Notes

P.S: His birthday is on October 7, but you can send him a card anytime, he doesn't mind. Send to: Archbishop Emeritus Desmond Mpilo Tutu, P.O. Box 1092, Milnerton, 7435, Cape Town, South Africa.

DAY 282

Today, a test of faith in humanity: deliberately abandon the Book in a public place and see if anyone returns it. They should find your details at the front, but for added security, feel free to write them a little message here outlining how much it means to you.

The truly paranoid may want to hide behind a tree and watch, but be warned: if you look at the world cynically, the world will match your low expectations.

....
....
....

Notes	

Let's Do Lunch

Today, dress in a smart suit and lunch in a fancy restaurant. After the meal, go round other tables introducing yourself as the owner, and thanking other patrons for eating at your establishment. Ask them how they found the food. Promise to send them a brandy on-the-house. Tell them their lunch is on you. See how long before you get ejected.

Notes	DAY 283	

BODYBUILDING DAY

You may not attend the gymnasium religiously, but you can still be ahead of the game by hyperdeveloping at least one muscle, one that very few so-called »bodybuilders« could even locate, let alone spell: the flexor digitorum profundus.

Sit on a bench.
Place forearms on thighs.
Grasp a barbell with an underhand grip.
Pull the barbell up with forearms.
Let down and hold
Repeat x10.

NOTES

Without the constant vigilance of fellow citizens, police forces everywhere are all too easily tempted to abuse their powers. Do your bit for democracy: follow a police patrol and make sure they respect suspects' rights.

You have the right to remain silent. Anything you say can and will be used against you in a court of law. You have the right to speak to an attorney, and to have an attorney present during any questioning. If you cannot afford a lawyer, one will be provided for you at government expense. (Police get really annoyed if you say this faster than they can!)

How can you tell a bad cop from a good cop?

A.

B.

Easy: The bad one's moral decrepitude will manifest itself in sloppy dress, like B's too-short pants.

What if you witness abuse?

If you sense that abuse is occurring or might be about to occur, do not hesitate to intervene. For instance, if police officers are running in pursuit of a suspected criminal, and seem to you a little too excited by the chase, run alongside them, reminding them of the alleged criminal's rights. It may help to video them if you have the equipment. When they catch the »suspect,« monitor how tight the handcuffs are, mentioning the Human Rights Declaration's ban on cruel and unusual punishment. Insist on accompanying the suspect back to the police station, and use the suspect's free phone call to alert your local civil liberties group to the situation. Occasionally, the police will pick on you as well at this point, asking you to leave the suspect's cell for example. If this happens, lie down and chain yourself to the nearest radiator in protest. You are now officially a political prisoner. Fight on!

NOTES

You don't need round-the-clock news

It needs you. Why allow yourself to be dangled in a permanent state of anxious suspense about matters that don't even directly affect you, like some remote murder enquiry, or even war?

Constant media-induced stress is addictive and prevents us from stepping back and seeing the big picture. You have nothing to lose but your remote. As long ago as 1854, Thoreau wrote in *Walden* about the pernicious dependence on the latest news: »I am sure that I never read any memorable news in a newspaper. If we read of one man robbed, or murdered, or killed by

accident, or one house burned, or one vessel wrecked, or one steamboat blown up, or one cow run over on the Western Railroad, or one mad dog killed, or one lot of grasshoppers in the winter – we never need read of another. One is enough. If you are acquainted with the principle, what do you care for a myriad instances and applications? To a philosopher all news, as it is called, is gossip, and they who edit and read it are old women over their tea. Yet not a few are greedy after this gossip. There was such a rush, as I hear, the other day at one of the offices to learn the foreign news by the last arrival, that several large squares of plate glass belonging to the establishment were broken by the pressure – news which I seriously think a ready wit might write a twelve-month, or twelve years, beforehand with sufficient accuracy.«

EXCLUSIVE! HAPPY END NEWS STORY!

ANNAPOLIS, MD–According to patrons of popular downtown Starbucks branch, teacher and father of two Robert Hindman, 41, narrowly escaped serious injury this morning, when he crossed the main drag without looking left.

»This guy just strolled across the street in the middle of rush hour without even looking,« said latte-drinker Kathy Peach. »It's like a total miracle he didn't get hit by a bus,« Peach added. »What an idiot.«

At an emotional press conference,

Hindman acknowledged he had failed to check for traffic, blaming pressure from work. »I was thinking about all those term papers I still had to mark by noon, and before I knew it, I'd just plain crossed Lafayette.«

Hindman and his wife Jackie hugged for the cameras, as he pledged never to repeat his mistake. »I'll never repeat my mistake,« he said. »But I came out of it alive, and that's all that really matters.«

OUT NOW!

It's official! No news is good new

Stacy Hoxburger of Buffalo, Wyoming, first realized she had a problem January 1998, five months after the death of Diana Princess of Wales. »At firs I thought it was still grief, that I hadn't dealt with it properly, but then I saw D Stanton and he told me about Media Addiction Disorder,« she confided.

Along with many others, Hoxburger was helped to cope with the loss of the Princess by the constant stream of news and features relating to her death. For weeks, much of the media led on the circumstances of her car accident, the alleged responsibility of the paparazzi, her troubled life, and even scurrilous speculation concerning the involvement of the British secret services. »It was kind of comforting seeing her on TV all the time, even though obviously it had to be old footage,« said Hoxburger. »It's as if she'd never gone away.«

When the coverage abated, most people returned to their normal humdrum lives. One person, however, found it difficult to live without her daily dose of Diana news. »It's like I needed my fix,« confirmed Hoxburger, a housewife and mother of three. »I'd wake up in the morning, switch on the TV and there'd just be some dumb item about the Bosniaks or whatever instead of Diana.«

»Jeepers,« she continued, »I called the damn network and gave them a piece of my mind, but the woman on the phone would just put me on hold for hours.

But I wasn't going to give up. I calle her every day for three weeks.«

After pressure from her husban Roger who claimed it was ruinir their marriage and increasing the phone bills, Hoxburger finally con sulted her physician. He referred h to Dr. Harold Stanton, who specialize in media-induced stress.

»Overexposure to the media is th no1 hidden cause of anxiety Americans today,« said Stanton. »A these stories of war and crime lead an adrenaline surge which the bod becomes addicted to. Stacy is a typ cal case. She got hooked on the who Diana thing and when it stopped, h hormones just went haywire.«

Dr. Stanton has written a book on th subject, called *Media Addictic Disorder: The News Behind th Headlines,* soon to hit the shelve Hoxburger says his advice has »totall cured« her: »I think he's a genius. I n longer even think about that Dian person one little bit. Now I spend m time monitoring the news and callir up when I feel their stories are takin over people's lives.«

Notes

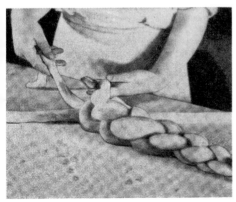

DAY 287
SEXUAL FANTASY DAY

It is said that we think about sex every 6 seconds. Today monitor your thoughts by writing them down as you go along, noting the sexual ones in capitals.

EXAMPLE: Must do shopping SEX! have run out of broccoli and SEX! now where did I leave that briefcase SEX! I wonder if it's raining SEX! hmmm, the veranda definitely needs repainting SEX! what time am I meeting Michael SEX! that's one ugly looking car SEX! Jenny must have finished choir practice by now SEX! can't believe how well that meeting went SEX! tra la la la the sky is blue SEX! I wish they'd take that billboard down SEX! what's on TV tonight SEX! oh here's mother.

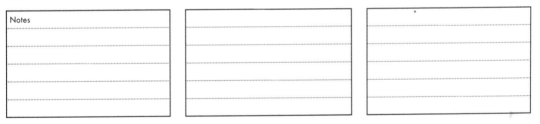

Notes		

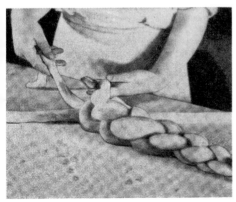

Day 288: How funny are you?
Today tell your favorite joke ever to several different people and note down how much they laugh on our FUN Scale™
....
....

FUN Scale™
Joke:..
....
....

Date.........................Hour...........................Subject.....................
Laugh YES/NO length.......................... depth...........................
sincerity...
Signature ....
Comments...
....

Conclusion
Based on the above measurements, it seems clear that:
- You should have your own TV show
- You're a pretty funny individual
- You can make people laugh if they're drunk
- You're just not very funny
- People laugh, but it's not with you
- You must have bought this book by mistake

Notes
....
....
....
....
....
....
....
....
....
....
....
....

FUN·O·METER

A FOOL OR A PROPHET?

According to Indiana-based »Church of the Holy Rapture«, the world will end today, at precisely one-half second to midnight, central Israeli time (7 p.m. GMT). Make all the necessary preparations just in case. But if you are still alive by 7.05 p.m., e-mail Bud Kramer on kramer89@hotmail.com to demand compensation for trauma.

WHAT TO LOOK OUT FOR:

»Jesus will come with a cloud of angels for his saints which know him and the fellowship of his deep sufferings... This will be heavensgate. Nuclear war will start the next 45 days of the wrath of the Lamb for those which are left within the doomsgate. Just prior to these events, the earth will shift, causing earthquakes and volcanic activity which will darken the skies and create worldwide chaos.«

Notes

Judge which one of your elderly relatives is most likely to have hoarded away a pile of cash and call them up out of the blue to get in their will.

True story! Marcus Grant, 32, was working as a checkout assistant for Wal-Mart in North Canton, Ohio, when his supervisor Russell Streiff called him to the phone. His great-aunt Lana Milova Granovskaia had just died at the age of 105. Lana had been a young painter of great promise just before the revolution, even said to be in line for a portrait of Tsar Nicholas II. Of course, her career ended as quickly as it had begun. Now, the only time Marcus had ever met great-aunt Lana was in 1995 in Moscow, when he had been backpacking around Europe and decided to drop in on her in her humble suburban flat. Then he had charmed the lonely old lady with his naive American ways, and his encyclopaedic knowledge of Cold War–era Bond films. Ironically, she later froze to death in her post-Soviet garret on the very day the new Russian courts accepted her claim to the Granovskaia estate outside Moscow, now worth a hefty $40,000,000. The rest of the Grant (ex-Granovskaia) clan having ignored her, she'd left everything to Marcus. Marcus has now quit Wal-Mart, and is living in San Fernando, California, pending the outcome of the court case with Lana's stepsister Magda, an off-shore tax accountant in Latvia.

Notes

DAY 291
Meeting!

These glamorous bars are designated *This Book Will Change Your Life* hangouts. Today go to the one nearest to where you live, and discuss your experience of the Book with friendly fellow owners. Bring your copy!

Rendezvous points

LOS ANGELES
THE WHISKEY BAR
1200 N ALTA
LOMA ROAD,
WEST HOLLYWOOD

SAN FRANCISCO
VESUVIO'S
255 COLUMBUS
ST, NORTH BEACH

Present your copy of the Book and demand a free drink

MIAMI
TOBACCO ROAD
626 S MIAMI AVE,
DOWNTOWN

NEW YORK
THE WHITE
HORSE TAVERN
567 HUDSON ST
AT 11TH ST

CHICAGO
GREEN DOOR TAVERN
678 N ORLEANS ST

LAS VEGAS
THE VOODOO LOUNGE
3700W FLAMINGO RD

NEW ORLEANS
MOLLY'S
1107 DECATUR ST

DES MOINES
BOB'S BAR
212 COURT AVE

NOTES		

PIGEON SHIT IS GOOD LUCK!

What pigeons look out for: the average pigeon likes a nice clean target, preferably a stationary or slow-moving bald head. *Women:* bright headwear also catches the pigeon's eye. It takes about two minutes for the pigeon to »lock on« to his target and maneuver into position, so stay patient and stand still. Resist the temptation to look up and check on progress as pigeon droppings are toxic to the eye, besides being aesthetically displeasing. A clear bull's-eye hit will yield roughly two weeks of good luck. Drippy muck on your shoulder is usually worth three or four days, whereas a near miss is actually bad luck.

NOTES

DAY 293

»EXPERIENCE IS THE NAME WE GIVE TO OUR MISTAKES« (OSCAR WILDE)

WRITE DOWN AND ACKNOWLEDGE YOUR BIGGEST MISTAKE IN LIFE. OR BE CONDEMNED TO REPEAT IT.

TODAY START A FIGHT

Top fight-starting lines:
Who you looking at?
Don't tell me that's your boyfriend
Big car, small penis...
What line?
Which is the kid which is the dog?
Hey, quit kicking sand in my face

NOTES		

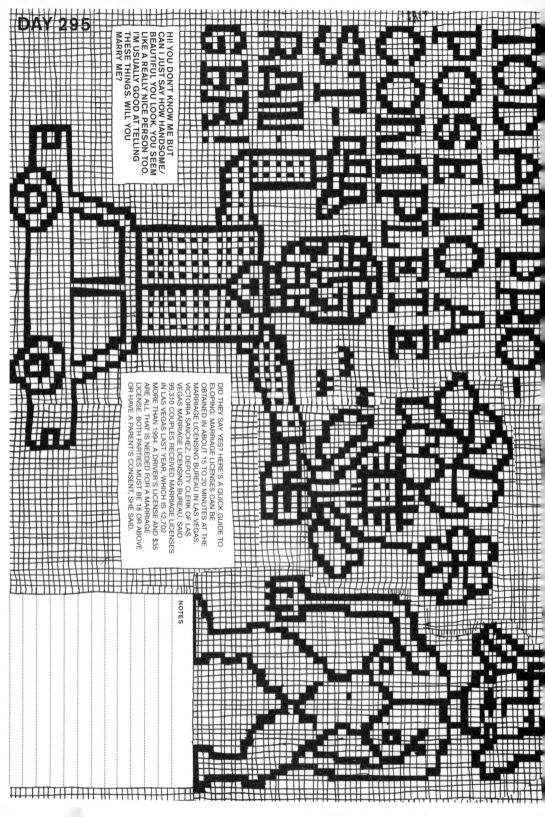

DAY 295

HI! YOU DON'T KNOW ME BUT CAN I JUST SAY HOW HANDSOME/BEAUTIFUL YOU LOOK. YOU SEEM LIKE A REALLY NICE PERSON TOO. I'M USUALLY GOOD AT TELLING THESE THINGS. WILL YOU MARRY ME?

DID THEY SAY YES? HERE'S A QUICK GUIDE TO ELOPING: MARRIAGE LICENSES CAN BE OBTAINED IN ABOUT 15 TO 20 MINUTES AT THE MARRIAGE LICENSING BUREAU IN LAS VEGAS. VICTORIA SANCHEZ, DEPUTY CLERK OF LAS VEGAS MARRIAGE LICENSING BUREAU, SAID 99,310 COUPLES RECEIVED MARRIAGE LICENSES IN LAS VEGAS LAST YEAR, WHICH IS 12,702 MORE THAN 1994. A DRIVER'S LICENSE AND $35 ARE ALL THAT IS NEEDED FOR A MARRIAGE LICENSE. BOTH PARTIES MUST BE 18 OR ABOVE OR HAVE A PARENT'S CONSENT, SHE SAID.

NOTES

Today earn a diploma

The Book have arranged a cooperative venture with
the UNIVERSITY OF HARVARD (Illinois) that
could procure you one of many prestigious
qualifications, based on your previous education, your
life experience and, of course, your knowledge of the
Book itself. Obtain a prosperous future, earning
power, and the admiration of all!

Here is a list of the qualifications you may
aspire to (along with »course« fees).

Bachelor of Arts with Honors BA (Hons) $2,000
Masters of Arts (MA) $3,000
Masters in Business Administration (MBA) $5,000
Doctorate (PhD) $5,500

All diplomas available in the field of your choice.
No required tests, classes, books, or interviews.
No one is turned down. Confidentiality assured.

NOTES

Receive your diploma within days!!!
www.thiswebsitewillchangeyourlife.com

How do you know you weren't adopted?

It is estimated that one in twelve people are adopted. Many never find out. If you have ever felt different from your parents or your siblings, seek out the truth today. Check by calling the National Adoption Information Clearinghouse (NAIC) on (301) 231-6512.

NOTES

»Book Club« Day

Here is the list of the top 100 masterpieces of Western literature. Work out how many you have read (no cheating now). Then work out how many you will have to read per year to finish them all.

1. Anonymous, *The Bible*
2. Aeschylus, *Oresteia*
3. Aristophanes, *Comedies*
4. Aristotle, *Politics*
5. Augustine, *Confessions*
6. Austen, Jane, *Pride and Prejudice*
7. Bacon, Sir Francis, *Essays*
8. Balzac, Honoré de, *Old Goriot*
9. Baudelaire, Charles, *The Flowers of Evil*
10. Beckett, Samuel, *Waiting for Godot*
11. Benrik, *This Book Will Change Your Life*
12. Blake, William, *Songs of Innocence and of Experience*
13. Boccaccio, Giovanni, *The Decameron*
14. Brontë, Charlotte, *Jane Eyre*
15. Brontë, Emily, *Wuthering Heights*
16. Bunyan, John, *The Pilgrim's Progress*
17. Camus, Albert, *The Stranger*
18. Céline, Louis-Ferdinand, *Journey to the End of the Night*
19. Cervantes, Miguel, *Don Quixote*
20. Chaucer, Geoffrey, *Canterbury Tales*
21. Chekhov, Anton, *Plays*
22. Conrad, Joseph, *Lord Jim*
23. Cooper, James Fenimore, *The Last of the Mohicans*
24. Cortázar, Julio, *Hopscotch*
25. Dante, *The Divine Comedy*
26. Darwin, Charles, *The Origin of Species*
27. Defoe, Daniel, *Robinson Crusoe*
28. Dickens, Charles, *David Copperfield*
29. Donne, John, *Poems*
30. Dostoevsky, Fyodor, *Crime and Punishment*
31. Eliot, George, *The Mill on the Floss*
32. Eliot, T.S., *Complete Poems*
33. Emerson, Ralph Waldo, *Essays*
34. Euripides, *Plays*
35. Faulkner, William, *The Sound and the Fury*
36. Fielding, Henry, *Tom Jones*
37. Fitzgerald, F. Scott, *The Great Gatsby*
38. Flaubert, Gustave, *Madame Bovary*
39. Freud, Sigmund, *The Interpretation of Dreams*
40. Frost, Robert, *Poetry*
41. Garcia Márquez, Gabriel, *One Hundred Years of Solitude*
42. Gibbon, Edward, *History of The Decline and Fall of the Roman Empire*
43. Goethe, Johann Wolfgang von, *Faust*
44. Hardy, Thomas, *Tess of the D'Urbervilles*
45. Hawthorne, Nathaniel, *The Scarlet Letter*
46. Hemingway, Ernest, *A Farewell to Arms*
47. Homer, *Iliad*
48. Homer, *Odyssey*
49. Hugo, Victor, *Notre Dame of Paris*
50. Ibsen, Henrik, *Plays*
51. James, Henry, *The Ambassadors*
52. Joyce, James, *Ulysses*
53. Kafka, Franz, *The Trial*
54. Keats, John, *Poems*
55. Lawrence, D.H., *Women in Love*
56. Machiavelli, Niccolo, *The Prince*
57. Mann, Thomas, *Buddenbrooks*
58. Maupassant, Guy de, *Stories*
59. Melville, Herman, *Moby Dick*
60. Montaigne, Michel de, *Essays*
61. Mill, John Stuart, *On Liberty*
62. Milton, John, *Paradise Lost*
63. Molière, *Selected Plays*
64. Ovid, *Metamorphoses*
65. Pascal, Blaise, *Pensées*
66. Pasternak, Boris, *Dr Zhivago*
67. Petronius, *Satyricon*
68. Plato, *Republic*
69. Plutarch, *Parallel Lives*
70. Poe, Edgar Allen, *Tales*
71. Proust, Marcel, *Remembrance of Things Past*
72. Rabelais, François, *Gargantua and Pantagruel*
73. Racine, Jean, *Phèdre*
74. Rilke, Rainer Maria, *Poems*
75. Rimbaud, Arthur, *Poems*
76. Rousseau, Jean-Jacques, *Confessions*
77. Sartre, Jean-Paul, *Nausea*
78. Shakespeare, William, *Plays*
79. Shakespeare, William, *Poems*
80. Shaw, Bernard, *Plays*
81. Sophocles, *Tragedies*
82. Stendhal, *The Red and the Black*
83. Sterne, Laurence, *Tristram Shandy*
84. Stevenson, Robert Louis, *Treasure Island*
85. Swift, Jonathan, *Gulliver's Travels*
86. Thackeray, William Makepeace, *Vanity Fair*
87. Thoreau, Henry D., *Walden*
88. Thucydides, *The History of the Peloponnesian War*
89. Tolstoy, Leo, *War and Peace*
90. Tolstoy, Leo, *Anna Karenina*
91. Turgenev, Ivan, *Fathers and Sons*
92. Twain, Mark, *The Adventures of Huckleberry Finn*
93. Virgil, *Aeneid*
94. Voltaire, *Candide*
95. Whitman, Walt, *Leaves of Grass*
96. Wilde, Oscar, *Plays*
97. Woolf, Virginia, *The Waves*
98. Wordsworth, William, and Coleridge, Samuel, *Lyrical Ballads*
99. Yeats, William Butler, *Collected Poems*
100. Zola, Emile, *Germinal*

Number left to read:...........................(X)

Number of years left (approx):...........(Y)

Masterpieces/year (X/Y) = ...

Notes		
	DAY 299	

Day 300: Say hello to everyone in the street today. Authorized variations:

DAY 301

BE THE LAST MAN STANDING TONIGHT!

Make sure to be asked to leave!

FAMOUS PARTY ANIMALS

REX (1965-1974)

BOOBOO (1912-1927)

SPARKY (1981-1999)

JULIUS (1883-1942)

NELLIE (?- 1976)

NOTES

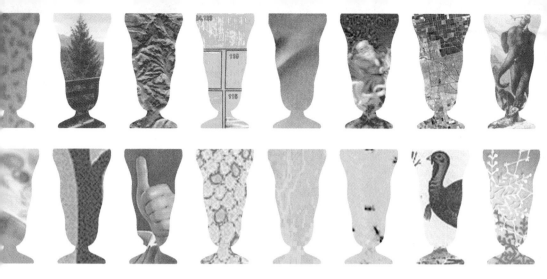

Day 302: Invent your very own milkshake and make a fortune

In 1933, little Ricki Putz got fed up with selling plain old lemonade on the street corner like every other schmucky kid in his neighborhood. So what does he do? He goes home to Ma, and he asks her for some leftover milk and a couple scoops of ice cream. Then he takes the cored-out pumpkin from Halloween the previous week, he mashes everything together in the garage real good, and hey presto, Putz's-Pokey-Pumpkin-O-Shake is born! Little Ricki himself unfortunately died of food poisoning not so long afterwards, God bless his soul, but his descendants today are rich on the proceeds.

notes	

REPORT A UFO SIGHTING	DAY 303
Website: www.ufodatabase.com	If over 10 people report sightings in the same area, a US government agency investigation is automatically triggered, anywhere on the planet.

Some typical UFO shapes:	

Characteristics of reported UFO (check all that apply):	Lights on the object ☐ Trail visible in the wake of the object ☐ Aura or haze around the object ☐ Beams emitted by the object ☐ Color changes visible in the object ☐ Object observed landing ☐ Sounds emitted from the object ☐ Aircraft chasing the object ☐ Electromagnetic effects observed near the object, such as a car engine stopping ☐	Methods of recording your evidence
What to do if you are abducted:	Remain calm. Aliens can sense panic telepathically. If it appears you are about to be sexually abused or dissected, focus on the positive side of the experience: you will be able to sell your story for hundreds and hundreds of dollars to the *National Enquirer*.	

Notes

SEE A SHRINK
EXERCISE
SPEED-DATE TEN PEOPLE
GO TO MASS
BAKE A LOAF OF BREAD
DONATE BLOOD
EXTEND FOREPLAY
WATCH HALF A MOVIE

DAY 304. TODAY SET AN HOUR ASIDE FROM YOUR SCHEDULE. HERE ARE SOME WORTHWHILE THINGS TO DO WITH IT.

Notes

Day 305: Draw attention to an unsung hero

In 1998, 27-year-old German Ute Schürings kidnapped the pet dog of the Venezuelan ambassador to Berlin, and sequestered it for nine weeks in her bedroom. At first, the police refused to take the case seriously but when Schürings began issuing demands, they investigated. After she was arrested following a tip-off from a neighbor, she explained that she had been trying to draw attention to the life of Josef Kunkel, a little-known 19th century zoologist. »I want my idol Josef Kunkel to be recognized at his true value,« she told a local news channel. »He practically invented sociobiology a century early with his work on giraffes. But he was from Pomerania and had mulatto blood, so no one took him seriously at the time.« The dog, a Weimaraner, was returned to its owner unharmed. Schürings was arrested but later released into care.

NOTES

US Presidential Election! Vote today! After the Florida 2000 chad debacle, the Book's authors have taken it upon themselves to design an improved ballot form. Not only does it offer more extensive options, but it can also be cast in advance! Just complete it and send it in to The White House, 1600 Pennsylvania Avenue NW, Washington, DC 20500, in time for the next election.

I wish to vote for the candidates

of the following party:

REPUBLICAN ☐

REFORM ☐

DEMOCRATIC ☐

SOCIALIST ☐

LIBERTARIAN ☐

GREEN ☐

SOCIALIST WORKERS ☐

DUNNO ☐

I have also put in brackets my second choice. I have put a little asterisk near my third choice. I have crossed out the ones I really really don't want. Thank you for taking this into account when you count it all up at the end.

To prevent any misunderstandings, I include my name and phone number here in case you're not sure which way I voted:..

....

Thank you for letting me know the results. My address is:...

....

....

Notes	
DAY 306	

DAY 307 RANDOM DAY

A) **COUNT THE NUMBER OF BUSES YOU SEE ON YOUR WAY TO WORK.**

B) MULTIPLY THIS NUMBER BY 3 AND DIVIDE IT BY 2.

C) **BUY AS MANY CANDY BARS.**

D) HAND THEM OUT RANDOMLY TO DIFFERENT PEOPLE.

E) **WRITE DOWN WHAT THEY TELL YOU – WORD FOR WORD – ON A PIECE OF PAPER.**

F) FOLD THE PAPERS AND PUT THEM EACH IN AN ENVELOPE. SEAL.

G) **FIND RANDOM ADDRESSES IN A TELEPHONE DIRECTORY.**

H) STAMP THE ENVELOPES AND SEND TO ADDRESSES.

I) WAIT AND SEE.

NOTES

EYESIGHT

Hold this text at arm's length. If you have trouble reading...

REFLEXES

Knock yourself on each knee with a small mallet. Your lower leg should jerk up.

HEARTBEAT

At rest: 50-100. After running on the spot for 20 minutes: 100-200.

NOTES

SPERM COUNT

Ejaculate onto glass, isolate 1cm³ of spermatozoa, and count them with a microscope. There should be roughly 100,000,000 of the little tinkers.

DAY 308: PERFORM A SELF-MEDICAL

Repeat every week and contact your doctor with any noteworthy variations

BREAST CANCER

FEEL FOR LUMPS (other than nipples).

TESTICULAR CANCER

Feel for lumps (other than testicles)

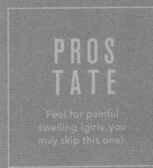

PROS TATE

Feel for painful swelling (girls, you may skip this one)

URINE TEST

Pee into a glass and use our color chart to check if it is within acceptable range

ACCEPTABLE

Drive a Ferrari!
The salesman will be only too happy to oblige you with a test drive. Just try not to crash it.

Book a suite at the Ritz!
Obviously call to unbook it tomorrow, as your private jet is unfortunately grounded.

Visit the casino!
Enjoy the free drinks without gambling and mutter about the dice being loaded here.

Millionaire!!!
Act like you're worth millions today. Only your bank manager will know the difference.

Notes

View a palatial mansion!
Look scruffy and estate agents will assume you're a rock star.

Call the president!
The White House number is (202) 456 1414. Leave a message to call back urgently.

Interview butlers!
A classified ad for a man-servant should attract plenty of potential minions.

TODAY PLACE FLOWERS ON AN OLD UNATTENDED GRAVESTONE

NOTES

Day 311
It's not all about you!
Ego Control Day!

Spend today thinking only about someone else and their life and problems for a change:

Bob Zuccione,
printer of this Book.

Bob was born in 1954 in Naples. He was a healthy baby, weighing in at a more than acceptable nine lbs. His mother Nina (née Panzani) originally came from Sicily but moved to Naples in 1945 when she married Gino Zuccione, fresh from the Eastern front. Gino had big plans for himself and his family. All the Zucciones until then had gone into the family business (pasta-shape mold-making), but not Gino, no way. Gino was going to make it big, in America! He was going to show them all. Anyway, after he got hit by a bus on the way to the gelateria, Nina remarried. Her new husband was Gino's uncle, Augustino, who hated Bob from the beginning. So Bob never got to go to America and live the Dream (except until last year on a cruise). Instead, he went to the local pasta-mold-making-apprenticeship school, run by Augustino, where the other boys made his life a misery for being the headmaster's stepson and Augustino made his life a misery for roughly identical reasons. Bob

longed wistfully for the day when he could leave home. But he was also quite lazy and so he didn't get round to it until the age of 28, by which time Augustino had become too arthritic to beat him much anyhow. Plus, Bob was now bigger, so there was that, too. Bob worked in the family »pastamodelleria« in the southern (rougher) suburbs of newly industrialized Naples. He was doing well, until in 1976 the local Camorra got in on the deal and tried to stuff the pasta forms with cocaine for export. Bob was unaware of this and boiled the experimental batch, ruining product with a street value of $2,000,000, a tidy sum in those days. Fortunately for Bob, the mob ordered the assassination of Augustino as revenge, so he didn't mind so much. It gave him a fright though, and he decided to leave the pasta business and head for a related field, printing, though the molds were different, shaped like letters as they are. In 1981, Bob got married to Julietta Pasqualini, a childhood friend who had correctly concluded that he represented her last chance of not ending up an old maid like her ugly sister Paola. They had clumsy sex a couple of times and agreed not to repeat the experience except when drunk. Bob tried going to a prostitute one time since, but after she

laughed at his request to be addressed as »Il Duce,« he chose not to return. Meantime, professionally things were going good for Bob, as he ascended the printing hierarchy, becoming deputy with special charge of inks in 1988. This was also the year that his beloved mother Nina died, aged 67, of deep vein thrombosis of the left foot. Bob was unconsolable. But in early February 1995, domestic unhappiness

notwithstanding, Bob was made head printer. His early pasta-mold-making had stood him in good stead. And in 2004,

with the successful printing of the Book, his career reached its apogee. But as he would be the first to admit, he does not consider himself fulfilled, and admits to lying awake at night thinking of cancer. And you thought you had problems. If you have any tips for Bob, write to him at:

Bob Zuccione
Via F Girardi 105
I – 80144
Napoli, Italy

NOTES

ER PENINSULA OF THE LEFT INNER EAR SENDS OUT THE FATHER OF MY BEASTS TO TAKE CARE OF THE MELANCHOLIC MELON AMONGST SACRIFIED WALMARTS. SODOMIZING THE WALLS RAISED ETERNALLY WITH CONCRETE SLABS AND WATER RUNNING OSE OF A RHINO IN THE BITTERSWEET TASTE OF MY MOUTH. CANCAN SALSA BUTTERBUG PANCAKE FROSTY FEMALE GLOBE- R STEELBENCH ON PARADE IN RIO. CYCLING BEATS RUNNING IF RUNNING IS WALKING AND WALKING IS WHAT KEEPS ME THINKING OF YOU. QUOTE UNQUOTE ANGLOSAXON VIKING WITH HYPOTHERMIA LOOKING FOR LOVE IN A CATALOGUE FOR ROENER AT HOME WITH HIS GNOMES. SCREAM, SAID THE CAT BUT HE KEEPS WALKING UP A TIGHTROPE FUNGUS CLOGGING Y BREATH AND TIME IS RUNNING OUT AND YOUR SCALP IS BITTER COLD AND PAINTED RED BY THE SUN. OCEAN RIPPLES COAG- S THE BEACH AND PARADES HISTORICAL KEYBOARDS MULTIPLIED BY FIVE THOUSAND CORIANDER BOTTOMS COVERED IN SNOW IT. PUTIN! PUTIN! CANNOT GET HOME THROUGH THAT RIP IN THE CLOTHING AND PIMPLES ALL OVER SIGNIFY A LOCAL TENDENCY P. OH SWEET RULING CLASS SPREADING SUNLIGHT IN THE ROBE I'M WEARING IN HONOUR OF BALZAC. LIGHTING A MATCH JU- S THE SHADOWS CLOSER TO ME. WHAT I THOUGHT WAS POSSIBLE IN SCHOOL WAS NOT. OPPORTUNITIES OF GOLD AND VACCOM ING UP TO WHAT I COMMONLY REFER TO AS "PROMOTING CAUSES THAT PROVOKES COMMON LANGUAGE". STOP NOW AND ST- OR THUMBS UP FOR A WHILE, THINK OF MOTHER THERESA IN A PICTURESQUE SETTING COMBING FLEAS OFF A BABYLON COW. E PEN TO SOME COMRADE CLAIMING TO BE AN ILL-RECIEVED FORMER MEMBER OF A BAND CALLED SUZY THE PANFLUTE IG BOZANOVA FAMILY AND LET HIM DRAW A BIG MAN WITH SMALL EYES ON THE INSIDE OF YOUR MOST TENDER THIGH... N WAS A CITY RATHER THAN AN ABSTRACT IDEA OF FREEDOM IT WOULD CERTAINLY CONTAIN LESS MOMENTS OF COMPLIC- TROKES OF BINARY PATHS IN SPACE. AUTOMATIC WRITING DAY. PROBE THE DEPTHS OF YOUR SUBCONSCIOUS TODAY. SIT DOWN A TABLE WITH A PEN AND A PAPER, PICK A FIRST LETTER AT RANDOM, AND START WRITING AS FAST AS YOU CAN WITHOUT TH- ABOUT IT. WARNING: IF YOUR AUTOMATIC WRITING ENDS UP SOMETHING LIKE THIS; "THE DEVIL PLAYS THE BANJO BETWEEN ECHEROUS LEGS OF MOTHER SUPERIOUR RAAAAGH I SPEAK IN TONGUES AT THE DAWN OF THE LAST DAY SCREW THE VEGE- AND LET THE UNIVERSE IMPLODE BOTTERCUPS BUTTERCUPS SUCK MY MANIFOLD ORIFICES!!!," YOU ARE EITHER UNHIN- A TEENAGER. GO DO YOUR HOMEWORK. ON THE CON-MAN! PISS ON A FLUTE! SPY ON A MALLORCAN! SATURE A MILLION. NOTH- N STAND IN MY WAY TO THE ETERNAL WISDOM OF A MAN WITH NO PAST AND NOTHING BUT HANDCRAFTED TOYS IN HIS POCK- LION ROWS YOUR BOAT. AND YOU'RE NOT HUNGRY. THE LIONS ARE CATS, YOU'RE JUST HUMAN. LIONS EAT ZEBRAS, YOU STICK TO ONCENTRATED GAFFER PENIS SUFFLE, HARBORING A TERRORIST UNDER EACH ARMPIT, SHOOTING BLUEBIRDS IN THE SKIES OF T LUDLUMS PRIVATE CINEMA. EVOLUTION IS NOT MISSING NOR WELCOME HERE. NEITHER IS STRAIGHT LINES OR THE LETTER T. VACY. THE SIGN OF THE FRONT PART OF THE GUITAR IS PULLING THE STRING THAT SUPPORTS THE LAUNDRY OF THE FIRST BL- AN TO GO TO THE MOON. NOW IS THE TIME TO UNRAVEL THE SONG THAT I'VE WRITTEN TO CELEBRATE THE ANNIVERSARY OF TH- RITHOUSE APPEARANCE BY THE PRINCE CAUGHT SHOPLIFTING A PAIR OF NEUTRAL-COLOURED LOAFERS IN A SHOP CALLED DALE, AFTER THE FAMOUS SINGER DAVID. INTERNATIONAL SCALPELS DRINKS DRUNKEN SAILORS LEFTOVERS TO COPE WITH OVE-VIRUS SPREADING FASTER THAN ITS COUNTERPARTS CARE TO CARE. PROLONG MY PICK-POCKET FRIENDS VISUMS TO N THE COUNTRY OF THEIR INFANTILE COUNTRY OF VIRGIN ORIGIN. FREQUENT VISITS FROM YOU KEEP ME CALM. FLAGS DON'T. THREATHEN ME WITH WITH BIRDS I WILL CONQUER YOU WITH SO 16-YEAR OLD VIRGINS PLAYING 50 CENT AND TRIVIAL PU- WITH A DWARF. NAIL ME TO THE WALL HIGH UP. CIRCLE IT WITH CHALK. ERASE THE SAME WITH A COMPUTER TELEPHONE. M IF YOU'RE A BABY, WHISPER IF YOU'RE A CHILD, AND IF YOU DON'T LIKE ME PREACHING, LOOK ME UP IN THE BOOK OF BELTS AND SMOKING GUNS AND YOU'LL SEE THAT I WAS THE FIRST TO SPEAK FRENCH WITH AN GEORGIAN ACCENT. AND VE IT, I'LL DIP TWO FURRY ANIMALS IN A KETTLE OF BOILING ASPHALT AND PRICE IT TO THE LITRE ACCORDING TO THE A-CONVENTION. IT IS ABOUT TIME NOW TO BE THE HERO OF MY OWN ACCORDS. CAN'T STOP FAILING IN THE AFTERNATH PLE WHO CLAIM THAT THE FOREST IS MADE UP OF MORE SPECIES OF TREES THAN ONE. SO SOD IT. JUST SHOOT. MUSTARD N MY VEINS LIKE POKER IN THE GAMBLER. PUNISHING MY MOTHER FOR STUFF THAT I DID OR AT LEAST WERE PARTLY ONSIBLE FOR IN A WICKED ROMANESQUE KIND OF WAY, AND YOU WERE SUPPOSED TO BE MY SISTER! DON'T TOUCH MY ! SORRY, DIDN'T MEAN TO GO SO FAR DOWN THE DIRECTORS INSTINCTS. GOT A BAD CASE OF PARADISE PRETENTIONS TING ENDLESSLY WITH OVERRIPE PRIMATES LOST FROM THEIR FLOCK. OH, I'VE SAID TO MUCH, GIVEN OUT TO MUCH, O MUCH. IT TELLS ME MORE ABOUT YOU THAN ABOUT ME IF YOU GOT THIS FAR. TWISTED MY ANKLE IN A LUMBERJACK TO ED WITH THE ROYAL DRAMA ABOUT THE POMPOUS WAR BETWEEN THE GOOD, THE BAD AND THE PEOPLE THAT ALWAYS UNNOTICED; THOSE OF THE PALSTERNAK TRIBAL UNIT SIXTEEN COUGHING IT UP BETWEEN THE TAKES OF SOME SE- OMMERSIAL FOR ELECTRIC RAZORS ON RETURN AFTER BEING DISHONOURED BY EU-REGULATIONS FOR OVER 200 BRI- LY HANDLED YEARS UP THE ASS OF A PEACOCK. MISS ME NOT, I'M SHAKESPEARE EXCEPT FOR THE TALENT INFLICTED BY TO BARRACUDAS WITH TEETH SHARP AS THE ICEBLOCKS ON THE

NOTES

COFFEINDRENCHED PARADIGM END AND THE TEENAGER OF CAPSULATE THE INNER EMO IMMEDIATE CIRCLE OF F- BUNCH OF PIMPS AND RE SOME EVIL VEGE- DAMN STEP YOU'VE STEAL MEDICAL AID OF A SHOPPING ST- CROSSING COMPL- TWO WAYS INTO CAN BE CONSID- LANGUAL JUSTI- SUSPENSE YOU PASADENA CAN A QUICK SET OF TED BY FEAR OF RAMMSTEIN. SCRA- ECIAL CRUMBS SO ED SLAPSTICK CUM. IF YOU CAN'T SEE REPRESENTATION OF RE SINCE I REALIZED FT OF MY MOST HATED TLY BRAGGING THAT HE WAS VIDEO. AHA TJOHO, ROCKETS TH-

JO PERSONS TRYING TO SOLVE A CRIME INVOLVING A BITTER EAR. EAT WITHOUT SCREAMING THEN, TAKE MY WHOLE BIN. AND SHOWCASE YOUR PRIDE TO THE ANCESTORS OF THE OS THAT YOU THINK IS TRUSTWORDY TO BE CALLED THE ES. DON'T OVERREACT AND BACK UP THE DATA BEFO- BITES YOUR COD AND MAKES YOU FORGET EVERY N TO REACH THAT GOAL OF SODOM AND GOMORRA. F A BUCKET YOU FIND STANDING ON THE MIDDLE FOLLOW THE YELLOW LINE TILL YOU COME TO A D AS A ZEBRA CROSSED WITH A POODLE, SEEING UCKING FUTURE, NARROWING DOWN TO WHAT GENETIKALLY IMPERFECT OR IN A SENSE BI- UNTS AND UNCLES USED TO THE BAD MUSIC OF LLY EXPECT FROM HOLLYWOOD BLOCKBUSTERS. E NEW FRESH START FOR YOU IF YOU ENJOY LES CONTROLLED BY A NAUTIC SENSOR OPERA- AID TO THE POOR MANDATE OF THE CITIZENS OF OUR ASS ANOTHER WAY. GOLD COLOUR YOUR SP- PARKLE OF BACKPACK PLURALISM AND DISGUIS- ES ARE GOOD FOR NOTHING IF YOU CAN'T SEE AND TEN KING FIUMATISATION AND HAVE TO RELY ON THE A CASSETTE. HERBS AND SPICES MEAN NOTHING NO MO ALIENS ARE HERE IN THE BACKYARD TO THE VERY LE- IBOUR, MAKING HIM EVEN MORE NERVOUS AND CONSTAN- IRST PERSON TO SEE MARTIN SCORSESES MEAN STREET ON AND PLUMS THERE. THE CAR WAS SPINNING OUT OF CONTROL WHEN I LEFT HIM TO THE FRONT ROW WITH THE FAU- TE THINNER STICK STICKING OUT OF YOUR EAR BUSTING THE BEAR COUGHING TOO LOUDLY AT THE MOVIES TRUST OW. STEP BY STEP. JEANS ARE BLUE, THE SUN IS YELLOW. YOU ARE PANICKING AWAY INSIDE CHILDRENS BOOKS OF A C LIBRARY IN MALTA BUILT FOR DISADVANTAGED BUILDERS AT THE TURN OF THE CENTRE. MANY DIED THERE, TRYING PULARIZE MOVEMENTS OF CAREERS ON ICE-SKATES THUMBLING AND FALLING TO COLLABORATE WITH CONSTABLES RNING TO DEMOCRACY AFTER A LIFE IN EXILE AND ABUSE OF THE FREEDOM OF SPEECH. CRYING FILLS THE SHELVES OF INSIDE PART OF A GUN NEVER TO BE USED BY ITS TRUE OWNER BUT BY PILGRIM STEPSONS OUT TO IMPRESS THE IR- S WITH GLASSES SHARPENED BY POSITIVE LIGHT. THE FIREBRIGAD WON'T GET HERE ON TIME IF YOU KEEP HANGING O THE DAGGER THAT POISONS THE GAP BETWEEN US TONIGHT WHEN DOGS AND FROGS GET ALONG BETTER THAN THE MARK ON THE EDGE OF A COUNTRY WON BY RETARDS. UNIFORMS ARE CLOTHES TOO, EVEN AT MCDONALDS. FIRES SPREADING AND YOU HAVE HOMOUS AROUND YOUR MOUTH. THAT'S WHAT GIVES ME THE URGE TO TOUGH YOU WITH A L-

DAY 313
TAKE ONE MEMORABLE PHOTO TODAY.
The most spontaneous-looking pictures are often those that require the most effort. Robert Doisneau had to wait all day for a policeman to walk past before taking this immortal shot. Today walk around with your camera, compose a great picture in your mind, and shoot it, no matter how long it takes you.

NOTES

FEEDBACK DAY

Today, feel free to ask the minds behind the Book any questions that may occur to you regarding its origins, contents, and philosophy. www.this-websitewillchangeyourlife.com/feedback

NOTES

Ideas for questions: »This is truly an amazing book. Isn't it?« »My life has changed. How can I thank you enough?« »Are you as pretty as you are funny?« »Why don't you run for presidents?« »If I was a girl, would you let me have your babies?«

 5/5   ½/5

DAY 315: JUST HOW GOOD IS YOUR DOCTOR?
Make an appointment to check he knows his symptoms:

TEST no 1: tell him or her you feel a large growing lump in the stomach, and have experienced hair loss along with bleeding from the anus. They should recommend you visit the emergency room within the next half an hour or so.

TEST no 2: don't say much, just groan and massage your stomach and head. When you do speak, sound drunk. They should recommend you stop wasting their valuable time.

TEST no 3 (advanced): how do they cope with unfamiliar symptoms? Tell them your left eyeball feels unusually mushy, your liver is palpitating, or your belly button is aching. How precise is their diagnostic and how many further tests do they order? Change doctors if you judge these insufficient.

NOTES

Day 316: We are each exposed to 2,000 commercial messages a day on average. Today count them.

TV commercials

Cinema commercials

Ads in newspapers

Classified ads

Posters

Radio ads

Ads on public transport

Ads in weird places

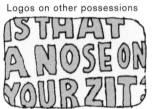

Logos on clothes

Logos on cars

Logos on other possessions

Shop signs

NOTES

Now go back and deface at least one of them for wasting your precious time.

DAY 317: DISCIPLINE DAY

Don't be a slave to your every impulse. Develop the willpower to overcome your body's inherent laziness and reap the rewards. You cannot master external circumstances, but you can begin to master your own mind. Follow this routine to enhance your self-discipline and get a grip on your life. Respect yourself and others will respect you.

SO:

Rise at dawn.
Take a cold shower.
Scrub behind your ears.
Scrub between your toes.
Brush your teeth for 3 mins.
Floss.
Cut your toenails.
Take your medicine.
Jog 5 miles.

Tighten your belt.
Straighten your tie.
Eat your sprouts.
Say »please« and »thank you.«
Look people in the eye.
Sit up straight.
Be in bed by 10pm.
Repeat every day.

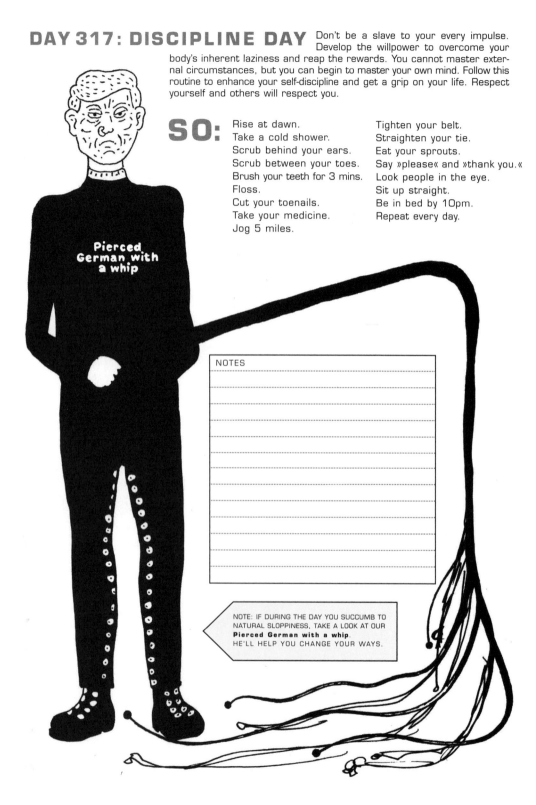

Pierced German with a whip

NOTES

NOTE: IF DURING THE DAY YOU SUCCUMB TO NATURAL SLOPPINESS, TAKE A LOOK AT OUR **Pierced German with a whip**. HE'LL HELP YOU CHANGE YOUR WAYS.

Day 318

Indulge Yourself

Today sample as many of the finest things
in life as your circumstances allow.

Champagne: Krug 1985 Clos du Mesnil ($560/bottle)

Caviar: Tsar Imperial Beluga ($1,500/lb)

Foie gras: Foie Gras Entier du Perigord ($142/20oz.)

Olive oil: Tenuta di Valgiano Extra Vergine ($56/bottle)

Smoked salmon: Wild Scottish ($30/lb)

Wine: Château Mouton-Rothschild 1945 ($8,450/bottle)

Truffles: Fresh White Alba Truffles ($1490/9oz.)

Lobster: large live Maine lobster ($48)

Chocolate: Neuhaus Belgian Pralines ($52/17oz.)

Whisky: Dalmore 62 Years Old Single Malt ($41,700/bottle)

Coffee: Jamaica Blue Mountain ($50/lb bag)

Cigar: Cuban Cohiba Churchill Esplendidos ($625/box of 25)

Prices may vary.

»Anyone who lives within their means suffers
from a lack of imagination.« (Oscar Wilde)

NOTES

_____

_____

_____

_____

_____

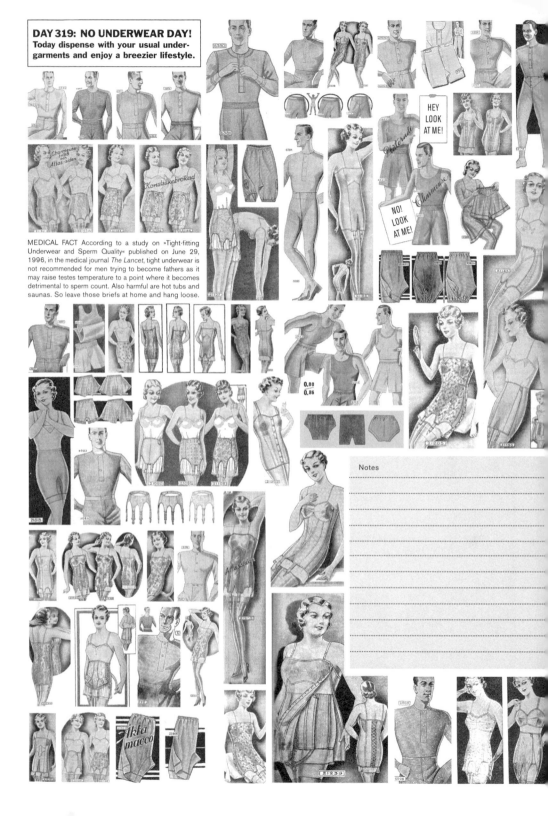

DAY 319: NO UNDERWEAR DAY!
Today dispense with your usual under-garments and enjoy a breezier lifestyle.

HEY LOOK AT ME!

NO! LOOK AT ME!

MEDICAL FACT According to a study on »Tight-fitting Underwear and Sperm Quality« published on June 29, 1996, in the medical journal *The Lancet*, tight underwear is not recommended for men trying to become fathers as it may raise testes temperature to a point where it becomes detrimental to sperm count. Also harmful are hot tubs and saunas. So leave those briefs at home and hang loose.

Notes

POSTERITY DAY

Don't sink into the oblivion of ages. Give humanity something to remember you by, whether it be a work of art, a feat of arms, or simply the sheer force of your personality. Today, decide what you want to be remembered for and set about writing yourself into History.

DAY 320

Notes	

Tip: one achievement is quite enough. Pity the novelists who diligently churn out one potboiler a year, when they could quite easily get away with one or two of a lifetime. Thackeray is famous for *Vanity Fair*, Proust for *Remembrance of Things Past*, Emily Brontë for *Wuthering Heights*. Tolstoy only needed a couple of decent novels to establish his genius. Paradoxically in our age of information overload, this has never been more true: spend ten years on something and you are presumed to be a thinker of the deepest ilk.

BAIL A STRANGER
OUT OF JAIL

FIND OUT IF YOU CAN TRULY TRUST IN MAN'S INNATE GOODNESS.
Every day thousands of petty criminals are available for release from jail pending trial, yet can't afford the relatively paltry sums necessary to post bail.

Call up your local courthouse and ask for suitable cases.

BEGINNERS: AVOID BAILING OUT SUSPECTS WITH ALLEGED VIOLENT PROCLIVITIES, AS THEY MAY TURN AGAINST YOU.

IF YOUR CHECK FOR BAIL GOES THROUGH, YOU WILL HAVE SOMEONE IN YOUR DEBT, A NEW BEST FRIEND FOR LIFE.

A NOTE OF CAUTION: BOUNTY HUNTERS.

If you post someone out of jail and they don't turn up in court, you may have a bounty hunter on your ass.

THESE GUYS ARE FOR REAL!

ASSIST THEM IN THEIR SEARCH FOR YOUR EX-NEW BEST FRIEND FOR LIFE, OR THEY COULD TURN NASTY.

BOUNTY HUNTERS ARE RECOGNIZABLE BY THEIR BURLY PHYSIQUES AND THEIR MEAN-SOUNDING FIRST NAMES, LIKE DOG, OR BEEF.

DAY 321
NOTES

Treasured Memories Day

Often, people find that they can remember the faces of casual acquaintances perfectly even years later, but not those of their departed nearest and dearest. Guard against the march of time by taking a good look at your loved ones' features today and committing them to memory.

NOTES

TAKE A COLD SHOWER

Historians of the future will no doubt trace the beginning of our civilization's decline to the universal availability of the warm shower, that enfeebling experience. Brace yourself this morning and prove your mettle by showering cold. Once the initial shock is over, it's actually quite invigorating. Plus you save on heating bills. Come on, are you a man or a mouse?

Look! It's so co that the of soap frozen t his body Amazing

I LIKE SHOWERS

CENSORED

NOTES

tudy this intriguing photograph today. What does it mean? What is the sausage doing there? What is it purpose? Who put it there? Write and send us your interpretation (max. 100 words). It will be published on our website and the best one will be rewarded.

DAY 324

NOTES	

Arabesque — Extend one leg directly behind the body in a straight line

pas de chat — Jump sideways, cat-like

entrechat — Jump crossing your feet in midair

jeté — Jump from one foot onto the other

NOTES

Day 325: Today learn a ballet step

Maria-Teresa Ludovinkha Petrovskavna's top tip for the beginner: »To become a prima ballerina assoluta, you just have to get the right name. As plain old Debbie G. Brookner, I was going nowhere fast. Then I simply changed my name, lost 80 pounds, and hey presto! here I am earning kazillions at the Bolshoi in world-famous Russia. Not bad for a girl from Poughkeepsie, huh?«

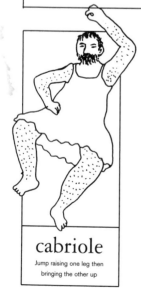

cabriole — Jump raising one leg then bringing the other up

pirouette — Turn on one leg with the other leg raised

éclat de genou — Raise both legs and jump backward, segueing seamlessly into a double pirouette

rond de jambe — Raise one leg with bent knee and circle the air with pointed toe

DO SOME DIY TODAY

LEVEL OF DIFFICULTY:

1

REPLACE A DEAD LIGHTBULB: UNSCREW OLD LIGHTBULB. SCREW IN NEW ONE.

LEVEL OF DIFFICULTY:

2

HANG A PICTURE HOLD PICTURE AGAINST WALL AND MARK CORNERS WITH PENCIL. HAMMER PIN-TYPE PICTURE HOOK INTO THE WALL EQUIDISTANT BETWEEN MARKINGS. HANG PICTURE.

LEVEL OF DIFFICULTY:

3

REPAIR A DRIPPING TAP. CUT OFF WATER SUPPLY. UNSCREW THE BELL-SHAPED COVER TO EXPOSE THE HEXAGONAL HEADGEAR NUT. UNDO WITH A WRENCH UNSCREW THE NUT HOLDING THE WASHER IN PLACE ON THE VALVE SEATING. FIT NEW WASHER AND JUMPER IF NECESSARY. GREASE THREADS ON TAP BASE. REASSEMBLE AND TURN WATER SUPPLY BACK ON.

LEVEL OF DIFFICULTY:

4

INSTALL A CHEMICAL DAMP-PROOF COURSE REMOVE SKIRTING BOARDS AND TAKE UP FLOORBOARDS. DRILL A HORIZONTAL ROW OF NOZZLE INTO THE FLUID CONTAINER OF YOUR DAMP-PROOF COURSE INJECTION MACHINE, INSERT ALL BUT ONE OF THE INJECTION NOZZLES INTO THE HOLES AND TIGHTEN THE WING NUTS. HOLD THE LAST NOZZLE OVER THE CONTAINER AND TURN ON THE PUMP. WHEN FLUID BEGINS TO FLOW, TURN OFF AND INSERT NOZZLE IN HOLE. TURN ON THE PUMP, UNTIL THE WALL BRICKS ARE SATURATED AND BEGIN TO SWEAT. REPEAT ACROSS THE ENTIRE WALL. LEAVE TO DRY FOR WEEKS.

3INCH HOLES INTO THE WALL ABOVE THE EXISTING DAMP-PROOF MEMBRANE (IF THERE IS ONE). 6INCHES ABOVE GROUND. PUT THE SUCTION

DAY 326

NOTES

Embrace mother earth.

Kiss the ground that supports life today. Mother Earth is not apart from us but of us and through us. We are at one with her, along with the plants, the other animals, the liquids, the minerals and the gasses. Mother Earth is covered in meridians, or leylines, which are sensitive to our healing caress (see map). The Cherokee people observed that upon kissing a leyline, the birds would often flock to that place, and vegetation sprout thereafter. Be part of that healing. We can all make a difference.

Day 327

Notes

....
....
....
....
....
....
....
....
....
....
....
....

day off

Leave the Book aside today and take a well-deserved break from its strictures.
Too much self-monitoring will drive you mad. In fact today, make a special
effort not to think about yourself at all. There, you've failed already.

Day 329
Today choose your motto and live by it

VINCIT VERITAS
Truth Conquers

IN FIDE ET IN BELLO FORTES
Strong In Faith And War

SOLI DEO GLORIA
Glory To God Alone

PRO MITRA CORONAM
A Crown For A Mitre

HOC MAJORAM VIRTUS
My Virtue Is From My Ancestors

GALATEA MEA VIRIDIS EST
My Helmet Is Green

SEMPER PATRIA SEVIRE PRESTO
Always Ready To Serve My Country

FELIS DEMULCTA MITIS
The Stroked Cat Is Meek

FINIS CORONAT OPUS
The End Crowns The Work

FORTI NON IGNAVO
To The Brave Man, Not To The Bastard

NEC TEMERE NEC TIMIDE
Neither Rashly Nor Timidly

NEMO ME IMPUNE LACESSIT
No One Provokes Me With Impunity

OMNIA VINCIT AMOR
Love Subdues All Things

FORTUNA JUVAT AUDACES
Fortune Favors The Brave

MANUS HOEC INIMICA TYRANNIS
This Hand Is Hostile To Tyrants

NEC TIMEO NEC SPERNO
I Neither Fear Nor Despise

PAREA NON SERVIN
I Obey But Not As A Slave

FORTIS EST VERITAS
Strong Is The Truth

FRUCTO COGNOSCITUR ARBOR
A Tree Is Recognized By Its Fruit

NECARE BARBAROS NOS DELECTAT
We Like To Massacre Others

GLANDIUM MUSQRUM NUTRIX
The Sword Is The Muse Of Muses

HONOS VIRTUTES SATILLES
Honor The Attendant Of Virtue

HUMANI NIHIL ALIENUM
Nothing That Relates To Man Is
Indifferent To Me

IN CRUCE SALUS
Salvation From The Cross

PRUDENS UT SERPENSSIMPLEX
UT COLUMBA PRUDENT
Careful As A Serpent
Simple As A Dove

PER ARDUA SURGO
I Rise Through Difficuties

PER MARE PER TERRAS
By Sea And Land

INDIGNANTE INVIDIA
FLOREBIT JUSTUS
The Just Man Will Flourish
In Spite Of Envy

REX PORCUS LARGUS EST
The King Is A Fat Pig

JUSTITIA ET FORTITUDO
INVINCIBILIA SUNT
Justice And Fortitude
Are Invincible

NIL DESPERANDUM
Never Despair

PRO ARIS ET FORIS
For Our Altars And Homes

AUT VINCAM AUT PERIAM
Either Win Or Perish

MALO MORI QUAM FOE DARI
Better Death
Than Disgrace

FACTA NON VERBA
Deeds Not Words

PATRIAE INFLICI FIDELIS
Faithful To My
Unhappy Country

Notes

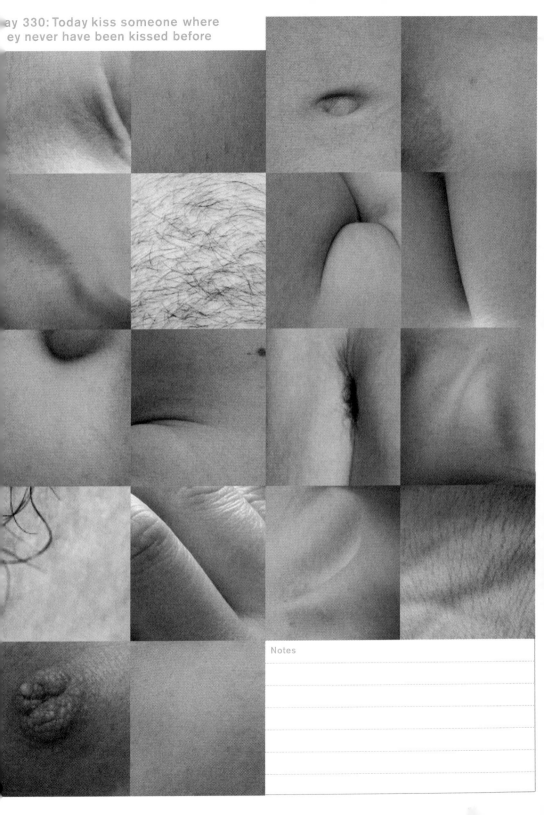

ay 330: Today kiss someone where
ey never have been kissed before

Notes

DAY 331

Hitchhiking has had a bad rap in the past, but it is one of the better solutions to the environmental pollution problems posed by cars, and a great way of generating a sense of community as well. Follow our guidelines to ensure safe and peaceable hitchhiking and hit the road.

DRIVERS: Pick up a hitchhiker today

Do not pick up anyone with a beard
Do not pick up anyone with fresh bloodstains on clothing
Do not pick up serial killer-types
Do not try to sexually engage with hiker (especially by pretending to confuse their knee for gearbox)

NON-DRIVERS: Hitchhike today

Do design a nice legible sign on some dry cardboard
Do hide any fresh blood stains on clothing
Do avoid mention of serial killer past
Do not try to sexually engage with driver (especially when they're driving)

Notes
....
....
....
....
....
....
....
....
....
....

Day 332

TONIGHT DATE YOURSELF

As Oscar Wilde noted, to love oneself is the beginning of a lifelong romance. You know you're special, and you deserve to be treated as such. Who better to cater to your every need but yourself? So today, come home early, run yourself a bubble bath, crack open a bottle of champagne, and treat yourself to a candlelit dinner where no one will bore you with selfish talk of themselves. And if the evening is successful, may we suggest you retire to the bedroom. Who knows, you might get lucky...

Notes

Telephone number home [   ]
Telephone number work [   ]
Telephone number mobile [   ]
Telephone number emergency [   ]
Telephone number of best friend [   ]
Fax number [   ]
Lottery numbers [   ]
Favorite number [   ]
Lucky number [   ]
Date of birth [   ]
Height [   ]
Shoe size [   ]
Collar size [   ]
Breast size [   ]
Penis size [   ]
Vision left eye [   ]
Vision right eye [   ]
Passport number [   ]
Credit card 1 number [   ]
Credit card 2 number [   ]
Credit card 3 number [   ]
Bank account number [   ]
Savings account number [   ]
Health Insurance number [   ]
Employee number [   ]
Current salary [   ]
Life insurance number [   ]
Home insurance number [   ]
Age [   ]
Age when first spoke [   ]
Age when first kissed [   ]
Age when first lost virginity [   ]
Age when married [   ]
Number of people slept with [   ]
Street number [   ]
Apartment number [   ]
Number of TV channels [   ]
Number of favorite TV channel [   ]
Number of siblings [   ]
Number of cousins [   ]
Number of children [   ]

Day 333:
Write down all the
numbers in your life

Numbers rule our lives.
As a society develops, more and
more numbers accrue to its individual
members. A fully evolved citizen
should easily be able to fill
in this chart.

Notes
....
....
....
....
....
....
....
....
....
....
....
....
....
....

Send some roses to your long-suffering mother

HOW MANY SHOULD YOU SEND?

START WITH 12, AND ADD OR DEDUCT AS FOLLOWS:

SHE BREASTFED YOU +3, SHE DROPPED YOU –4, SHE GAVE UP PROMISING CAREER FOR YOU +2, SHE OVERPROTECTED YOU –2, SHE TRIED HER BEST +1, SHE SMOKED DURING PREGNANCY –3, SHE'S STILL YOUR BEST FRIEND +5 (WOMEN) –5 (MEN).

NOTES

Day 335: Become a master of wine

Why remain a philistine when you could enjoy your drink more and impress society with your savoir-vivre in four easy steps:

1. SWIRL

Hold your glass at a steady angle then swirl it in a controlled movement, so it doesn't ruin your shirt and credibility (practice at home first if unsure). Look out for its color (light/deep) and its legs (how long it clings to the inner side of the glass).

2. SNIFF

Stick your nostrils over the freshly swirled glass (swirling frees up the smell) and take a deep nasal breath. Does it smell fruity/old/fresh/of shit (good red burgundy)/of cat's pee (good sauvignon blanc)?

3. TASTE

Still considered a key part of the wine experience. Rinse around your tonsils as you would mouthwash, then (and this is the clever bit), open your mouth slightly while the wine is still there and breathe in to let the flavor oxygenate. At first you will choke, and then spew all over soft furnishings and make a fool of yourself. Persist.

4. SPIT

The toughest step for many, but essential to convey professionalism. The trick is to form a semi-solid gob that hits the spittoon with a metallic clink, rather than a shower of particles, 90% of which miss the target entirely. Voilà!

NOTES

Day 336: Disappear
Don't you sometimes wish you could start all over
again? How difficult would it be just to walk away
from your life, and begin afresh somewhere else?
Test the waters by spending the day on the run from
your friends, family, and colleagues.

RULES OF SPACE TOURISM. The Book authors take it upon themselves to regulate space tourism to prevent it from spoiling the galaxy. RULE 1) No casting of empty cans, beer bottles or other trash into deep space. RULE 2) If everyone took a bit of the moon home, soon there'd be none left. RULE 3) Safety: to avoid muggings, do not walk on the dark side of the moon unaccompanied. RULE 4) Do not feed the aliens. RULE 5) No »my space helmet's leaking aaarrrgghh!« jokes. Photography no-no: pics of Planet Earth are such a cliché. How exactly are yours going to be different?

NOTES

Today dig at the end of a rainbow

Myths often survive throughout the ages because
they contain a grain of truth. Find out if this one is
true today, and you may reap huge rewards, and very
possibly get to marry Cinderella as well.
1) Call up your local weather office for information on
probable occurrences of rainbows in your area, based
on satellite imagery of cloud formation.
2) Triangulate the exact coordinates of the rainbow's
end, and track them down using a portable GPS system.
3) Secure the area and excavate a 1 acre site, aiming
for an average drilling depth of 3 metres. Use a
magnetometer to establish an electromagnetic and
geophysical profile of the zone.
4) Sift for any pots of gold. Be sure to have legal
help-at-hand to assert your right of ownership and
patent the »Rainbow-Digging« process.
Warning: if the rainbow happens to end on
a bank, find another one.

NOTES

24k Gold

Carnivorous Day! Today eat nothing but red meat!

Man is a carnivorous mammal, who owes his domination of the earth to a diet of high-protein raw meat. This is all too often forgotten in our anaemic vegetarianistic limp-wristed times. Regain some of those red blood cells with this man-sized feast.

BREAKFAST: 6 sausages with ketchup and/or mustard.

LUNCH: fry yourself 2–3 burgers (easy on those fatty sauces now).

DINNER: a nice big roast.

MIDNIGHT SNACK: nothing like a couple of meat pies to help you sleep.

Do something kinky today
Here are some little-known kinks to trigger your imagination.
Please note that illegal ones are marked with a star.

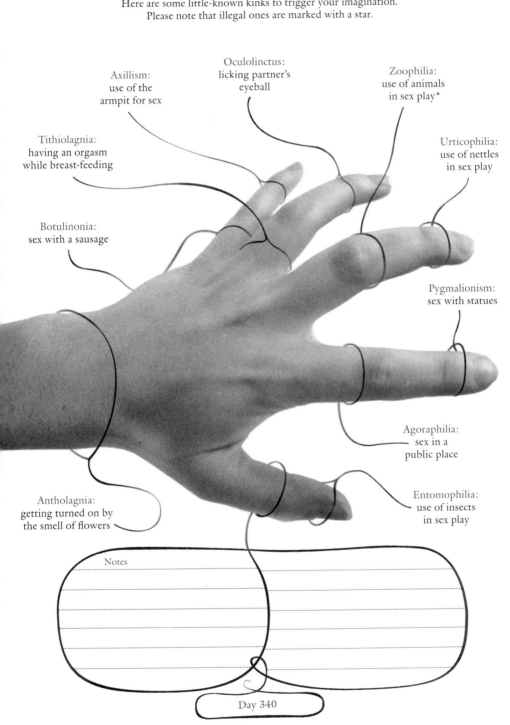

Axillism:
use of the
armpit for sex

Oculolinctus:
licking partner's
eyeball

Zoophilia:
use of animals
in sex play*

Tithiolagnia:
having an orgasm
while breast-feeding

Urticophilia:
use of nettles
in sex play

Botulinonia:
sex with a sausage

Pygmalionism:
sex with statues

Agoraphilia:
sex in a
public place

Antholagnia:
getting turned on by
the smell of flowers

Entomophilia:
use of insects
in sex play

Notes

Day 340

Day 341
Magic of Xmas Day:
Make a kid's day by convincing them Santa does exist!

Choose from the following foolproof arguments depending on how precocious the kid is.

»Simple« kids:
Where do you think presents come from then, you little mook?

Average kids:
How do you know he doesn't exist?

Snotty kids:
Of course Father Xmas could deliver gifts in millions of chimneys at once; quantum physics has proven that particles can be in more than one place at a time, unless someone is watching in which case their quantum waveform collapses. QED.

PRE-FEMINISM DAY

The most radical change of the twentieth century has been in the relationship between men and women. It is the first time in history that women have been even approximately treated as equal. Today, revert to pre-feminist behavior to measure the difference.

WOMEN:
1) Make sure you look your best
2) Don't speak unless spoken to
3) Stay at home and do the housework
4) Cook a nice dinner
for your man
5) Ask him for some pocket
money for a new dress

MEN:
1) Open doors, stand up, take your hat off
2) Buy your lady some flowers on
your way back from work
3) Compliment her on her cooking
4) Sssshhhh her if she
voices a foolish opinion
5) Skip foreplay, roll over and snore

DAY 342

Notes	

Swap jobs with a friend just for today Make sure you get your coworkers on board: say Bob couldn't make it today unfortunate but he's delegating to you his most trusted friend and he's explained how to do it in detail. Now what are those red dials for agai

Notes

Day 344
We have hidden $1,000 in this tree. If you recognize it today, the money is yours for the taking!

CLUE:
the tree is situated
in a park, not far from
the park entrance.

Notes

Today collect your belly button fluff and send it in.

WE WILL USE IT TO KNIT A MULTICOLORED SWEATER FOR THIS DOG.
»What if I have an outie?« About 10% of the population have an »outie«, so you are not alone. Doctors disagree as to the cause of the condition. The most popular current theory is that they are caused by an umbilical hernia: a small circular defect in the baby's abdominal wall that fails to heal during the first few years. The condition is essentially harmless, but unfortunately it means you will never have belly button fluff.

Day 345

NOTES

Day 346
Today plan for your old age

Prudent financial planning is indispensable to ensure a decent income in your sunset years. The earlier you start the better. Work out your needs with this simple formula.

How much you need
Mansion $1,000,000
Yacht $200,000
Cosmetic surgery $20,000
Golf $5,000/year
Viagra $5,000/year
Trip down Nile $5,000/year
Medical care $10,000/year
Prepaid funeral expenses $5,000

Total T

How many years before you retire R

T/R=how much you need
      to save a year

Typical example:
Photocopier technician Pete Donnelly is 42. He wants to retire at 60 and die at 90. His total T is therefore $1,975,000. Divide by number of years until he retires (R=18), which means Pete needs to save a mere $109,800 a year to retire in comfort. Good luck Pete. Now how about you?

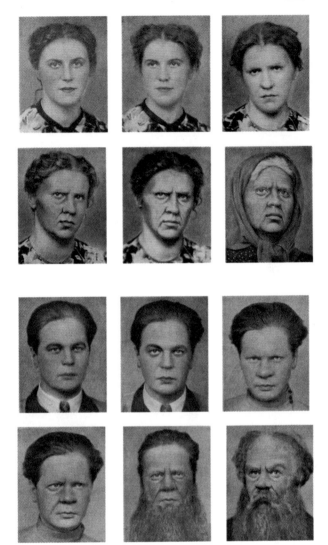

Notes	

TODAY MAKE A SPEECH

NOTES

HECKLER PUT-DOWNS
A good speech will attract hecklers. Here's how to deal with them subtly but firmly.

»Have you missed your medication again?«

»Is that your face or did your neck throw up?«

»The alcoholics anonymous meeting is the next door down.«

»Hey, I could have been your Dad but the dog beat me over the fence.«

»Shut up! Shut up! Shut! Up!«

What's the point of having opinions if you don't share them with your fellow countrymen? A good speech can jilt a conscience, start a revolution, move you to tears, sometimes even get you laid. Choose a suitably public spot, stand on a box of some kind, and spew forth on a controversial topic.

DAY 348
WHAT GOES AROUND COMES AROUND: A STORY.

START TO A TRAMP
GIVE $20

WITH $20, THE TRAMP WILL HAVE ENOUGH TO SPEND THE NIGHT IN A HOSTEL, AND A LITTLE TO SPARE.

WITH THAT LITTLE TO SPARE, HE WILL BE ABLE TO AFFORD A NICE WARM COFFEE.

IN THE COFFEESHOP, HE WILL SIT NEXT TO A RICH FAT MAN AND HIS FAT YOUNG SON AND HEIR.

THE FAT YOUNG HEIR WILL DROP HIS EXPENSIVE FOUNTAIN PEN ON THE WAY OUT.

THE TRAMP WILL NOTICE, PICK IT UP AND FOLLOW THEM OUT TO RETURN IT.

THE RICH MAN WILL TAKE FRIGHT UNTIL HE REALIZES THE TRAMP MEANS WELL.

HE WILL THEN REWARD THE TRAMP, BUT PROBABLY NOT WITH $20. THE END

NOTES

TODAY
DON'T ANSWER
THE PHONE

When Bell invented the telephone in 1876, people predicted it would never catch on; being summoned by a ring wa strictly for servants. And indeed, why let others dictate your movements? Strike a blow for personal freedom by ignoring th confounded machine.

NOTES

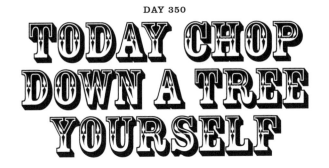

HOW TO FELL A TREE PROFESSIONALLY

Today, join the  Freemasons

Freemasonry: world-dominating conspiracy or well-meaning brotherhood of man? There's only one way to find out and that's to sign up! Today, send in your petition to become a Mason to your nearest Masonic Lodge (address it to the Worshipful Master).

Ancient, Free and Accepted Masons

I, the undersigned, a firm believer in the existence of a Supreme Being, respectfully request that I be considered for initiation unto the secrets of the masonic order. I hereby give my word that am not motivated by mercenary or other unworthy motives; that I am prompted by a favorable view of the Institution and a desire to learn of its mysteries; and that, if chosen, I will conform to the various usages and codes of the order.

Name...

Age...

Profession...

Wealth...

....

Are you of sound bodily health?.....................

Do you have any physical defects?....................

Are you loyal to your country?........................

Have you an upright heart and mind?................

Sign here twice...

....

Recommendations by two existing Masons

I am a member of ....masonic lodge and have been since...... I have personally known the petitioner for ....years, and vouch him to be a well-disposed candidate who will reflect well on our institution.
Signed..

I am a member of ....masonic lodge and have been since...... I have personally known the petitioner for ....years, and vouch him to be a well-disposed candidate who will reflect well on our institution.
Signed..

What happens next? Your local lodge will contact you in due course and speak to your family and employers, to ascertain your good standing in society. If accepted unanimously by the existing members, you will receive your first degree (the Degree of Entered Apprentice), learn a catechism covering your degree and be examined by your fellow Masons. You will then be taught the secret handshakes and start making steady progress in your political career.

Notes

Go into a bookshop and discreetly sign a few books by classic authors to enhance their value. Some famous signatures to emulate: *Tolstoy, Proust, Shakespeare, Dickens, Jane Austen, Cervantes, Goethe, Kafka.*

NOTE ON VERISIMILITUDE: insofar as possible, try to use contemporaneous writing materials, e.g. ink and quills rather than ballpoint pens, markers or pencils.

Notes

Reward your lover with a small sum, proportionate to the efforts exerted. After the initial surprise, they will appreciate the gesture, as well as the extra cash, and perform more keenly in the future in the hope of similar tips. Many staid relationships have been transformed overnight by this simple little trick, and some have even been saved!

Etiquette:
Do not plonk the money down on the bedside table ostentatiously as you would with a common whore or gigolo. Rather, give your loved one a naughty wink and slip it into their bra or jockstrap (try to use banknotes rather than coins). How much should you give? Current recommended rates are $5/hour, plus tax where applicable.

NOTES

NOTES
_____
_____
_____
_____
_____
_____
_____
_____
_____
_____
_____
_____

Day 354
celebrate life by drinking
nothing but champagne!

8. Sunrise. Champagne breakfast.

9.

10.

11. What a beautiful morning! Champagne!

12.

13. Lunch. Friendly colleagues, good food, and champagne of course...

14.

15. That meeting went very smoothly!!!! Glass of champagne anyone?!

16.

17. Hurrah! Work. End of. Celebrate!

18.

19. Dinner is time already?! bubbly bubbles pop pop pop barf!

Day 355: Challenge everyone you meet to
a game of tic-tac-toe. By the end of the
day you will know how mentally agile you
are relative to your social circle.

Notes

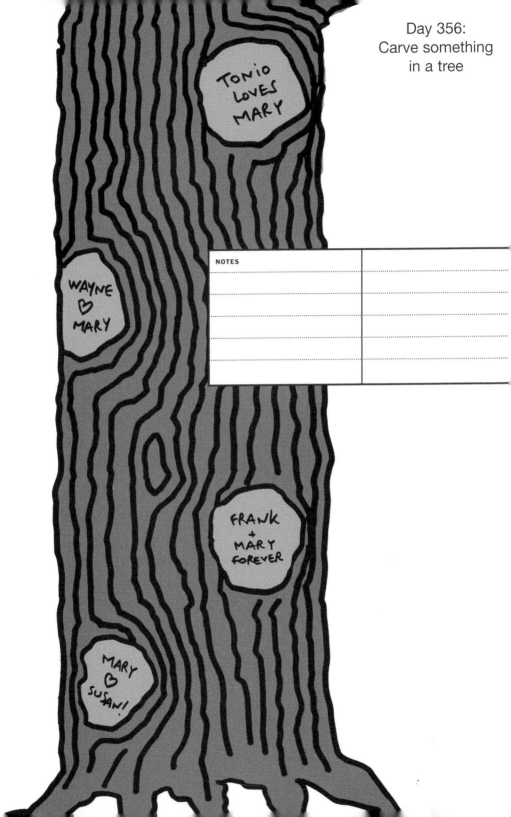

Day 356:
Carve something
in a tree

NOTES

Day 357

Today come out as a Book-owner

Wear one red sock and see if there's anyone else out there. If you spot someone sporting a red sock today, engage them in conversation. You may assume straight off that as Book-owners they are bright discerning individuals with a good sense of humor and finely honed critical faculties, and therefore well-worth knowing. They are not going to respond to some oafish overture like »nice sock!« wink-wink. To help, here are some recommended witty ice-breakers that will help establish kinship. »At the risk of putting my foot in it, may I compliment you on your sock« »Together we're quite the pair, wouldn't you say?« »I'll be darned if we haven't met before!« »If you don't want to chat , do tell me to put a sock in it…«

NOTES

DAY 358: SKETCH SOMEONE OPPOSITE YOU ON PUBLIC TRANSPORT AND SEE HOW THEY REACT

Notes

In case of violent reaction, show them this:

The bearer of this document has been mandated by the public transport authorities to effect paper likenesses of individual users of aforesaid public transport facilities for the purposes of national security. Civilians are asked to cooperate with enquiries under pain of prosecution.

Today, hand deliver all your e-mails

No one denies e-mail is a convenient business tool, but it cannot replace face to face interaction, source of ideas and team spirit. Today, get the best of both worlds by printing out your e-mails and taking them round personally.

Notes

DISINHERIT A RELATIVE!

Does your teenage daughter monopolize the phone? Does your brother still call you Junior? Does your annoying cousin persist in claiming he has better barbecuing technique? Today, cut an undeserving relative out of your will, raising the stakes with expressions such as »I renounce you,« »You are no longer my mother,« or »I can't believe you are the fruit of my loins.«

NOTES

STARTING
POINT

MUMMY! DADDY!
IF YOU DON'T LET ME
PLAY THE LITTLE ANTS
GAMES I WILL GROW
UP AND BECOME
LAZY IN SCHOOL
AND A BIT
OF A DIRTY
KNEE!

What is this ant trying to say to you?

If the pattern seems mainly circular, the ant is establishing a rapport with you.

If the pattern seems essentially diagonal, the ant senses danger. Beware.

If the pattern seems hexagonal, that is one clever ant.

If the pattern seems phallic, you probably need psychiatric assistance.

If the ant leaves the page, he's saying he has better stuff to do than talk to a dumb-looking schmuck of a human being such as you. Kill it to teach it a Darwinian lesson.

NOTES

Today imagine what it would be like to be this person.

Are you fulfilled? What is your job? Do you break down and sob quietly in the middle of the night? Are you sex-mad? What is your dream in life? Have you ever known true love?

NOTES

Increase your tolerance to »hot« food.

Most Westerners are used to bland seasonings, though with a bit of exercise they could get used to the spicier diets that other civilizations enjoy. Today, work out your current limits.

The heat level of a dish can be graded thanks to the Scoville Organoleptic Test, originally developed for chilli peppers. The hottest chilli pepper in the world, the Red Savina Habanero, weighs in at a whopping 577,000 Scoville units.

chilli markings table

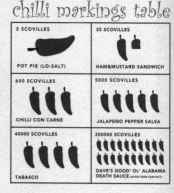

2 SCOVILLES	25 SCOVILLES
POT PIE (LO-SALT)	HAM&MUSTARD SANDWICH
600 SCOVILLES	5000 SCOVILLES
CHILLI CON CARNE	JALAPENO PEPPER SALSA
40000 SCOVILLES	200000 SCOVILLES
TABASCO	DAVE'S GOOD' OL' ALABAMA DEATH SAUCE (AVOID SKIN CONTACT)

We asked Mexican gourmet Alberto Rodriguez Sr his opinion of a typical Western dish, macaroni cheese: »This is very boring for me, just mushy mush, I had to pour a whole bottle of tabasco in before it even registered on the taste buds. And this you call a great delicacy? *Madre de dios* etc etc...«

THE SECRET OF CHILLIES: CAPSAICINOIDS! Chillies get their supernatural heat from chemicals called capsaicins, compounds from the vanilloid family. They bind themselves to pain receptors on the tongue, causing a flow of calcium ions between molecules that translates into a burning sensation. In concentrated form, capsaicin can reach 16,000,000 scovilles, over 25 times as hot as the hottest chilli pepper ever recorded. Pure capsaicin is a highly dangerous irritant: chemists who work with it have to wear full hooded protective suits to avoid inhaling it accidentally. One milligram on the skin would lead to instant severe blistering! Here is how to extract it. Purée a dozen habaneros in a blender with a large quantity of ethanol. Leave overnight. Filter the resulting sludge and evaporate (do not use naked flames!), until a brick-red oil is precipitated on the surface. Suck off the oil with a pipette. It should be 40% capsaicin. Do not ingest or touch.

DAY 364

Try one of these sexual positions
Beginners: 2, 3, 8. Intermediate: 1, 7, 9.
Advanced: 4, 5 ,6. Porn star: 10–16.

NOTES

DAY 365:
»NEW YOU« PARTY

Well done! You have completed a full year of life-changing instructions. By now, you should be a completely different person. Throw a party where you will unveil the »new you« to your friends and acquaintances.

You will probably find that your entourage no longer suits the new you. Where once you were quite happy to discuss last night's reruns of *Cheers*, now you crave conversation of a more cultivated nature, like some light badinage about Brecht perhaps? Two solutions offer themselves to you. First, give all your old friends a copy of the Book so they can catch up with you. Second, discard them and acquire some new ones.

NOTES

CONGRATULATIONS!

You have lived with the Book for 365 days now, 365 days of rollercoaster emotion that will no doubt have transformed your life in a million different ways (or more). So well done for sticking with it. As a token of our gratitude and admiration, here is a *$100 Coupon,* which you may redeem against a one-in-a-million chance* to enter the draw for our top prize!!!

*One applicant in a million gets the chance to be selected for the draw. Selection at the discretion of Benrik Ltd. Top prize to be announced.

Visit www.thiswebsitewillchangeyourlife.com
to register your achievement!
No, don't thank us. It is we who thank you.

The history of the Book

Most readers will be surprised to learn that the Book is not entirely new. The present authors have endeavored to bring it back to life. But it has a long and rich history, which Dr. Gunther Pedersen of the Bern Institute of Cultural Studies (Kulturelles Zentrum, Bern) has researched for this edition.

The precise origins of THIS BOOK WILL CHANGE YOUR LIFE are a matter of academic dispute. So divided are scholars even as to its original title, the truth may never be conclusively established. Over the centuries it has been known variously as »The Book of Days,« »Fate's Very Own Calendar,« »Perish Ye Whom Glance Herein,« »365 Rollickin' Rides« and »Die Entdeckung der Weltgeschichte« – amongst many others. Nevertheless we will attempt to outline in broad terms its history, pointing out inconsistencies and gaps in our knowledge, bearing in mind along the way that, as the great Carlyle has said, ultimately »history is but a distillation of rumor.«

The first mention of the *Book* is to be found in Herodotus, the Greek »father of history,« writing in about 450BC. He refers to »the curious custom practiced by the Pelasgians of following everyday of the calendar rites written on their oracle's tablets« (*Histories*, VI.56). Herodotus discusses the derivation of this custom: »I may say, for instance, that it was the daughters of Danaos who brought this ceremony from Egypt and instructed the Pelasgian women in it.« (II. 171). The Pelasgians, of course, mentioned both by Herodotus and the more reliable Thucydides, are recognized as the majority tribe within the nomadic population of Greece and the Aegean, before their gradual assimilation by the Hellenes. There is therefore a strong case to suggest that the very origins of the *Book* can be traced beyond the classical age and back to Egyptian civilization, the ultimate cradle of our culture.

Indeed, some have seen fit to speculate on the influence of the (as yet nameless) *Book* on Egyptian history. Could Pharaoh Akhnaton's contempt for age-old tradition, for instance, stem from his worship of the *Book*'s ancestor? Certainly much has been made of the fact that when his sarcophagus was opened by the American amateur Egyptologist Theodore Davis in 1907, the dusty and unreadable remnants of twelve papyrus scrolls were found at his side. But in truth there is no solid evidence to back this claim.

At this point we should attempt to shed some light on two contentious issues. First of all, which of the multifarious versions is the genuine *Book*? Fakes and translations are legion. For our purposes, the real *Book* is the so-called Greek version, as found in Constantinople in 1422 by scholar Giovanni Aurispa

(of whom more later). Both in depth and in originality, it stands out as the truest incarnation of the *Book*, as anyone who cares to study it at the British Museum will surely agree (by appointment with the British Museum Special Finds Dept, London WC1B 3DG). We call it the »Original *Book*,« though no one has managed to pinpoint its ultimate authors (many have tried; see for instance H. Beckenbauer, *»The origins of the Book: Atlantis revealed?,«* Eon Press, 1954).

Secondly, why is there so little mention of this ancient text in conventional histories? The answer will become readily apparent as we proceed; the *Book* is essentially an instrument of radical change, unleashing forces too powerful for authorities to control. Thus it has been ignored and hidden away in official accounts; for those who know to look though, its footprints are everywhere.

Following Herodotus, The *Book* resurfaces now and again in Greek fragments, mostly concerned with Orphism. Anaximander, for instance, tells us of γμγενειζ, »loosely translated as »The Book Of Days« It is perhaps then no coincidence that Plato is the first to refer to it at any length, for we know he spent 12 years in Egypt and a deep understanding of Orphic cosmology permeates his works (his contemporary Krantor in fact accused him of lifting the *Republic*'s political hierarchy straight from the Egyptian caste system). In a little-known appendix to his *Symposium*, he has prophetess Diotima of Mantinea argue the following: »What do you think, Socrates, of the study that Euthydemus and others make of that Phoebean text in which their pursuits are commanded day by day? Haven't you noticed how the course of their existence is varied, when so many people in Athens repeat everyday yesterday's actions again. Don't you agree?«

»By Zeus I do!« said [Socrates]. »Well then, [said Diotima], can we say that this text is a medium for messages between mortals and the goddess Fate?« Socrates then goes off on something of a tangent regarding the parentage of said goddess Fate; but it is clear from this that the *Book* was in use round about 400BC. It is also surely more than mere coincidence that it is mentioned in the course of the *Symposium*, famous for its emphasis on homosexual relations between adult males and young men. Could some early *Book* injunction to experiment sexually have caught on in Greek culture?

The *Book* then enters a long period of obscurity, along with so many classical masterpieces. True, there is the odd reference to it in Roman texts; Cicero associates it uncritically with Epicureanism, accusing it of being »so easily grasped and so much to the taste of the unlearned« (*Tusculan Disputations*, IV, 3). But in truth it was more suited to the imaginative Greek spirit than to the more plodding organizationally-minded Roman outlook, and so never really caught on.

Of course throughout Antiquity the *Book* was very much intertwined with religion. Early versions might have enjoined Phoenicians to sacrifice goats and suchlike. Indeed it is probable that the religious trend for issuing arbitrary instructions, such as the Ten Commandments, was derived from that very source. But it is with its rediscovery and adaptation in the Renaissance that it enters the modern age.

The *Book* re-emerges – where else? – in Florence. Under Coluccio Salutati, Chancellor of Florence from 1375 to 1406, there came a new yearning for knowledge of the classical past. Very few authors remained in circulation, with some quasi-extinct; there was only one known manuscript of Catullus in existence anywhere, for example.

In 1392 Coluccio himself found Cicero's »Epistolae Familiares,« which signalled the beginning of an intensive search for classical manuscripts. It was directed by Niccolo Niccoli, with the help of his right-hand man, the irrepressibly enterprising Poggio Bracciolini.

In the summer of 1416, Poggio visited St Gall, a 7th century Benedictine monastery 20 miles from Constance in Switzerland. He asked to visit the library, which turned out to have been grossly neglected, »a most foul and dimly lighted dungeon at the very bottom of a tower.« As he leafed through the dusty old manuscripts, mostly in deplorable condition, Poggio's excitement grew. Here he had found a complete manuscript of Quintilian's *Training of an Orator*, substantial portions of Cicero, and a partial damaged Roman copy of something enigmatically named the »codex diei,« the book of days.

Poggio stayed at the monastery and copied it out himself with goose quills and inkhorn over 56 days. He then sent his copy back to Florence for which we must be grateful, as the original was lost in a monastery fire 7 years later. We are also in his debt for making it readable; the original, like most old parchment manuscripts, was copied out in minute Gothic text, which he exchanged for his own much rounder script (which in due course became the basis of modern handwriting).

It would be false to claim that the Florentines immediately recognized the value of the *Book*, which is why it is hardly mentioned in contemporary accounts. This was partly because the Roman version they inherited was very much incomplete. Fragments such as »Today abandon all your pursuits in favour of the greatest good of them all ....chariot!« left them bemused rather than amazed. This all changed in 1423 when Giovanni Aurispa arrived in Italy with a vast hoard of original Greek manuscripts, 239 in all, including most of Greek literature: the *Iliad*, the *Odyssey*, Aeschylus, Sophocles, Euripides, Herodotus, Plato, and countless others, all of a sudden given to Florence, along with of course the original Greek copy of the *Book*... This treasure chest of classical culture was seized, debated and lectured upon avidly by the Florentines. The young Greek scholar Marsilio Ficino translated Plato and the *Book*, declaring the latter to be »one of the crowning achievements of classical civilization.« Indeed, his famous inscription in the hallway of the Academy, where the leading lights of Florence used to meet, was meant to bear witness to its influence: »Rejoice in the present.« Every citizen had a copy; Lorenzo de Medici had his bound in gold leaf. In retrospect, it is hard to resist the conclusion that the *Book* contributed substantially to the conception of the individual that flowered in Quattrocento Florence. It enshrined the notion of »complete man,« one who realized all his innate qualities. It also chimed with the new Renaissance perception of time. The agricultural and monastical societies of the Middle Ages moved to the slow rhythm of the seasons and eternity. With their eye firmly fixed on the afterlife, they cared little for daily upheaval. But the Florentines were a manufacturing and trading people, to whom time was precious, to whom indeed time was money. It is no coincidence that a Florentine, Brunelleschi, invented the alarm clock (in between painting masterpieces and building his famous dome). The Renaissance man lived for the here and now, and prized every moment. The *Book* was part and parcel of this Weltanschauung.

Along with so much else in Florentine civilisation, the *Book* met its nemesis in the form of Dominican friar Savonarola, who took Florence by storm in the 1490's with his apocalyptic preaching of hellfire and brimstone against the corrupt citizens who had abandoned the gospels for more wordly pleasures and values. In Savonarola's vision of Florence as the new Jerusalem, there was no room for the impious free-thinking *Book*. And in 1497, he tried to make sure all copies were burnt in his infamous Bonfire of the Vanities, along with copies of Boccaccio, Petrarch, paintings by Botticelli and other masterpieces. Almost all *Book*s were thus consumed by the flames, and none would likely have survived if he had held power much longer. But in 1498 he finally went too far and was excommunicated by the Pope, then hanged in the Piazza della Signoria and thrown on a bonfire of his own. The Florentine Renaissance was at an end.

Thankfully one of the factors in its downfall also guaranteed its survival. When Charles VIII and the French Army invaded Italy in 1494, precipitating the demise of the Medici dynasty, they were spellbound by the scale and beauty of the Florentine achievement: the Medici palace, the sculptors and painters, the tapestries... And so as conquering king, he shipped back to Amboise 21 artists and craftsmen, manuscripts, pictures, over 34 tons of marble – effectively transplanting the Renaissance back to France.

The *Book* went with him of course. It was in large part because the French held the original copy that Leonardo da Vinci accepted Francois I's offer to move to France from Italy in 1516, so that he could study it. For the next few centuries, under the absolutist reign of the Bourbon kings, the *Book* held a much lower profile, and was considered mostly a quaint, even frivolous curio. Voltaire though saw its subversive potential and in 1778 translated it into French, none too scrupulously, adding much of his own trademark irony in the process.

CE LIVRE VOUS CHANGERA LA VIE, as it had become, then re-emerged in aftermath of the French Revolution in the unlikely hands of Donatien Alphonse Francois Marquis de Sade. Sade, of course, was an indefatigable scribbler himself and it will readily be perceived how the LIVRE's mix of arbitrary dictates fired up his imagination. A dozen days he wrote survive. The least unprintable enjoin followers to copulate variously with goats, toads, dwarves and grandmothers (the conceit here being to precipitate a fatal heart attack). Baudelaire claimed to have read the full-year Sadean version, describing it in his correspondence as a »veritable *Kamasutra* of pain.« No copy alas is extant.

The original *Book* fell victim to Sade's notoriety and excesses. On March 6, 1801, Parisian police arrived suddenly to search the premises of Sade's publisher Nicolas Mosse, in hot pursuit of an obscure pamphlet, »*Zoloe*,« which Sade had allegedly penned against Napoleon and Josephine. The accusation turned out to be false, but the police nevertheless seized all the remaining stock of his novel *Juliette*, and of course his copy of the *Book*. Napoleon, it seems, was ungrateful for this new acquisition, for he had Sade imprisoned without trial, and later transferred to Charenton insane asylum, where he stayed locked up until his death in 1814. In 1810, Napoleon punished him further by signing a decision to

keep him in detention and forbidding all communication with the outside world, depriving him also of any writing materials. Whether this fate would have befallen him without the *Book* is quite possible, but it is clear that Napoleon's unlawful confiscation of such a valuable manuscript helped consign the Marquis to political oblivion.

There is no record of Napoleon himself directly referring to the *Book*, but there is no doubt he would have perused it; it is known that he liked books – even in difficult times at St. Helena he had 3370 books in his library. But as Madame de Remusat informs us, he was »really ignorant, having read very little and always hastily.« The *Book*'s clear and concise orders would have suited his military temperament.

Few of his career-defining decisions can be traced directly to the *Book*'s dictates, with one exception: the Louisiana Purchase. Historians have always been somewhat puzzled by Napoleon's agreement to suddenly relinquish French possession of what was then called Louisiana but in fact encompassed 13 current states and over 900,000 square miles, for a relative pittance (15 million dollars). This was one of the greatest real estate deals in history, doubling the size of the United States, transforming it into a world power and effectively ending France's dreams of worldwide presence overnight. No one was more surprised than Napoleon's finance minister, the Marquis de Barbe-Marbois, when he was instructed to reverse official policy on the morning of April 4, 1803. Perhaps if he had known that day's *Original Book* entry, he would have been wiser: »Aujourd'hui, débarrassez vous d'une source d'ennui« (Today, get rid of something tiresome). Thus was the whole course of 19th century geopolitics and the destiny of nations transformed in one stroke.

On a more general note, it is surely not coincidental that the year Napoleon acquired the *Book* corresponds to that when his ego exploded: he was already First Consul by 1801, but by 1802

he had made himself Consul for Life, and by 1804 he was Emperor. Perhaps he took the *Book*'s emphasis on extreme individualism at face value. Some historians even posit he kept it close to his heart in his famous Imperial greatcoat, hence his famous position right hand tucked inside the tunic. Certainly he took it with him on all his major campaigns, and indeed this is how it was acquired by its next owner, one Alexei Fedrovsky. As Napoleon retreated across the Berezina in December 1812 after his disastrous invasion of Russia, one of his staff officers, a Bordelais by the name of Ramballe, was hastily put in charge of the Emperor's remaining possessions as Bonaparte fled back to Paris in a fur-laden sleigh.

Ramballe was immortalized by Tolstoy in *War and Peace*, where we find him ragged and near-delirious with his orderly Morel sharing a campfire with Russian soldiers near Krasnoe. Alas, he never made it back to Bordeaux. Like so many thousands, both French and Russian, worn out by the sub-zero temperatures and incessant gales, he froze to death drunk in the knee-deep snow on the roadside near Orsk, only ten miles from the Prussian border. The *Book* was found amongst other papers by a band of pillaging cossacks, more interested in mens' boots than any obscure bundle of documents. They dumped the lot at their local billet, the castle of Alexei Fedrovsky, a count exiled from Moscow for political reasons in 1807. Alexei was famous for his imaginative cruelty: on at least one documented occasion, he sent his servants out early one morning to the local weekly village market, ordering them to buy up all the food available so that his peasant neighbors would have to starve for the week.

Fedrovsky was an early exponent of Russian political dissent, a radical before his time and more by temperament than ideology: he advocated the overthrow of Tsar Alexander on the grounds that his beard was not sufficiently manly. Rather like Sade, he was exiled at the insistence of his family, who kept finding their relative the laughing stock of Muscovite society. Nevertheless, Fedrovsky maintained links with the early precursors of Russian dissent. Though he did not make much use of the *Book* himself (except when following its edicts could annoy his loved ones), he did pass it on upon his death in 1827, along with copious notes on facial hair throughout history, to his anarchist friend Bakunin. Bakunin, at the time, was not yet quite the international firebrand and scourge of governments worldwide that he became in the 1850s. But he was still too impetuous and restless to sit down and take orders from a mere manuscript. He was also permanently penniless, and so it came that he gave the *Book* away in exchange for some cabbage soup at the house of a friend of his in 1832.

Fortunately, this friend was none other than literary critic Vissarion Grigorievich Belinsky, perhaps the man most deserving of the *Book* anywhere on the planet at the time.

By the early 1830s, Russia was a moral and intellectual vacuum. The burgeoning young intelligentsia was desperate for spiritual nourishment, caught between the dumbly repressive autocracy of Nicolas I on the one hand, and the illiterate groaning peasant masses on the other. With no native role models to look up to, the Russian youth avidly absorbed every Western notion with a hint of revolutionary change. This was fertile ground for the *Book*, and no one took it up more forcefully than their effective spokesman, Belinsky, the »conscience of the

Russian intelligentsia« as Isaiah Berlin so aptly terms him. To Belinsky, books and ideas represented salvation from the grim material philistine circumstances of Russian life. His was a philosophy of engagement; a man's life should reflect his beliefs, however much of a struggle was involved. Behavior had to follow on from ideas. He lived in a state of permanent moral frenzy, of constant searching after the true ends of life. It is no surprise that the *Book*, with its zeal for unending revolutionary experimentation and disregard for social conventions, appealed to him immediately. He copied out some of the more extreme days like »Go up to a member of the ruling classes and tell him how ignomious he is« or the religious-themed »God is dead. Make a small clay model of him and bury him in your back garden« and disseminated them amongst his friends and fellow radicals. He even penned a few pages of his own on the subject of serfdom (»Grab the nearest serf and run for the woods to free him,« »Paint ›serfdom is the doom of the human spirit‹ on the wall of the Kremlin«). This sort of sentiment did not endear him to the Tsarist police as can readily be imagined.

And indeed it is reading out these pages of Belinsky's (and not merely his more famous 1847 »*Letter to Gogol*«) that got Dostoevsky condemned to death and sent to Siberia. By then Belinsky had alas died of consumption. But such had been his influence that he can legitimately be called one of the founders of the movement that led to the Russian Revolution.

After his death the *Book* continued as one of the underground texts that fuelled the revolutionary fire across Russia and in the various places of exile where Russian radicals congregated. Though it has to be said that Belinsky probably best understood the essence of the *Book*, which is its permanent encouragement of the flowering of the individual human spirit, the expression of the whole of man's nature, unfettered by the shackles of tradition. Later generations of revolutionaries were to put it to far more prosaic use. For the rest of the 19th century the *Book* passed from radical to radical. It is difficult to know its exact history during this period as its successive owners were understandably publicity-shy and left few traces of their whereabouts and activities. The Populist-turned-Marxist leader Plekhanov seems to have recuperated it sometime in the 1880s. He in turn entrusted it to his star pupil Lenin, who found its radical tone of great comfort during his lonely years abroad in Geneva and Paris. Indeed it played a direct part in the Russian Revolution. During the 1905 uprising, Lenin had decided to stay abroad, obeying his more prudent instincts. When it came to the February 1917 uprising though, he consulted the *Book* on February 12, which urged him thus: »Today plan a surprise trip somewhere hot.« Immediately he resolved to set off for Moscow in the famous sealed train and changed the course of the revolution, ending with the Bolshevik takeover in October 1917.

More generally, it is clear that the nature of Lenin's rule was influenced by the *Book*, as reflected both in his ruthless drive and in the speed of his decisions. By the time Lenin died in 1924, he had grown mistrustful of both his comrades Trotsky and Stalin, and so bequeathed the *Book* to Nicholas Bukharin, whom he called in his testament »the greatest and most valuable theoretician of the party.« His theorizing was no real match for Stalin's peasant cunning though, and the *Book* soon got Bukharin into trouble. To be fair, it was no easy task to Sovietize what was essentially an individualistic bible, no matter how glorious its part in the history of the Revolution. Whole schools were given special versions, with tasks such as »Today, work to achieve the goals of the Five-Year-Plan« or »Dispose of ten kulaks by lunchtime!« (at the height of the collectivization hysteria in 1929). Yet this did not go far enough for Stalin. Unintentional lapses such as »How much do you love Comrade Stalin on a scale of 1 to 1000?« were seen as perilously close to inviting dissent, and undoubtedly contributed to the downfall and eventual execution of Bukharin. But there was worse to come for the *Book*, or rather its bastardized Stalinist form. By the early 30s, such was Stalin's paranoia and fear of »Trotskyist contraband« that everything published (not just the *Book*) was expected to be rewritten in his own personal style. Half the days in the 1934 *Correct edition* were about Stalin directly (»Compose a realist poem to the glory of the Revolution and its leader and nail it to an enemy of the working classes«). The other half were merely written in his plodding repetitious pseudo-scientific manner (»Today help organize your local communist associations with a view to undermining international capitalist superstructures«). Eventually fault was found with this edition too and its supervisor Sokolnikov was purged in the »Trial of the Seventeen« in 1937. Thus ended the sorry saga of the Soviet *Book*.

Fortunately for us, the original emerged unscathed. Trotsky, who had seen which way the wind was blowing, managed to

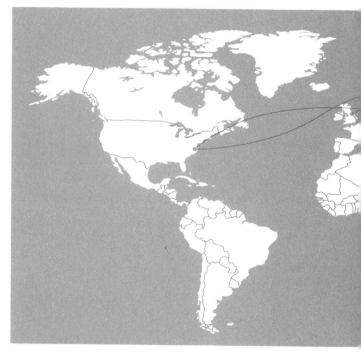

procure Bukharin's copy and took it with him in exile in 1929. He wandered about for years, persecuted at a distance by Stalin who still feared his moral authority, until he eventually landed in Mexico. There he found a house in Coyoacan near Mexico City with his wife Natalia Sedova. The Mexican Communist Party was strong but deeply divided into Stalinist and anti-Stalinist factions. Trotsky soon settled in, making friends with local sympathizers. He was particularly close to revolutionary muralist Diego Rivera and even closer to his painter wife Frida Kahlo. Rivera had helped Trotsky gain asylum in Mexico; they were comrades until 1938 when they split over ideological differences, and rumors of an affair between Trotsky and Kahlo.

Finally history caught up with him when Spanish communist and Stalinist agent Ramon Mercador smashed his head with an alpine pickaxe on August 20, 1940 while he was writing an accusatory biography of his nemesis. Rather gruesomely, he did not die from the blow but stood straight up, screamed, and started pelting his assassin with everything within reach, including his dictaphone. His eventual death the next night went relatively unnoticed, as the world was otherwise preoccupied at the time.

Trotsky's wife Natalia couldn't find the *Book* after her husband's traumatic death. She suspected Stalin's agents had stolen it back, but the truth was closer to home. Frida Kahlo had indeed had an affair with Trotsky, in the course of which she'd borrowed the *Book*. When the two of them broke up under suspicion from their spouses, she never returned it. Trotsky would not have been best pleased with her behavior after his death: both her and Rivera showed little sympathy for him, seeking readmission to the Stalinist Mexican Communist Party and denouncing Trotskyism. Kahlo added insult to injury by slandering Trotsky as a thief and a coward. Her last painting was an unfinished portrait of Stalin, started

Communist sympathizers, and Trotsky's copy of the *Book*, no doubt regarding it as some kind of timing masterplan for global insurrection.

The investigation into Kahlo's anti-American activities eventually petered out for want of firm evidence. No mention is made of the *Book*, for the simple reason that Hoover kept it to himself. Like so many powerful men before him, he fell under its spell. Perhaps to those used to the hubris of arbitrary authority and unquestioning obedience, submitting to the *Book*'s straightforward orders represented something of a liberation.

In any event, its influence on Hoover was more tragicomic than machiavellic. The entry that particularly caught his eye was March 24, 1958: »Experiment with forbidden fantasies.« The result saw him attending at least two gay orgies at the New York Plaza Hotel in 1958, wearing »a fluffy black dress with flounces and lace stockings and high heels and a black curly wig« according to one witness. He was introduced as »Mary« and allegedly engaged in sex with boys as the Bible was read to him, throwing the Good Book down at climax. The latter claim is not considered reliable; but certainly the episode explains why the FBI had limited success against the Mafia during his long tenure. With blackmail material such as this, underworld bosses Frank Costello and Meyer Lansky had little to fear from J. Edgar.

The *Book* has lain in Hoover's classified files since his death in 1972. Under Exec. Order 11152 it was meant to be declassified 30 years

after the dictator's death in 1953, and interrupted by Kahlo's suicide in 1954. By one of those minor quirks of which history is fond, the *Book* then ended up in the hands of the FBI. Kahlo had died at the height of the McCarthyite hysteria in the US. Under heavy political pressure, all government security agencies were looking for reds under the American bed, particularly writers and artists whom everyone knew were susceptible to communist leanings at the best of times. Mexico was America's backyard. Naturally the spotlight fell on Rivera and Kahlo, artists of international renown with documented links to one of the chief instigators of the Russian Revolution.

J. Edgar Hoover himself, head of the bureau since 1924 and vehement anti-commie, took an interest in their activities, so that immediately upon Kahlo's death FBI agents in Mexico raided her house and made off with addresses of supposed

later in May 2002. The FBI claim a clerical error prevented it from being found until November 2002, when it was finally made available to the public, and even then it languished at the bottom of a box in the FBI archive hall in Washington. It is only by amazing luck that the present authors, whilst engaged in a much larger authoritative study of the JFK Roswell cover-up, found it and decided to dust it off and update it for the benefit of the present generation. As with so much pertaining to this incredible artifact, it is impossible to tell whether the delay was deliberate.

One thing that history teaches us is certain: the *Book* has always threatened various powerful groups by its very existence. May this new edition continue to do so.

Dr. Pedersen (1956–2003)

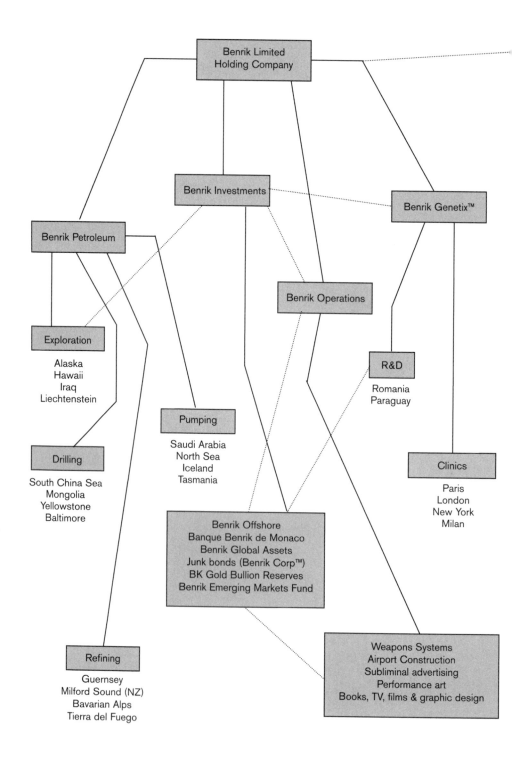

Benrik Limited
Holding Company

Benrik Investments

Benrik Genetix™

Benrik Petroleum

Benrik Operations

Exploration

Alaska
Hawaii
Iraq
Liechtenstein

R&D

Romania
Paraguay

Pumping

Saudi Arabia
North Sea
Iceland
Tasmania

Drilling

South China Sea
Mongolia
Yellowstone
Baltimore

Clinics

Paris
London
New York
Milan

Benrik Offshore
Banque Benrik de Monaco
Benrik Global Assets
Junk bonds (Benrik Corp™)
BK Gold Bullion Reserves
Benrik Emerging Markets Fund

Refining

Guernsey
Milford Sound (NZ)
Bavarian Alps
Tierra del Fuego

Weapons Systems
Airport Construction
Subliminal advertising
Performance art
Books, TV, films & graphic design

Chairman: Benrik
Chief Executive: Benrik
Vice presidents: Ben Carey, Henrik Delehag
Executive directors: Simon Trewin, Claire Scott, Leo Hollis, Trena Keating,
Scott Waxman, Shailesh Gor, Chris Clarke, Jonas Jansson
Non-executive directors: Richard Carey, Prue Carey, Kenneth Delehag, Anna-Lena Delehag.
Consultants: Lana Ivanyoukhina & Räkan, Kathy Peach, Katy Follain, Antony Topping, Stefanie and
Charlotte Drews, Jamie Colonna, Sophie Hewat, Mark Cole, Fiona Couper, Gaby Vinader, Joel Chovet, Clelia Uhart,
Sarah Woodruff, Charlotte Davies, Elizabeth & Alex Carey, Aunt, Eugene, Edwin Lee, Trevor Franklin,
Emily Haynes, John Hamilton, Chris Callard, Clare Pollock, Grainne Ashton, Hjalmar & Lovisa & Elin Delehag,
Jonas Delehag, Farmor & Farfar & Mormor & Morfar, Claes Kjellström, Marc Regan, TBWA STHLM,
Åsa Fridh, Rasmus Nilsson, Lilja Ivanyukhina & Alexander Ivanyukhin, Alan Payne

PLUME
Published by the Penguin Group
Penguin Group (USA) Inc., 375 Hudson Street, New York, New York 10014, U.S.A.
Penguin Books Ltd, 80 Strand, London WC2R 0RL, England
Penguin Books Australia Ltd, 250 Camberwell Road, Camberwell, Victoria 3124, Australia
Penguin Books Canada Ltd, 10 Alcorn Avenue, Toronto, Ontario, Canada M4V 3B2
Penguin Books India (P) Ltd, 11 Community Centre, Panchsheel Park, New Delhi – 110 017, India
Penguin Books (N.Z.) Ltd, Cnr Rosedale and Airborne Roads, Albany, Auckland 1310, New Zealand
Penguin Books (South Africa) (Pty) Ltd, 24 Sturdee Avenue, Rosebank, Johannesburg 2196, South Africa
Penguin Books Ltd, Registered Offices: 80 Strand, London WC2R 0RL, England

First published by Plume, a member of Penguin Group (USA) Inc.
First Printing, November 2003
5 7 9 10 8 6 4

® REGISTERED TRADEMARK—MARCA REGISTRADA
ISBN 0-452-28489-9
Printed in the United States of America.

Where the work is not property and copyright of the authors, all reasonable attempts have been made by the
authors to contact correct copyright holders. The authors would like to gratefully thank for permission to include
the following within this edition: Day 13 photo of Richard Ramirez permission courtesy the Associated Press;
Day 34 logo © Amnesty International; Day 75 Gino's photography layout and copy © Gino Marino (thanks again Gino!);
Day 114 photography © Johan Warden; Day 121–2 photography © Getty Images/Paul Weber; Day 131 Thanx illustration
© Rasmus Nilsson; Day 137 illustration © Getty Images/Michele Warner; Day 146 photography © Getty Images/Shuji
Kobayashi; Day 188 photography © Charlotte Davies; Day 207 photography © Getty Images/Ron Chapple;
Day 272 thank you to HarperCollinsPublishers for the extract from The Diceman © George Cockcroft 1971;
Day 298 photography © Getty Images/Laurence Monneret; Day 313 photography © Robert Doisneau/
Rapho; Day 324 photography © Jonas Delehag; Day 353 photography © Lana Ivanyoukhina;
Day 362 photography © Lana Ivanyoukhina. If there is further enquiry, please contact the authors c/o:
PFD, Drury House 34-43, Russell St, London WC2B 5HA, England.

www.thiswebsitewillchangeyourlife.com
Publisher is not affiliated with the authors' website, and assumes no responsibility for its information or use.
Although the authors have endeavored to provide accurate telephone numbers and Internet addresses at the time
of publication, neither author nor publisher assumes any responsibility for errors or changes.